Practical Approach to Educational Psychology

Practical Approach
to
Educational Psychology

Bharti Satsangi

RANDOM PUBLICATIONS
NEW DELHI (INDIA)

Practical Approach to Educational Psychology

ISBN 978-93-5111-480-2

Published in 2015 in India by

RANDOM PUBLICATIONS
4376-A/4B, Gali Murari Lal, Ansari Road
New Delhi-110 002
Phone : +9111-43580356, 011-23289044, 011-43142548
e-mail: sales@randompublications.com,
info@randompublications.com, randomexports@gmail.com

Reprinted 2025

Type Setting by : Friends Media, Delhi-110089
Digitally Printed at : Replika Press Pvt. Ltd.

Preface

Educational psychology is the branch of applied psychology, which observes the educational activities in schools and learning centres and presents the solutions for problems, faced during learning process. It not only helps in improving the performance of students but it also helps teachers and educational planners, in their way to achieve best education system, healthy learning atmosphere and healthy learning growth of students. The knowledge of educational psychology is important as it provides teachers with some basic skills and guidelines to solve the problems of teaching- learning process. The scope of educational psychology is as vast as education and psychology are themselves. With the rapid changes in social life and especially the role of information technology have brought great impacts upon educational process. New and modern situation needs new approaches to deal with educational matters.

Practical Approach to Educational Psychology opens up the broad discipline of educational psychology with an emphasis on helping students and teachers to understand the concept and theories of the subject and making them expertise in both teaching and learning. Carefully edited and structured as such that the presentation of the subject, the order of topics and the treatment is well-suited to those who require a basic understanding of the subject. The book is based on the assumption that educational psychology is an applied psychology, comprises many different facts of the educative process from the practical and applicational points of view. Readers are introduced to concepts, theoretical formulations and many new fields of study concerned with educational psychology that are assumed to have implications for education. Besides ideally suited for educational courses, the book will also serve as a valuable reference for teachers, teacher-trainees and other professionals at various levels of education.

Author

Contents

1

What is Educational Psychology?

Educational psychology is defined as the branch of psychology that is concerned with the study of the mental processes and behaviors associated with human learning and instruction. Educational psychologists ask questions about the nature of learners and learning, the characteristics of effective teaching, and how the nature of classrooms affects learning. They study a wide range of phenomena associated with learning, both in the laboratory and in the classroom. Over the last thirty years, however, educational psychologists' interest in classroom learning has increased dramatically. In 1999, the *Journal of Educational Psychology* reported the results of studies investigating the teaching and learning of writing, mathematics and problem solving, and reading. In addition, some studies investigated questions about the effects of technology on learning, individual student differences affecting school achievement, and the effects of social influences on students. When educational psychologists ask questions about learning, they apply the methods of science, careful observation, and rational analysis to answer their questions. The answers to their questions are used to formulate and assess theories that teachers use in their decision making.

Teaching is a complex activity, and effective teaching requires a complex set of knowledge and skills. These characteristics have been organized into various sets of standards that are used by many states in the certification of teachers, such as those developed by the Interstate New Teacher Assessment and Support Consortium (INTASC), shown in Table 1.

Table 1. INTASC Standards

1. Content Pedagogy	The teacher understands the central concepts, tools of inquiry, and structures of the discipline(s) he or she teaches and can create learning experiences that make these aspects of subject matter meaningful for students.
2. Student Development	The teacher understands how children learn and develop, and can provide learning opportunities that support their intellectual, social, and personal development.
3. Diverse Learners	The teacher understands how students differ in their approaches to learning and creates instructional opportunities that are adapted to diverse learners.
4. Multiple Instructional Strategies	The teacher understands and uses a variety of instructional strategies to encourage students' development of critical thinking, problem solving, and performance skills.
5. Motivation and Management	The teacher uses an understanding of individual and group motivation and behavior to create a learning environment that encourages positive social interaction, active engagement in learning, and self-motivation.
6. Communication and Technology	The teacher uses knowledge of effective verbal, nonverbal, and media communication techniques to foster active inquiry, collaboration, and supportive interaction in the classroom.
7. Planning	The teacher plans instruction based upon knowledge of subject matter, students, the community, and curriculum goals.
8. Assessment	The teacher understands and uses formal and informal assessment strategies to evaluate and ensure the continuous intellectual, social, and physical development of the learner.
9. Reflective Practice and Professional Growth	The teacher is a reflective practitioner who continually evaluates the effects of his/her choices and actions on others (students, parents, and other professionals in the learning community) and who actively seeks out opportunities to grow professionally.
10. School and Community Involvement	The teacher fosters relationships with school colleagues, parents, and agencies in the larger community to support students' learning and well-being.

A glance at the principles that make up the INTASC standards will give you an idea of how important an understanding of psychology is to teacher effectiveness. Effective teaching results in student learning. Learning is a psychological process, and to influence this process teachers must understand the nature of this process and their students.

Scientific Theories

Science is a method of studying the world. This method includes the collection and analysis of data and the generation of logical explanations for the data that have been gathered so far. These logical explanations are called theories. The effectiveness of teachers' decisions depends on their ability to understand their students and classrooms. Developing this understanding is the goal of reflective practice. As the quote by John Dewey suggests, the scientific approach provides teachers with one of the most effective means of achieving this understanding.

In general, a *theory* is a set of beliefs about how the world works, or at least how some part of it works. Such beliefs help explain the world and allow us to make predictions and modify the world to achieve our objectives. For every aspect of our day-to-day lives we have sets of beliefs that we use to understand our situation and guide our response. Therefore, in a sense, anybody who tries to solve a problem begins with a theory. For many people, such beliefs take the form of informal intuitions developed from their encounters with similar problems. These informal beliefs are sometimes referred to as common sense or *implicit theories* . Teachers might have implicit theories about how students learn, how they are motivated, or the causes of students' misbehaviors. Research has shown that the implicit theories of teachers do influence their teaching practice.

Scientific theories are a set of formal statements that describe variables and relationships that are important to the understanding of some part of the world. For example, information-processing theory proposes that the rate of learning is limited by learners' ability to pay attention. That scientific theories comprise such a set of formal statements is important because it makes it easier to test the accuracy or preci-sion of the described relationships. By testing these relationships, we develop a more accurate understanding of the world and are able to make more accurate predictions. For instance, a researcher might investigate what kinds of distractions are most likely to influence the rate of learning. In general, experts are more likely to use these types of formal theories when they solve problems within their domains of expertise.

It is important to note that scientists don't think of their theories as *the truth.* Theories are the best explanation they have so far. The development of theories is an evolutionary process. Theories compete to explain what we know, and as new information comes to light, some theories are modified and survive, whereas others are abandoned. The theories of educational psychologists are subject to these same evolutionary forces, meaning that as we learn more about human nature, the theories of educational psychologists change. Driving this evolutionary process is the scientific method.

Scientific inquiry begins and ends with a theory. After developing a theory the researcher uses the theory to formulate research questions. Ihe questions that a scientist tries to answer are influenced by the scientist's theory. To answer these questions, scientists conduct research. The research is designed to gather information in a way that helps answer the research question. After planning their research, researchers make observations and gather data. The data are then analyzed to answer the original question. Sometimes the result of this research strengthens the theory that generated the question, but often the results of research require that the theory be refined or modified in some way. Frequently, the research process causes researchers to ask new questions and the process begins again. This cyclic process is illustrated in Figure 1.

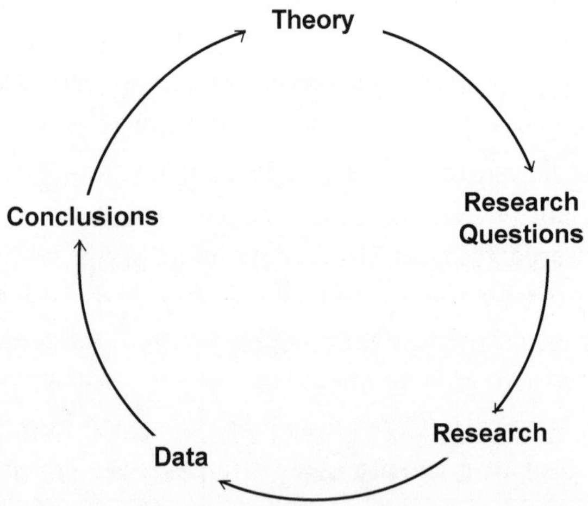

Figure 1. The Theory/Research Cycle

Comparing Theories

Teaching is a complex task and classrooms are complex environments. To study this complexity, researchers tend to focus on limited aspects of the teaching task or classroom environment. Generally, they choose their research topics based on their individual knowledge and interests. As a result, no single theory of teaching and learning exists. An important task for teachers is to compare various theories and select that theory that is most appropriate for a given situation.

Theories may be compared along three dimensions.

- The theory's characteristics, including the scope of the theory as well as the constructs and processes of the theory;
- Epistemic value, or the theory's potential to explain and make predictions about the world; and
- Applicability, or the theory's ability to guide people's decision making in everyday problem situations.

Characteristics of Theories

Because human beings arc so complex, psychologists often focus on some restricted aspect of human nature. Their research concentrates on answering questions about a small set of psychological phenomena, and the resulting theory tries to explain these phenomena. This characteristic is referred to as the scope of the theory. The *scope* of a theory refers to the type of phenomena that the theory attempts to explain. Because of this, it is important to consider the focus of different theories when making comparisons. For a teacher, the question becomes, "What classroom situations will this theory help me understand?" Consider the science teacher who wishes his or her student to learn how to use an analytic balance. This teacher needs a theory that describes the process of learning and the factors that affect it. Alternatively, a teacher evaluating a character-education curriculum might need a theory that specifically describes the factors that affect children's empathy and their ability to understand other people's perspectives.

All theories describe some aspect of the world, and psychological theories attempt to describe the human mind and human behavior. These theories involve the description of psychological constructs and psychological processes. A *psychological construct* is a hypothetical human characteristic that is used to explain patterns of behavior. Learning style, intelligence, mood, and personality are examples of psychological constructs. *Psychological processes* are actions that create or modify psychological constructs. Learning, motivation, and development are three psychological processes that are of particular interest to educational psychologists and teachers.

Psychological constructs may vary in terms of their permanence. A *trait* is a psychological construct that represents a relatively permanent and consistent mental characteristic. Personality and intelligence are typically described as traits. For instance, you may have friends who have been very outgoing for as long as you have known them. They enjoy meeting new people, and they like to interact socially with other people. You might explain the person's behavior by saying that she or he is friendly or extroverted. In other words, you seem to believe that there is some underlying psychological trait that explains this consistent pattern of behavior. A mental characteristic that arises from a specific situation and then goes away when the situation changes is called a *state.* Many emotions are examples of states. In psychologically healthy people, fear or anxiety are mental states brought on by some situation. For instance, a student may feel anxious before an important test, but when the test is over, the anxiety subsides. The emotion is tied to the student's situation.

Different theories may use different psychological processes and constructs to explain the same event. These differences produce different ways of understanding a situation. For example, developmental theorists may use the psychological construct of readiness and the process of maturation to explain differences in children's academic performance and behavior across grade levels. From this perspective, if a child is having trouble in school, the problem may be that the child is just not mature enough to achieve at the expected level. The solution would be to provide the students with tasks that are appropriate for their levels of development. On the other hand, learning theories might explain students' performance in terms of the psychological construct of knowledge, which results from the psychological process of learning. Learning theory would explain a child's academic problem as indicating a lack of knowledge and suggest that instruction be designed to make use of what the child already knows to develop the knowledge necessary to achieve in the classroom.

Epistemic Value of a Theory

Howard suggests that scientists judge a theory based on its contribution to understanding the world, guided in their judgment by what he has termed epistemic value. *Epistemic value* refers to the power of a theory to contribute to our understanding of a specific situation or the world in general. Epistemic value includes the following:

- Predictive accuracy, or how closely predictions derived from a theory match real world outcomes; Internal coherence, or the degree to which the constructs and processes proposed by a theory are logically related;
- External consistency, or how well the theory describes objects and events in the real world;
- Unifying power, or the ability of a theory to identify, incorporate, and explain similarities in data from different fields of research; Fertility, or the ability of the theory to inspire and guide research that results in useful information; and
- Simplicity, or the number of constructs or processes comprising the theory. All things being equal, simpler theories are preferred.

Practical Application

The practical application of the theory is a final comparison point for theories. Some theories provide attractive descriptions of situations, but are weak in terms of their applicability. Practitioners need theories that provide explanations and suggest a course of action to solve the problems they face. In some cases an older theory may simplify a problem even though the theory is known to be an incomplete, narrow, or inaccurate description of the world. For example, sailors still use a system of celestial navigation based on the assumption that the earth is at the center of the universe and the stars are in fixed positions relative to each other in space. These assumptions are incorrect, but by making these assumptions the calculation of their geographic position is simplified with no noticeable loss of accuracy. One way to judge the practical application of a theory is to consider the types of principles that can be developed from that theory. By making predictions and testing the accuracy of the predictions, we are able to make judgments about the accuracy of our theories. When repeated test results reveal a consistent relationship between specific situations, actions, and outcomes, the relationship may be stated as a principle. For instance, cognitive learning theory proposes that learning depends on the active participation of the learner. This being the case, one prediction that might be made is that learners' intentions affect what they take away from a learning activity.

This prediction has been supported by numerous studies. A principle that can be derived from these consistent research findings is: Learning is an active, goal-directed process.

Principles serve an important role in the application of theory. Principles often serve as the foundation for making decisions and formulating a solution to a problem. A good decision maker uses a theory to understand a problem. This understanding allows the decision maker to select the relevant principle. The principle then serves as the basis for a solution to the problem. This is how Ramona Mahoney applies this approach.

Sometimes students need help in this area. One way to help the students is to begin with some activity designed to encourage them to set appropriate goals for the lesson. For instance, for my science unit on electricity I begin by having students observe the deflection of a compass needle when it is placed near a wire connected to a dry-cell battery. The students are always surprised, and the unexpected behavior of the compass needle arouses their curiosity. They then set out to discover what is causing this effect.

Using Theory and Research to Improve Teaching

As a teacher, you will make hundreds of decisions daily. As you plan for your classes, you must decide what to teach, how to teach, and how to assess your students' learning. As you deliver your lessons, you must decide if students are motivated and learning, or if a change of plan is required. To manage the classroom effectively, you must decide how to respond to the unique problems and behaviors of each student. After you have presented a lesson, you will probably start thinking about how to improve future lessons. Other decisions are associated with the administrative and housekeeping actions required by schools, districts, and other governmental agencies. Teaching is the act of making decisions, acting on those decisions, and evaluating the effects of those decisions.

Teachers make their decisions in complicated environments. Classroom teaching requires the successful completion of many different types of tasks, a concept known as *multidimensionality*. Teachers are managers, instructors, mediators, counselors, and at times medics. They are responsible for teaching a wide-ranging curriculum that includes facts, skills, problem solving, as well as interpersonal skills and attitudes. In addition, they must be able to relate effectively to their students and the adults in their students' lives.

The variety of the decisions that teachers face makes teaching complex and demanding. However, the teacher's task is made even more complex because teachers' decisions are rarely independent of decisions made previously. For example, a teacher deciding what concepts or skills to teach needs to consider the concepts and skills that were previously taught. A teacher deciding how to respond to a student's disruptive behavior may need to consider the student's past responses to similar situations.

The multidimensionality of teaching means that knowledge of a single theory may be insufficient for all the situations faced by teachers. No single theory is likely to be the most useful theory in all situations. Part of the decision-making process for teachers, therefore, is the selection of the theory that is most useful for a given situation. To make an informed selection of a theory, you need some method for comparing theories, and you need to know something about the nature of the educational research behind the theories.

Contribution of Research to Teacher Decision Making

What people know or believe plays a central role in how they think and act in any given situation. This applies to teachers and their decision making. Teachers' beliefs about the nature of their students and how they learn, about the purpose of education, and about themselves as teachers all influence their decision making. Specifically, teachers' knowledge and beliefs influence how they set goals in their classrooms, which student characteristics they identify as critical, and the instructional and management strategies they apply.

The theories that result from the scientific study of teaching and learning can be valuable tools that help teachers organize and clarify their thinking, thus improving the quality of their decisions and teaching practice. Much of what expert teachers know and believe about teaching is grounded in personal experience; and their decisions are often based on the intuitions derived from this experience. However, even experienced teachers may be stumped by unfamiliar circumstances or an unusual problem. In these situations, the results of the scientific study of teaching may be helpful.

For new teachers, understanding the insights derived from the scientific study of teaching can be even more valuable. As a new teacher you may lack the experiences and intuitions of experienced teachers; however, you will be required to make decisions the moment you enter your first classroom. Where will you begin? The theories derived from a scientific study of teaching can provide a valuable starting point for your decision making. Your purpose in studying educational psychology is to develop a theoretical base in preparation for making decisions in your future classroom.

Theories and Decision Making

How do theories affect the decision-making process of teachers? To answer this question, we first need to think about the nature of decision making and what makes a good decision maker. Then, we need to think about how theory might assist the decision-making process.

Decision Making as Problem Solving

Making a decision is a form of problem solving that usually means choosing a course of action. Psychologists who study human problem solving typically identify a series of steps in the process of solving a problem. These steps include

(a) understanding the nature of the problem,

(b) developing a plan to solve the problem,

(c) implementing the plan, and

(d) looking back and evaluating the effectiveness of the planned solution.

To understand the nature and role each of these steps plays in the problem-solving process, researchers have compared the problem-solving performances of experts and novices. An expert is someone who has demonstrated a great deal of proficiency in solving problems in a particular area, such as classroom teaching, chess, physics, mathematics, and so on. A novice is someone with limited experience within a specific domain. Typically, experts are better able to understand the important characteristics of a problem and formulate effective solutions more efficiently than are novices.

What accounts for these observed differences? Experts' ability to understand and solve problems in their domain of expertise seems to be related to their extensive and well-organized knowledge of the problem domain. Experts' knowledge makes them especially sensitive to important relationships among the elements that define the problem situation. Having an effective theory allows them to:

- Identify the important characteristics of the problem situation and ignore unimportant characteristics;
- See the underlying pattern of relationships in the problem situation; and
- Identify principles that can be used to guide the generating of a solution.

To illustrate these points, consider how an expert teacher might use her understanding of behavioral learning theory to respond to a child whose talking is disrupting learning. First, she focuses on the misbehavior as part of a sequence rather than as a single event. By taking this focus, the teacher is able to identify those factors that trigger the misbehavior. Perhaps the student's talking only occurs during certain types of activities or when the student is with a particular student or students. By seeing the student's misbehavior as a sequence, the teacher also focuses on the consequence of the misbehavior. The teacher may try to determine what rewards the student receives for the misbehavior.

By understanding these cause-and-effect relationships, the teacher may try to use principles derived from behavioral learning theory to modify the disruptive behavior. For instance if the student talks when with certain students, the teacher can arrange for these students not to be together. Alternatively, she may arrange her class to make some other behavior more attractive than talking.

Expert teachers' theories about teaching also influence how they perceive a problem and the principles that they apply in the classroom. You probably already have developed some of these theories, and certainly others will develop as you gain experience as a teacher.

A lot is required of teachers as decision makers, and your authors believe that the scientific study of teaching can help you make more effective decisions in your multidimensional world. One approach that scientists frequently use when studying a complex process is to break the process into parts and study the parts separately. Once the parts of the process have been adequately described, the scientist may then study the relationships between the parts. The advantage of this approach is that it makes it easier to ask and find the answers to specific questions. To simplify the discussion of the kinds of decisions teachers make, your authors have decided to divide the teaching process and the types of decisions teachers make into three areas, referred to as *decision points*. The three decision points are

1 *Planning decisions.* These include decisions that are made before a specific interaction with the learners occur.
2. *Teaching and managing decisions.* These decisions include those made while interacting with the students.
3. *Assessment decisions.* These decisions are made to assess the effectiveness of an interaction with a student.

This division aids our discussion of how the various psychological theories may help your practice as a teacher, but it is important to keep in mind that all types of decisions are interconnected. Decisions that are made while planning a lesson often determine the types of interactions you have with the students. For instance, if you decide to have your students do group work, you are presented with a set of opportunities and challenges that differ from those you would have face if you had decided to do a lecture. Group work may present you with more opportunities to monitor students' understanding one on one than will a lecture. The challenge of keeping the students focused and on task is also likely to be greater if you decide to do group work rather than present a lecture. Relationships also exist between the decisions you make when planning and the decisions you face when assessing the effectiveness of your lesson, and between the decisions you make while teaching and your assessment decisions.

Teachers and Research

The development of theories is an evolutionary process, that is, theories change as new information becomes available. This means that for teachers to get the most benefit from theories, they must keep up with current developments in the field. In other words, teachers should be aware of and use current research to expand and modify their understanding and application of theory. Although the actual impact of educational research on classroom teaching can be debated, we tend to believe that a conceptual understanding of educational research can be beneficial to teachers in two ways: as consumers of research and as researchers in their own right.

Teachers as Consumers of Research

First, teachers may benefit as consumers of the information produced by others. Teachers have multiple sources of information about learning and teaching in classrooms. They are exposed to interpretations of educational research in their college classes, through on-site training experiences, through informal conversations with colleagues, through professional journals, and through other outlets such as the Internet. It is important that you become critical consumers of the information you gather. A critical interpretation of research helps you understand and appropriately apply the results of research to your own teaching.

Teachers as Researchers

Research is not an activity limited to professional researchers. Teachers conduct research every day in their own classrooms. When they evaluate the effectiveness of new ideas, instructional techniques, or materials, teachers are conducting a form of research. For example, a teacher who is trying different instructional approaches to help a student who is having trouble grasping the course content is conducting research. While not formally stated, the teacher is testing a hypothesis about the nature of learning and the learner. The results of this informal research may help the teacher improve his or her ability to teach the learner and improve professional skills.

A more formal approach to teacher research in classrooms is action research. *Action research* is defined as teacher-initiated, school-based research. Consider how an action research approach might bc used in the example given in the preceding paragraph. First, the teacher would use the information the teacher had about the student, the course content, and the teacher's beliefs about learning to make an explicit statement of the problem. The statement might include information about the student and the learning situation that the teacher believed was relevant. The statement would also describe the current state of the student's learning and a description of what a solution would accomplish. Here is an example of a problem statement developed by Jane Forbes for a student in her tenth grade chemistry class:

> William is not doing well on his chemistry examinations. He seems to be bright and motivated, but doesn't volunteer to participate much in either large group discussions or when working within his lab group. I talked to him about his work and he seemed embarrassed. He appeared to understand chemistry concepts at a very basic level, but had difficulty discussing what he knew. He says he finds the textbook and class discussions hard to follow. I talked to some of his other teachers and they have confirmed that his reading skills are poor. The school psychologist has told me that William's performance on tests of reading comprehension are below average, but that he doesn't have a disability. I believe if I can improve his comprehension of the text and class discussions, he will do better on the tests.

Next the teacher would identify specific instructional modifications that might help the student and apply the modifications and collect data through appropriate observational techniques to determine which modifications yielded results that were closest to the desired solution. Here's how Jane Forbes decided to handle William's situation.

> I've talked to William and he has agreed to try a new reading comprehension strategy called concept mapping. I will teach him how to construct concept maps, then for each reading assignment I will require him to create a map from the main concepts of the assignment. At first I will identify the concepts for him, but eventually I want him to find the main ideas for himself. I will also provide him questions for each reading assignment. He will justify his answers with reference to his concept map. He has a study hall during my prep-period so he will stop by to discuss his map and answers before class starts. In addition to monitoring his performance on quizzes and test, I will keep track of how often he contributes to class and group discussions.

Finally, having determined which techniques were most effective for the student, the teacher would apply the technique more generally to the instruction of that student. This is how Jane Forbes accomplished this last step.

> It took a while for William to master the concept mapping techniques, but his maps gradually improved. As his maps improved so did his answers to the assigned questions and his ability to explain his answers during our pre-class meetings. I kept a record of William's participation in class discussions and found that as his maps improved he seemed to be participating more in the class discussions and lab groups. His test scores have also improved, but not to the level I would expect. Maybe he needs help in developing some test-taking strategies. The concept mapping approach seems to have worked, and I have suggested he try it with some of his other classes. I have talked to Bob Carson, William's history teacher, and he is enthusiastic about Bill's concept mapping in his class also.

As can be seen, action research is typically more focused on the specific problems and decisions of a teacher or group of teachers. As with all forms of research, action research is a systematic approach to problem solving and decision making in the classroom. Gay and Airasian identify four steps in the action research process: (1) problem/ topic identification; (2) data gathering; (3) decision making; and (4) action.

The problems that teachers identify derive from their own unique situations, but the teacher's perception of a problem and the questions the teacher asks are influenced by the teacher's theories about learners and learning.

In action research, the decision leads directly to action on the part of the teacher. Action research is based on a specific classroom and directed toward solving a specific problem or answering a specific question within that classroom. For this reason the decision made is more likely to lead to a specific teacher action. The teacher's action leads directly to another question; that is, was the action effective? With this question the whole process begins again.

General Insights about Educational Research

Your authors would like to help you in your interpretation and application of educational research by providing some general insights gained from our own reading and interpretation of educational research:

- Different research questions require different data collection procedures.
- An effective understanding of classrooms requires both qualitative and quantitative data.
- There can be multiple competing explanations for the same data.
- The range of differences among individuals, even within the same group, is greater than the range of differences between groups.

Learning is complex, and classroom learning must be understood in the context of many interacting variables.

Varied Data Collection Procedures

When teachers or researchers ask a research question, they must decide what type of data would be most useful in answering the question, and the best way to gather those data. Three commonly used data collection procedures are helpful for different types of questions: direct observation, performance assessment, and self-report.

If researchers or teachers want to know how often, how long, or under what circumstances a behavior occurs, they might use direct observation techniques.

Direct observation techniques require an observer to record those behaviors as they occur. If researchers wanted to know how often teachers ask questions during an hour, then it makes sense to use direct observation techniques. The researcher might sit in the back of the room or watch a videotape of the classroom. Each time the teacher asks a question, the researcher might make a mark on a recording sheet. If a teacher wants to know how often a student participates in class, she might move a token from her left pocket to right pocket with every instance of participation. Later, a count of the chips in the right pocket provides an estimate of the amount of participation. If researchers and teachers want to know if students understand and can apply what they have learned, they might employ performance assessments.

Performance assessments evaluate students' learning by having them complete a predetermined task. For example, if a science teacher wants to know if students can correctly prepare a microscope slide, then that teacher could evaluate students as they prepare a slide. If researchers want to know if students can apply some problem-solving skills, then they could have those students problem solve and observe the desired skills. If researchers and teachers want to know how people feel, or what they are thinking, they may want to use self-report techniques.

Self-report techniques ask people to report or discuss their perceptions, beliefs, and thought processes. For example, teachers or researchers who want to understand students' math problem solving might ask students to talk aloud about their thinking as they solve problems. If they want to know how students feel about themselves, they might ask them to fill out a self-esteem inventory or survey.

Obviously, the three techniques can be used for other purposes than those included in these examples, and other data collection techniques exist besides these three. The purpose is to show how a data collection procedure should be matched to the type of research questions being asked. As researchers, we want to make sure we collect the data we need for decision making.

Qualitative And Quantitative Data

Ourquestions determine the types of data collection techniques we use, and the data collection techniques determine the types of data that result from our procedures. There are two general categories of data, qualitative data and quantitative data.

Qualitative Data are observations of essential characteristics or differences and often take the form of verbal descriptions of a person, group, or situation. *Quantitative data* are a measure of the quantity or amount of something and are expressed as numbers such as scores or counts.

Collecting qualitative data is more than recording observations; it also involves an interpretive process. Through this interpretive process, the researcher tries to understand the significance of observed events. In his book, *Life in Classrooms,* Philip Jackson noted that when elementary school students raised their hands to attract the teacher's attention, they often supported the raised right arm by placing their left hand just under the elbow. The significance attached to this observation was that the arm was heavy, and children must often keep their hand up for long periods of time before the teacher responds. These qualitative data were combined with others to help understand classrooms as crowded places with limited resources. Extending this interpretation still further, Jackson concluded that in elementary schools children must learn to wait and be patient.

The process of collecting quantitative data often begins by creating an *operational definition* that describes the characteristic being measured in terms of a score or some other type of numerical observation. For example, in assessing the effectiveness of a specific instructional method, the researchers Jane Stallings and Eileen M. Krasav-age collected quantitative data on (a) the quality of instruction, (b) student engagement during instruction, and (c) student learning. To assess the quality of instruction, trained observers assigned a score to teachers' classroom performances. The students' engagement during instruction was operationally defined by the proportion of time students were observed to be *off-task* (chatting, disrupting, waiting, etc.) during a class period. The researchers addressed students' learning by the change in their performance on standardized achievement tests.

Quantitative and qualitative data each have advantages and disadvantages. Quantitative data can be analyzed using powerful statistical methods to find patterns and make comparisons across many observations. As a result, the conclusions drawn from quantitative data are often more generalizable. The *generalizability* of a conclusion refers to the number of different situations to which the conclusion may be applied. A disadvantage of quantitative data is that sometimes important details are lost.

For example, consider a teacher who is assessing his students' mathematical problem-solving skills. One approach might be to give the students a set of word problems and ask them to solve the problems showing all their work. The quantitative data that may result from this might be a score indicating the proportion of problems correctly solved, or partially correct. However, the information that might be lost is the types of errors that the students are making. Examining the students' responses qualitatively may reveal patterns that point to students' misconceptions about various parts of the problem-solving process. This kind of information may allow teachers to give specific help to some students or alert them to problems with the way the problem-solving concepts and skills have been taught.

Qualitative data allow the researcher to preserve the fine details of observed situations. This often leads to important and interesting insights about the situation being studied. The trade-off is that qualitative data are often so specific to a particular situation that the researcher can only draw valid conclusions about the particular person or group being studied.

Returning to the previous example, through a qualitative analysis of students' problem-solving performance a teacher may identify a student's misconception. But, do all the students in the class share the same misconception? Because many student differences may affect whether or not a particular student develops a similar misconception, it would be dangerous to assume that all the students have the same problem. The question cannot be answered without completing a qualitative analysis of each student's response to the problem-solving exercise.

Multiple Competing Explanations

To explain their data, researchers try to make logical connections between the data and other knowledge possessed by the researcher, including theoretical knowledge. Researchers want these explanations to be valid. *Validity* refers to the quality or the correctness of an explanation or a decision. Researchers try to increase the likelihood that their explanations are valid by considering alternative explanations for their data. By eliminating alternative explanations, researchers can have more confidence in the conclusions they draw from their research.

Once researchers have collected and analyzed data, they are ready to draw some conclusions. Frequently, the researcher's conclusion is an explanation of the results. The idea that the same observation or data can have multiple explanations is an important idea for both teachers and researchers. It helps us avoid jumping to incorrect conclusions.

Consider a hypothetical study of the effectiveness of a new classroom management program in a school. The program is introduced enthusiastically by the principal, who states that this program will work and that discipline referrals to the principal's office will be a measure of its effectiveness. Not surprisingly, referrals to the principal's office do decrease once the program has been instituted. Certainly, the decreased referral rate could be attributed to the program. However, another plausible explanation is that teachers stopped referring discipline problems because they thought it would make them look bad to the principal. What other data do you think could be collected to evaluate which of these two hypotheses is correct?

Teachers also must consider the various plausible explanations for their observations. If their explanations are incorrect, they may select interventions that don't match the problem. For example, one explanation for why a student does not turn in his homework is because the student doesn't care. Obviously, there are other explanations, such as the student doesn't understand the lessons, or his home is so chaotic he can't complete his homework. Can you see how failure to consider alternative explanations in this case might prevent you from making good choices about how to help your student?

Within-group and Between-group Differences

Within-group differences and be-tween-group differences are ideas that are borrowed from statistics. The *within-group differences* are how much members of the same group differ from each other. *Between-group differences* are how much members of one group differ, on average, from members of another group. In research as well as in classroom teaching, it's helpful to remember that the within-group differences often equal or exceed between-group differences. This is particularly important for issues of learner diversity. For example, although children with different ethnic backgrounds may differ in important (between-group) ways, there are also important differences within each ethnic group. Assuming all the children from the same ethnic group learn the same way can cause problems for both researchers and teachers. Researchers may miss important subgroups they need to study, and teachers run the risk of stereotyping individual students from a particular group.

The Complexity of Learning

Much of the research conducted by educational psychologists and teachers is focused on answering questions about how instruction influences student learning. Trying to answer this question is a complex problem. Many factors affect how and what a person will learn in any given situation. In an effort to make sense of this situation, Jenkins (1979) proposed a model of learning research called the theorist's tetrahedron or simply *the tetrahedral model.* The tetrahedral model is a model of four key instructional variables and how they affect each other.

A tetrahedron is a three-sided pyramid. In the model proposed by Jenkins, each of the four points of the pyramid is an important variable that affects learning. The four variables of the tetrahedral model are orienting tasks, materials, criterial tasks, and subjects. *Orienting tasks* refer to the type of instruction and learning activities being used by the teacher. For example, is the student to memorize a list, summarize the gist of a poem, and so on? *Materials* are the way in which the learning task is presented. Is it presented orally, on a computer, through earphones, and so on? *Criterial tasks* refer to the way in which learning is to be assessed. Will the teacher assess learning by asking learners to recognize learned materials, to recall learned materials, or to complete some more complex performance? *Subjects* refer to the learners. In any learning situation it is important to consider any learner characteristics that might influence the learning process. Some of the important learner characteristics include abilities, interests, knowledge, and purposes.

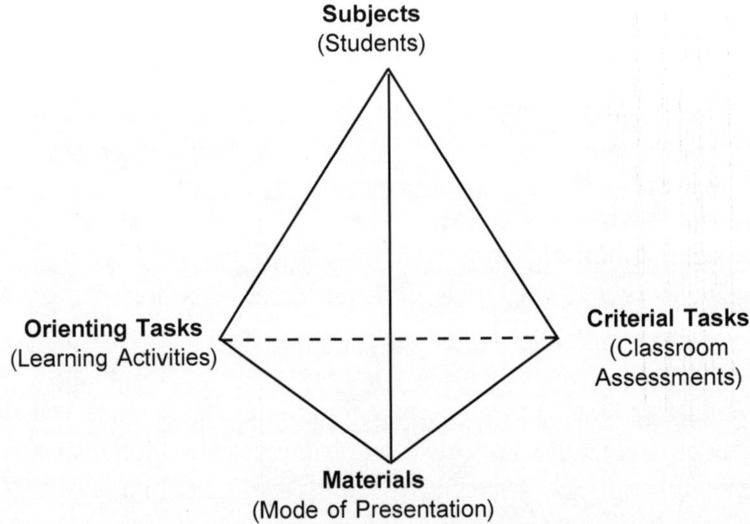

Figure 2: Adapted Tetrahedral Model

A second important characteristic of the tetrahedron is that each point of the tetrahedron is connected to each of the other three points. Jenkins was trying to show with his model that a comprehensive understanding of classroom learning requires that we consider how each variable interacts with the other three. For example, the criterial tasks should make sense with the type of learning that is being studied.

Jenkins proposed the tetrahedral model as a way to conceptualize the key variables in learning research. However, the tetrahedral model can be adapted to describe and guide understanding of classroom situations. In your classroom setting the orienting tasks refer to the actions you expect of your students during a lesson. These expected actions might include taking notes, manipulating materials, or discussing a concept. Materials refer to the type of media you use in your lessons, for example, videos, diagrams, or books. It is interesting to note that as the teacher you may be considered part of the media from which your students are expected to learn. Criterial tasks refer to the way you test your students and assign grades. The subjects are your students and their diverse characteristics.

Both teachers and researchers can use the tetrahedral model to frame important questions. Both might be interested in how learner characteristics interact with different forms of media. For example, do some students do better with computerized instruction than others? Both might be interested in how learner characteristics interact with criterial tasks or assessment procedures. For example, are there important gender or cultural differences that affect performance on some forms of assessment? The tetrahedral model provides a useful framework for considering how different variables affect learning.

Research and Textbooks

By knowing about and understanding theory teachers are better able to understand how and why their students learn. This allows them to make better decisions when planning lessons, when delivering a lesson, or when evaluating and improving on the effectiveness of a lesson. Knowledge of research allows teachers to understand the latest techniques and strategies and to incorporate those strategies and techniques into their own classrooms. However, it is not only teachers who can benefit from an understanding of learning; students may also benefit from such understanding. Good learners are, in a sense, their own teachers and make good decisions about what and how to study. By learning about how good readers learn from text you can help your students use their textbooks more effectively.

Mayer suggests that there are three different types of readers and that these types may be classified by how well they are able to learn from the texts they read. After reading a passage from a textbook some learners remember only a small amounts of the information and are unable to apply the information from the reading to new situations. Other learners can remember many of the facts and details of what they have just read, but are nevertheless unable to apply the information to new situations. Finally, some readers remember the main ideas from the reading and apply what they've read to new situations. The difference in these three groups seems to be in the way they mentally process the concepts from the material they are reading.

Starting from a constructivist/information-processing theory Mayer suggests that meaningful learning depends on how well learners perform three cognitive activities:

(a) selecting important information,

(b) organizing the information selected, and

(c) integrating the organized information with what they already know.

Readers who fail to select important concepts within the text are able to remember very little of what they read. Readers who are able to select the important ideas are able to recall what they read, but if they fail to organize and integrate the new material, they will not be able to apply the material to new situations.

Selecting Information

Selection refers to the process of focusing attention. In any situation, what is learned is determined by how attention is directed. Things we attend to are likely to be remembered, and things that do not attract our attention are more likely to be forgotten. Whether or not a reader focuses on some idea or concept depends on the reader's knowledge and the characteristics of the material being read . If the reader is familiar with a topic he or she is able to select important ideas from what is read. When the information presented is new, then the selections are likely to be less efficient. Authors can assist readers unfamiliar with the material by providing cues within the text that signal the importance of the concepts presented. In the current text, we signal the importance of a concept by changing the font, for instance, using either bold or italicized letters, by separating important concepts by bul-leting and by questions in the margins that can be answered by attending to specific facts or concepts within the text. As you read this text, attending to these cues will help you select those ideas that are most important. This in turn will prepare you for the next learning process, organization.

Organizing Information

Organization refers to the learner's creation of logical connections among ideas and concepts presented in the text. Research suggests organizing the information presented in a text helps learners form a mental representation or model that increases their ability to recall and apply what they remember. As with selection, organization also depends on the knowledge of the reader. But in addition to knowledge of the content, readers' abilities to organize the information from a passage also depends on whether or not they are able to recognize the underlying structure of the text. If readers are able to recognize these structures, they are better able to organize the new information.

Science texts, such as the one you are reading, have organizational structures that are different from those found in narratives. Cook and Mayer investigated whether training readers to recognize structure in scientific texts lead to better understanding. They found that even good readers benefited from learning how to recognize some of the common ways in which science books organize information. Some of the structures that appear in our text book include:

- *Generalizations.* This structure is built around a topic sentence that presents a main idea or concepts. Additional information in the passage describes various aspects of the main idea or provides examples. The key to organizing this type of passage is to identify the main idea and then understand how the additional information relates to that idea.
- *Sequence.* This structure describes a series of events or steps of a process. To organize information from this type of structure you first identify the topic, then list the steps in the sequence, and finally describe the change that occurs from one step to the next.
- *Classification.* This type of structure organizes facts, concepts, or events into categories. The structure is often hierarchical in that the passage may describe subcategories within categories. To organize this

information you first need to identify the main class or category, then find the subcategories, and note what distinguishes each subcategory from the others at the same level.

- *Compare and Contrast.* These structures identify the similarities and differ ences between two concepts. To organize this structure, you first must identify the two concepts being compared. Then list their similarities and differences.

Looking for these structures and using them to organize the information being read have been shown to increase readers' ability to recall and apply what they have read. As you read this text, be on the lookout for these types of structures. Headings, bullets, diagrams, and tables have been included to provide you with clues to help you find these structures and organize what you are reading. Developing coherent organization for the facts and concepts you have learned allows you to take the next step toward meaningful learning, integration.

Integrating Information

Integration refers to actions that learners take to find connections between new facts and concepts and things that are already known . As with selection and organization, the ability of readers to integrate new information depends on the reader's initial knowledge base. Obviously, readers cannot connect what they've learned with things they don't know, but even when readers have knowledge that could be usefully connected with the information presented in a text, readers may still fail to make the connection. In this case, there are text features that can help readers remember what they already know and make the connections. Examples of some of the text features that serve this function are analogies, examples, cases, and questions that remind readers of previously presented materials. You will find features such as these in this text. Remember, the purpose of these features is to help you integrate the information being presented.

Selection, organization, and integration are all actions that are under the control of the learner. What this means is that the meaningfulness of what you learn depends on choices you make. This text provides some your guidance for your choices and additional guidance is likely to come from your instructor. But ultimately, you must make the choice to learn and invest the effort needed to select, organize, and integrate what is presented.

References

Detterman, D.K. (1993) The case for the prosecution: Transfer as an epiphenomenon. In D.K. Detterman & R.J. Sternberg (Eds.), *Transfer on trial: Intelligence, cognition, and instruction*(pp. 1–24). Norwood, NJ: Ablex.

James, W. (1983). *Talks to teachers on psychology and to students on some of life's ideals.* Cambridge, MA: Harvard University Press.

Lucas, J.L.; Blazek, M.A. & Riley, A.B. (2005). The lack of representation of educational psychology and school psychology in introductory psychology textbooks. *Educational Psychology*, 25, 347–51.

Perkins, D.N. & Grotzer, T.A. (1997) Teaching intelligence.*American Psychologist*, 52, 1125–33.

Thorndike, E.L. (1912). *Education: A first book.* New York: MacMillan.

Woolfolk, A.E.; Winne, P.H. & Perry, N.E. (2006).*Educational Psychology* (3rd Canadian ed.). Toronto, Canada: Pearson.

2

Educational Psychology for Effective Teaching

There are certain things that make up a good teacher. Effective instruction (teaching) is a matter of one person with more knowledge than another transmitting it to the other. It is important for a teacher to:

- task-motivate their student
- merge the classroom
- assess prior knowledge of the students
- communicate ideas effectively
- take into account the characteristics of the learners
- assess learners outcomes
- review information

Good teaching can be taught. It has to be observed and practiced, but there are principles of good teaching that teachers should know. These can then be applied in the classroom. These major components are:

- Knowledge of the subject and teaching resources
- Critical thinking and problem solving skills
- Knowledge of students and their learning
- Teaching and communication skills

There are certain things that make a teacher outstanding at what they do. One of these things is called intentionality. Intentionality means doing things for a reason, or on purpose. Intentional teachers are those who are constantly thinking about the outcomes that they want for their students. They think about how each decision they make moves their students towards this outcome. They realize that being a good teacher and teaching a lot to a student does not happen by chance. They constantly ask themselves:

- What goals they and their students are trying to accomplish?
- Whether each portion of their lesson is appropriate to the studentsknowledge, skills and needs?
- Whether each activity or assignment is clearly related to a valued outcome?
- Whether each instructional minute is used wisely and well?

An intentional teacher uses a wide variety of methods, experiences, assignments and materials to be sure that their students are achieving all sorts of cognitive objectives. Along the way a teacher will make sure that a student is learning knowledge, creativity, application of knowledge, and affective objectives such as love of learning, respect for others and personal responsibility. The way that a teacher can become an outstanding teacher is related to teacher efficacy. Teacher efficacy is a teacher thinking that he or she is making a difference, and is at the heart of what it means to be an intentional teacher.

Educational Psychology and Teaching

It could be said that the educational psychology is the study of learners (students), of the process of learning and of teaching. It is the study of what makes a good teacher, the role of research in education, effective program development, development, theories of learning, the diversity of students, motivation and learning environments.

The role of research in educational psychology is to carefully examine certain questions about factors that may contribute to learning. For example, a research study may examine what type ofteaching method works best, and what decision a teacher may make about a problem or issue, to be most successful. Various teaching programs and theories of how to teach are also examined.

Computers used in the classroom are becoming a common strategy - especially when meeting the diverse needs of students. In a way the computer works as a tutor to present information, give students practise, assess their level of understanding and provide more instruction if needed. The question here is how effectively can computers teach? Most research done on this topic concludes that it has small to moderate positive effects on achievement. It is effective when used in addition to regular classroom instruction and has less effective results when it entirely replaces classroom instruction.

The way in which teachers are educated and supported to meet the challenges of the 21st century has become a contended issue. In raising alarm, criticizing the status quo, and making recommendations, various study groups and blue ribbon panels have focussed on economic issues, equity and excellence, the need for more rigorous subject matter preparation, and on the restructuring of incentives and the career ladder for teachers.

Although considerable agreement exists about the need for improvement in teacher education and professional development, wide differences of opinion are apparent about where to concentrate limited resources. These differences of opinion will probably persist as the recommendations and mandates of the 1980s become the legislation, regulations, and redesigned teacher preparation programs of the 1990s. But whatever programs and designs emerge from the present period of scrutiny, research, and revision in teacher education, we are confident that each route to certification will include substantial attention to learners, learning, and human development. For, in the broadest sense, the roles and purposes of teachers will continue to focus on the facilitation of learning and development by each student, to the practical limits of teachers' abilities. Consider what one portrait of future teachers implies about their knowledge of learning and development. Such teachers would

> possess broad and deep understanding of children, the subjects they teach, the nature of learning and schooling, and the world around them. They exemplify the critical thinking they strive to develop in students, combining tough-minded instruction with a penchant for inquiry. ...Competent teachers are careful not to bore, confuse, or demean students, pushing them instead to interact with important knowledge and skill. Such teachers interpret the understandings that students bring to and develop during lessons; they identify students' misconceptions, and question their surface responses that mask true learning.

The above quote portrays a teacher who has deep knowledge of the psychology of learning, development, and instruction; who is able to apply and draw on this psychological knowledge in her own teaching; who is able to transform this knowledge when necessary to adapt to new learning situations and learners; and who is continuously adding to and developing psychological knowledge through informal inquiry, as well as through formal education. Thus, knowledge of the domain of educational psychology is central to the teaching enterprise and to the preparation of teachers.

It was less than a century ago that William James, in his *Talks to Teachers*, made the argument for including psychology in the preparation of teachers. At that time, psychology was an infant science with only the sketchiest understanding of the human learner and human cognition. Since then, educational psychologists have filled in much detail in the explanation of human cognition that James put forth:

The gist of the matter is this: Every impression that comes in from without, be it a sentence which we hear, an object of vision, or an effluvium which assails our nose, no sooner enters our consciousness than it is drafted off in some determinate direction or other, making connection with the other materials already there, and finally producing what we call our reaction. . . . The impression arouses its old associates; they go out to meet it; it is received by them, recognized by the mind. . . . It is the fate of every impression thus to fall into a mind preoccupied with memories, ideas, and interests, and by these it is taken in. This way of taking in the object is the process of apperception. . . . The apperceived impression is engulfed in this, and the result is a new field of consciousness, of which one part (and often a very small part) comes from the outer world, and another part (sometimes by far the largest) comes from the previous contents of the mind.

Although James' vision of the learner anticipated much of the work by contemporary educational psychologists on cognition and instruction, today educational psychologists have more to contribute to the teaching-learning enterprise than they did a century ago. For example, in the last decade research on learning has revealed a great deal about students' conceptions and misconceptions and has shown how the knowledge that students bring to the teaching-learning situation affects substantially what and how students learn. William James' broad and general claims about learning have been supported and elaborated by subject-matter specific research on teaching and school learning.

Although one prominent source of proposals for reform of teacher preparation, the Holmes Group, drew significantly on recent theory and research in the psychology of learning and teaching in portraying the ideal teacher, their report left the re-formulation of educational psychology as a course of study undefined. The Group's only caveat was that "professional courses of study in education should meet the standards of the core disciplines from which they derive; that is educational psychology must be sound psychology." Now that many institutions are attempting to build on such general recommendations to reform their teacher education programs, faculty need to begin to explicate, more specifically, the learning and teaching of educational psychology in the preparation of teachers for the 21st century.

Teaching of Educational Psychology

How should educational psychology be conceptualized in the new teacher preparation programs being developed in the United States and elsewhere? As we reflected on this question, we found that we drew heavily on the recent scholarly writing and theorizing of educational psychologists in the area of cognition and instruction. Moreover, we sense a growing awareness among educational psychologists of the need to reexamine their own discipline. Such a reexamination needs to focus not only on the learning and teaching of educational psychology but also on understanding how educational psychology as a course of study influences the knowledge of candidates in teacher preparation. The content and methods of educational psychology courses seem to be determined largely by the scope and sequence of educational psychology textbooks, which seem to reflect a static conception of educational psychology as a "foundation" in teacher education. Our reading of recent research and theory in cognition and instruction led us to begin to question this unexamined metaphor.

We found that what emerged was not a new "scope and sequence chart" for the teaching of educational psychology, but rather several interconnected questions and problems that might provoke our thinking and that of our colleagues as we begin to consider how educational psychology should be incorporated into revised teacher education programs. Each suggests inherent dilemmas for the learning and teaching of educational psychology. Some of these dilemmas may be resolved or managed by appeal to empirical research on teaching and learning. Others may yield to practical constraints or to local traditions, norms, and preferences. In any case, the time is upon us, as educational psychologists, to engage in thoughtful dialogue about what knowledge our field has to offer to future teachers and how that knowledge might be taught well.

Our questions confront both educational psychologists and teacher educators with four persisting problems of practice in preparing professionals for a changing profession: the problem of transfer or application of psychological knowledge, the problem of balance between general and content specific knowledge about school learning, the need to consider the knowledge and beliefs of prospective teachers, and the challenge of applying knowledge about teachers' learning to the teaching and learning of educational psychology. In short, the curriculum and the instructional approaches appropriate for creating an educational psychology for teachers in tomorrow's schools need examination in light of recent research on teaching and learning. In what follows, we use these problems to frame a discussion of issues to be considered in rethinking educational psychology as a foundation in teacher education.

Educational psychology is taught as a foundation course in most teacher education programs, and at least one course on the psychology of human learning is typically required for teacher certification by most states. Typically, in most colleges and universities teacher education majors take a course or courses in the psychology of learning, development, and instruction prior to taking their methods courses, practicum experiences, and to doing their actual teaching in schools. The pattern, sequencing, and methods of teaching educational psychology make implicit assumptions about teachers' knowledge about learners and learning. An underlying rationale for the timing and format of educational psychology courses is that teacher education majors need the basic factual information and conceptual knowledge of the psychology of learning, development, and instruction to be able to apply this knowledge in their clinical teaching experiences, in their methods courses, and, eventually, in their classroom teaching. Thus, the teaching of educational psychology as a foundation in teacher education has rested on certain classic but typically, unquestioned, psychological assumptions about the learning and the transfer of learning of the prospective teacher to teaching.

Educational Psychology as a Foundation of Teaching

From early attempts to extrapolate laws of learning from laboratory studies of animal learning to the present writers of contemporary educational psychology textbooks who still harken back to some "rather obvious principles known since the beginning of this century," educational psychologists have framed the problem as one of transfer of learning from one situation to another, or from in school to out of school. Gagné introduced the concepts of vertical transfer and horizontal transfer—two concepts that have affected significantly the content and methods of teaching educational psychology for the past two decades. In his theory of *vertical transfer*, Gagné posited the idea that learning of lower level skills in a learning hierarchy facilitates the learning of higher level skills in the hierarchy because they serve as prerequisites for those higher level skills as follows:

> In vertical transfer, intellectual skills exhibit transfer to "higher-level" skills, that is, to skills which are more complex. . . . The intellectual skill of multiplying whole numbers, for example, is a part of the more complex skills of dividing, adding, and multiplying fractions, finding square roots, solving proportions, and many others. Transfer to the learning of these more complex skills is dependent primarily on the *prior learning* of the simpler skills. The more basic skills must be "mastered," in the sense that they can be readily retrieved, in order for transfer to take place to the learning of the more complex intellectual skills. This principle is illustrated by the learning hierarchy.

While Gagné's description of vertical transfer seems to pertain more to the learner's procedural knowledge, Bloom et. al's *Taxonomy of Educational Objectives* sets forth a similar hierarchical model with the application of factual knowledge being dependent on prior learning of propositional knowledge and factual information. Thus, in an educational psychology course the prospective teacher might be taught the "definition of learning" prior to being taught the "principle of learning" on the assumption that the propositional knowledge—the definition—is necessary to learn the principle.

Gagné identified a second kind of transfer as lateral or horizontal transfer. He defined lateral transfer as generalization by the learner of what is learned in one situation to a new situation that differs from the situation in which the learning occurred. An example of lateral transfer in teaching would be learning a principle of child development in an educational psychology course and then applying that principle in teaching practice. Gagné argued that "There is evidently some advantage to having the learner practice the application of the skill to a *variety* of situations or problem contexts." By implication there must exist a knowledge base in educational psychology, including psychological facts, principles, and theories, of learning, development, and learners that the teacher education student would learn and then would be able to apply and transfer to the actual teaching situation.

In some ways, this dilemma is similar to that posed in the design of curricula for learning and teaching of reading and mathematics in elementary schools (e.g., should students memorize and learn basic number facts before they learn to use the number facts to solve real mathematics problems?). To illustrate, and to illuminate the choices faced by educational psychologists, we discuss briefly the learning and teaching of elementary reading and mathematics.

Learning Hierarchies and Transfer

In the past, most teaching in elementary reading and mathematics has rested on the assumption, derived primarily from task analyses and behavioral psychology, that students must learn the lower order facts and skills before going on to master higher order problem solving and application skills. In contrast, recent theory and research from cognitive psychology call this idea into question:

> This assumption—that there is a sequence from lower level activities that do not require much independent thinking or judgment to higher level ones that do—colors much educational theory and practice. Implicitly at least, it justifies long years of drill on the "basics" before thinking and problem solving are demanded. Cognitive research on the nature of basic skills such as reading and mathematics provides a fundamental challenge to this assumption.

For example, computational skills may not exist as lower order prerequisites for higher order mathematical problem solving, but rather are learned in relation to, and as part of, the problem solving activity. Ample evidence also exists that both top-down and bottom-up processes are involved in reading.

An important point is that new information to be learned and taught needs to be related in a meaningful way to knowledge and information that the learner already knows. Thus, instructional content and practices ought to relate new knowledge in a meaningful way to the knowledge that students have already developed. This means, for example, that reading should be taught with a basis in meaning and that mathematics computation should be taught in the context of problem solving. What does this rethinking of elementary reading and arithmetic teaching and learning imply about educational psychology for prospective teachers? If learning involves both top-down and bottom-up processes, then a hierarchical model in which educational psychology is a prerequisite or a foundation in teacher education is inconsistent with the best psychological research and theory.

Researchers are also questioning the notion of horizontal transfer and the relationship of in-school and out-of-school learning. For example, researchers have discovered instances where students have learned and can perform complicated mathematical procedures with understanding in an out-of-school setting. In contrast, mathematical procedures that students learn in school often do not transfer to the out-of-school setting. This notion of knowledge as contextually situated calls into question the basic notions of how to facilitate learning in school being used and applied later by the student in real-life situations.

Although concepts of vertical and horizontal transfer have affected the teaching of educational psychology as a foundation for at least two decades, we need to reconsider them as well as the content and methods of educational psychology in light of several alternative framing assumptions that have emerged from recent research on cognition and instruction. These include the notions that thinking and cognition are situated in physical and social contexts, that thinking and learning are situated within the contexts of personal and social epistemologies, beliefs, and understandings; and that learners have "strong potential capabilities for cognitive growth that enable complex and subtle processes of construction of knowledge and thinking skills." These alternative framing assumptions are related not only to the substance of what is traditionally taught and learned, but also to the methods by which learning is presumed to take place. Given these alternative framing assumptions, researchers have begun to think differently about knowledge and about the thinking and learning of children and youth in school and out.

Just as we are beginning to think differently about the development of children's knowledge and about the learning and thinking of children, we may also need to begin to think differently about the development of teachers' knowledge about learners, learning, and development and about how we facilitate the learning and thinking of teachers through teacher education. In doing so, we need to consider how these alternative framing assumptions fit with our developing understanding of the psychology of teachers' knowledge and thinking and the contextualized nature of that knowledge and thinking.

TEACHERS' KNOWLEDGE OF LEARNING

An important beginning question is how to think about teachers' knowledge of the principles and theories of learning and development that define much of the domain of knowledge in educational psychology that is relevant to teachers. Such knowledge is what comprises most of the texts currently used in educational psychology courses for teachers. It includes what Shulman has referred to as knowledge of learners and their characteristics—as well as aspects of what he has identified as pedagogical content knowledge:

> The conceptual and procedural knowledge that students bring to the learning of a topic, the misconceptions they may have developed, and the stages of understanding that they are likely to pass through in moving from a state of having little understanding of the topic to mastery of it. It also includes knowledge of techniques for assessing students' understandings and diagnosing their misconceptions.

The above knowledge clearly concerns the psychology of learning even though it is embedded within a specific subject or content area. Relevant knowledge also includes teachers' content-specific cognitional knowledge or teachers' awareness of the mental processes or cognitions by which learners acquire subject-specific knowledge through classroom learning.

To illustrate a possible way in which educational psychologists might think differently about the knowledge that teachers need to develop about the psychology of learning, we use as an example from recent research that Peterson conducted with her colleagues Thomas Carpenter and Elizabeth Fennema at the University of Wisconsin-Madison. In this study researchers tried to make accessible to teachers some knowledge from psychological research on children's learning of addition and subtraction. Because recent research had shown the importance of initial knowledge, researchers began by asking to what extent teachers already have this knowledge:

(a) What do teachers know about the distinctions that young learners naturally make between addition and subtraction problems types? and

(b) What do teachers know about the strategies that children use to solve different addition and subtraction word problems?

They assessed teachers' knowledge through questionnaires and an interview and found that, in general, most of the 40 first-grade teachers were able to identify many of the critical distinctions between addition and subtraction word problems and the primary strategies that children use to solve such problems. However, teachers' knowledge generally was not organized into a coherent network that related distinctions between problems, children's strategies, children's solutions, and problem difficulty. Given that it took many years of research for psychologists to arrive at such knowledge, perhaps it is not surprising that teachers did not have this in-depth and coherent network of knowledge of young childrens' learning of addition and subtraction.

In a subsequent experimental portion of the study researchers showed that by working with these teachers and giving them access to recent research knowledge from on childrens' thinking processes in learning addition and subtraction, the teachers' knowledge base was enhanced. Rather than teaching addition and subtraction facts and computations, experimental teachers taught addition and subtraction within the context of story problems. Experimental group teachers were more knowledgeable about childrens' learning processes than control teachers who had not participated in the workshop. By observing these teachers in their classrooms during the following year, researchers found that experimental teachers were able to use this knowledge to assess their childrens' thinking and to modify their instruction in addition and subtraction. Children in experimental teachers' classes were better at solving complex addition and subtraction story problems than were children in control teachers' classes and were more confident of their ability to do so. Children in experimental teachers classes also knew the addition and subtraction facts as well as did children in control teachers' classes.

These research findings have two implications for our present discussion of the knowledge of educational psychology that is relevant to teachers. First, the research demonstrates that there is new, emerging knowledge of the psychology of children's learning of mathematics. By being given access to this knowledge, teachers modified their knowledge and understanding of children's mathematics learning, changed their classroom instruction, and improved their childrens' mathematics problem solving and learning of number facts. The research demonstrates the importance of contextualized or situated knowledge of the psychology of childrens' learning to the continuing education of teachers who are then able to facilitate the meaningful learning, understanding, and problem solving of their students. Left for further thought and discussion is the question of how to provide such integrated knowledge and practice in the education of prospective teachers who typically do not have daily access to teaching young learners and who typically do not learn educational psychology within the context of their actual teaching.

Second, the findings suggest a possible evolution in the boundaries of the domain of educational psychology that is relevant to teachers. According to this conception, educational psychology would include subject-matter-embedded knowledge of the psychology of learning and development, as well as more general knowledge of theories of learning and development. A related implication is that in teaching educational psychology, educational psychologists need to work more closely with subject matter specialists, just as they have in the development of this knowledge through research. Although the above discussion refers to the psychology of learning mathematics, the same argument might be applied to other subject areas, for example, reading and science.

Third, the research of Peterson and her colleagues was based on the idea that children's learning of addition and subtraction is a process of active construction of knowledge. In working with the teachers they took the same view of teachers' learning as a process of active construction of knowledge. Such a view presents an interesting dilemma for educational psychologists who have often used a lecture approach to teach constructivists theories of learning.

Active Construction of Knowledge

Over the past decade, educational psychologists studying children's learning and cognition have provided extensive evidence that "problem solving, comprehension, and learning are based on knowledge, and that people continually try to understand and think about the new in terms of what they already know." More and more psychologists are viewing learning as a process of active construction of knowledge by the learner. Such a constructivist view of learning stands in sharp contrast to passive reception or absorption psychological models of learning that have dominated educational practice for decades. Most of this research on knowledge has focused on young learners and has dealt with the specific content areas of reading, science, or mathematics such as in childrens' learning of arithmetic. Although researchers have done some cognitive analyses of the subject matter knowledge of teachers, they have not yet done similar cognitive analyses of the prior knowledge and learning of educational psychology by teachers. Such research might be conducted to understand how students in teacher education come to construct knowledge actively in the domain of educational psychology.

In addition to the assumption of learning as active construction of knowledge psychologists have proposed, as a framing assumption, that thinking and learning are situated in contexts of beliefs and understandings about cognition. Thus, for example, a teacher's learning is situated within the context of her beliefs and understandings of what she considers knowledge and understandings to be. We return to an example from our own research to illustrate one way in which psychology knowledge might be connected to teaching through the teachers' active construction of knowledge. Our example also illustrates how teachers' learning and thinking were situated within the context of their beliefs about children's knowledge and their own beliefs about what knowledge and understanding are. Although others have attempted or are attempting similar endeavors, we provide this example because it is one of which we have personal knowledge.

In the yearlong activity described above, Elizabeth Fennema, Thomas Carpenter, and Peterson worked with a group of first-grade teachers to change their practice of mathematics in teaching addition and subtraction in ways compatible with recent findings from psychology. From clinical interviews with children, psychologists have found that before young children enter school they have significant knowledge and abilities to solve many simple word problems by using counting strategies that they have already developed. Although the researchers worked with teachers through a traditional mechanism of a staff development workshop during this summer, the staff development activity itself was unusual because they focused the workshop on giving teachers access to knowledge about a wide variety of word problems and the informal knowledge and strategies that young children have to solve these problems. Teachers were then encouraged to use the knowledge, think about it, construct their knowledge, and plan and change their first-grade mathematics instruction based on this knowledge. The research findings shared with teachers were rather precise—a taxonomy for thinking about types of word problems that reflect both psychologists' and childrens' thinking about these problems, as well as, examples of strategies that children use to solve these problems. The researchers did not prescribe precisely the way in which teachers would take this knowledge and construct their own classroom instruction.

In the work with first-grade teachers described above, researchers viewed the staff development workshop with teachers as only the beginning of a process of knowledge construction and learning for the teachers. During the workshop, teachers viewed videotapes of actual children solving problems in addition and subtraction. Then each teacher interviewed a child, gave the child different types of word problems, and then asked the child how he or she solved the problem. Thus, beginning in the workshop, the teachers gathered evidence and tested for themselves to ascertain that children entering first-grade *do* have knowledge and strategies for solving word problems. When teachers began teaching addition and subtraction to their own classes, they further tested these ideas with their own students.

During the summer when viewing the videotapes, many teachers regarded some of the videotaped children as exceptional and were skeptical childrens' informal knowledge and abilities to solve certain kinds of problems. However, when teachers began posing problems to their own students in the fall and, listening carefully, and seeing for themselves their own students' abilities to solve problems, they found out that the children they had seen on the videotapes during the workshop were not exceptional and that their children had knowledge and strategies for solving many types of word problems.

Teachers came to see that children can solve different problems by counting or modeling the quantities and relationships between the quantities and the problem with physical objects. This knowledge then served as a "hook" into expanding teachers' understanding of children's informal and formal mathematical knowledge and thinking. Teachers' beliefs about children's knowledge changed most fundamentally as a result of asking kids to solve word problems aloud during class and then listening to the strategies that children use to solve those problems.

The teachers who became most knowledgeable about their own students' mathematics knowledge and strategies in solving word problems and who also held most constructively oriented beliefs about childrens' knowledge tended to adopt a personal and active constructivist view of the learning process and of childrens' mathematics understanding. An example is Ms. Jennings who seemed to redefine her work as a teacher "to include on-the-spot clinical research into the way a learner thinks about something." In an interview, Ms. Jennings gave an almost up-to-the minute description of the knowledge of a particular first-grade child in her class:

> I was working with Cheryl the other day, and she had 12 cubes in her hand. The problem was Ms. Riva had 12 carrots, and she made three carrot cakes. She needed to divide them equally into each cake. And you know, Cheryl had these cubes, and go, go, go—she snapped it off real quick. I said, "How did you get that so quickly?" And she goes, "Oh, you know the numbers, you know—first there were three. If you put three cakes, three carrots in each cake, and then I had nine. But if I add one more, that would be four." So they [the children] are thinking. It's just so sophisticated. It just seems to come together for them.

Teachers who experienced the workshop differed in the extent to which they knew and believed that children enter first grade with useful problem-solving knowledge. Some teachers like Ms. Jennings, Donaldson, Taylor, Miller, and Pruitt clearly knew and believed that children have their own knowledge. For example, Ms. Pruitt referred specifically to children's knowledge as their own, and Ms. Jennings described the sophistication of her students' own knowledge. Donaldson noted how questioning, listening to, and observing children's problem solving strategies made her "realize how many children can do these things [problem solving] in different ways" and that "we were trying to mold them into one of way of doing that. It's exciting to see what they [children] can do without us molding." In a very real sense, these teachers began engaging in psychological research into their own students' mathematical thinking.

These five teachers were the highest among the 20 workshop teachers in having cognitively based or constructivist-oriented beliefs about children's knowledge. However, even these teachers varied in the extent to which they were in classroom process. We did find that these five teachers were significantly higher than the other teachers in the amount of time they spent listening to processes that their students were using to solve problems. These teachers were taking seriously the processes the children use to solve problems and were attending to the knowledge that their students had. Ms. Jennings, the most constructivist teacher in her classroom practice, clearly listened to determine the knowledge of mathematics that her students had, and then she used that information to decide what to teach, given where the child was in his or her thinking.

Providing an insight into how very personal and experiential this knowledge, Ms. Jennings also illustrates clearly how her own thinking about children's knowledge is situated within the context of her understanding of what it means to understand mathematics. Before the workshop, when asked what kinds of problems she had her first graders solve, Ms. Jennings said only that she had her students work problems that could be solved by answering the question, "How many do you have altogether?" In order to solve these problems, she said that she would teach the kids to focus on the word "altogether" and what that means. Interesting, psychologists as well as mathematics educators have sharply criticized this "key word approach" because it focuses on a mindless or rote approach to problem solving rather than on conceptual understanding of the problem. When asked why she had her students learn that kind of word problem in addition and subtraction, Ms. Jennings replied, "Because I didn't learn how to solve them; and word problems were always hard for me. It was like, `how do you even attack a problem like this?'"

The kinds of thinking in which teachers engaged are similar to the kinds of examples that Donald Schon provided in describing teachers' reflection-in-action. Magdalene Lampert and Eleanor Duckworth reported similar insights into teachers' thinking and on-the-spot clinical research into the way a learner thinks about something. They described the thinking, beliefs, and understandings of teachers engaged in the Teacher Development Project at the Massachusetts Institute of Technology organized around the concept of teacher as psychological researcher. This project is another example of an alternative approach to connecting psychological knowledge to teaching. In this project two cognitive psychologists, Jeanne Bamberger and Eleanor Duckworth, endeavored to make Piaget's theories and research accessible to teachers. They constructed musical, mathematical, and physical tasks for the teachers (for example, keeping track of the changing phases of the moon) that were meant to make teachers more conscious of the usefulness of their own intuitive knowledge. They demonstrated clinical research methods with children, and they led discussions with teachers of the use of these methods in the classroom.

One of the important similarities between the projects is that in both the Wisconsin project and the Teacher Development Project teachers came to understand a constructivist viewpoint *not* through being lectured to about Piagetian or constructivist learning theory. Rather, teachers' learning was situated within the context of specific activities and tasks. Often teachers worked on these activities together in groups. In both projects teachers began to ask questions intended to illuminate how their students were thinking; to ask questions that would help them as teachers understand how students were interpreting a problem and to capitalize on the knowledge that students' have; and to think of students' questions as a way of gaining insight into how a student was making sense of an experience or situation. In both projects the emphasis was on understanding children's conceptions, *not* misconceptions. This may be an important difference between these projects and others that focus on changing students misconceptions.

For example, Monk and Stimpson found that teachers' focus on students *mis*conceptions rather than students' conceptions tended to be related to teachers' desire to "teach" or "tell". They noted, as did Lampert in describing the Teacher Development Project teachers, that teachers had found it difficult to assume the role of researcher as one of diagnosing or understanding students' intuitive knowledge and how the student was making sense of something. Teachers tended to focus on students' *mis*conceptions rather than students' conceptions and intuitive knowledge. They often felt a need to assume their role of teacher when they construed as telling formal knowledge or as alleviating students' misconceptions.

These examples demonstrated how teachers' learning was situated within the context of their personal epistemologies. In these projects, what teachers were learning in psychology was inseparable from how they were learning and was connected inextricably to their insights into their own leaning. The growth of teachers knowledge in these projects demonstrates the development of thoughtful teaching of the kind portrayed in recent reform reports.

Psychology of Teachers' Learning

In their recommendations for reform in teaching and teacher education, both the Carnegie Forum Task Force and the Holmes Group portray the new vision of thoughtful teachers as ones who are engaged continuously in the process of learning; are "able to learn all the time"; and who view learning and development as a lifelong process for themselves and their students. Just as the field of educational psychology has been affected by advances in cognitive psychology, the field of developmental psychology has been transformed in recent years by a life-span developmental perspective that argues for a view of teachers as professionals who continue to learn and develop throughout their teaching careers.

In developing this capacity for continuous learning, teachers may benefit by knowing not only something about how other teachers learn, but also by reflecting on their own processes of learning. If teachers are to become thoughtful professionals, they need to have both meta cognitive knowledge for classroom learning as well as meta cognitive knowledge for classroom teaching. The former involves learners' self-awareness of their own cognitions through which they acquire information, gain understanding, and learn in the classroom. Metacognitive knowledge for classroom teaching includes self-awareness and ability to reflect on one's own cognitive knowledge for classroom learning, as well as ability to reflect on knowledge about classroom teaching. Although little research has been done on such metacognitive knowledge of teachers, many researchers, including educational psychologists, are now suggesting that teachers' self-awareness and deliberate action are important aspects of teaching expertise that need to be studied.

The above discussion illustrates the centrality of knowledge of the psychology of teachers' learning. In reflecting on this topic, we propose three points for consideration: first, that the psychology of teachers' learning constitutes an important new domain of knowledge in educational psychology; second, that the knowledge of theories and research findings on the psychology of teachers' learning may be meaningful and important for students in teacher education, and further, may enhance their teaching practice; and finally, that knowledge of the psychology of teachers' learning may enhance the ability of faculty to teach educational psychology more effectively in teacher preparation programs.

Although the subject of teachers' learning was the focus of some early studies by educational psychologists learning to teach more than a decade ago, educational psychologists have tended not to focus on teachers' learning as an important area of study. Only in the past decade have educational psychologists turned their attention from the study of teachers' behavior to the study of teachers' thinking, cognitions, and knowledge. The studies by Leinhardt and Putnam (of networks of teachers' knowledge and script theory) and of Lampert (on the role of teachers' understanding of subject matter and interpretation of what students mean) are most salient. One can begin to see that research why and how teachers come to behave as they do. This literature and that of other researchers on teacher thinking have explored the many ways in which teachers think, plan, and decide, and how teachers' work is constrained by the world in which teachers operate. Using psychology to understand the teacher in this way might make contact with teachers in powerful ways. Such psychological windows into teachers' thinking or psychological lenses for examining teaching also open up new possibilities for metaphors that convey new ways of thinking about how to connect psychology to teacher education.

Researchers studying teachers' thinking and teachers' knowledge have typically used cross-sectional rather than longitudinal approaches and thus have not examined teachers' learning or the development of teachers' thinking over time. More recently, educational psychologists and teacher educators have begun working together to conduct a longitudinal study of how teachers' learn to teach. They are studying the development of teachers' knowledge, skills, and dispositions related to teaching writing and mathematics in 11 different teacher education programs over a three-year period. They are also examining teachers' beliefs including their conceptions of knowledge. This research represents an ambitious new effort and the methods as well as the findings may be useful to educational psychologists who want to study the learning of students in their own teacher education program.

Because both research on teachers' thinking and research on teachers' learning is relatively recent, not much of the content and findings from this work have appeared in contemporary educational psychology textbooks. Even though findings from this research have not yet appeared in textbooks, these topics may constitute an important content domain that should be learned and taught in educational psychology in teacher preparation programs. Knowledge of the psychology of teachers' learning might contribute to the effective teaching of educational psychology in two ways. First, such knowledge would be useful as educational psychologists begin the process of conceptualizing the learning and teaching of educational psychology in the preparation of teachers for the 21st century. Second, such knowledge would be particularly informative as educational psychologists think about the possibility of adapting the content and methods of educational psychology to the individual learner.

Teachers and Adaptation of Educational Psychology

A final question concerns how to adapt the content and methods of educational psychology to the individual learner—the teacher—to facilitate the meaningful learning and application of that learning to teaching practice. The problem of transfer is central to this discussion. Although some deeply entrenched notions of transfer have dominated the teaching of educational psychology for two decades, recent research on cognition and instruction suggests the need to think differently about it. For example, if cognitive research suggests that first graders come to know and understand addition and subtraction best within the context of a real-world story problem relevant to their lives, then the teacher should begin with the story problem to teach the addition/subtraction number facts and problem solving. The student is simultaneously learning number facts (what would have been called a lower order skill) while solving a story problem (what would have been called a higher order skill). Similarly, the story or word problem (which would have previously been conceptualized as a transfer or application activity) serves as the context for learning computation and problem solving (which would previously have been thought of as the in-school skill.)

The use of word problems as the context for children's learning of addition and subtraction has come from years of comprehensive research on children's learning of addition and subtraction. Unfortunately, similar research has not yet been done on *teachers'* meaningful learning and application of educational psychology. Recent work on everyday learning, learning outside of school, and the contextualization of cognitive tasks has demonstrated the importance of context in affecting meaningful learning, task performance, and application to a work environment. Thus, we can only speculate and propose the following for consideration: Just as childrens' meaningful learning and application of mathematics skills is facilitated by teaching-learning within the context of real-life mathematics problems, teachers' meaningful learning and application of knowledge and theories in educational psychology may be facilitated by teaching and learning educational psychology within the context of real-life teaching-learning problems or cases. Recently, some educational psychologists have suggested that the study of cases may serve as a basis for meaningful learning and teaching in teacher education. Cases have long been used effectively in the education of lawyers as well as physicians.

In the context of the learning and teaching of educational psychology, a case might represent a realistic learning-teaching problem in a classroom. Thus, such cases for teachers in educational psychology would be similar to the real-life story problem experience of the first grader learning addition and subtraction (or of the medical student or law student learning to problem solve in a complex, uncertain task environment). Cases might take the form of print, text, video or audio recordings, jointly witnessed field experiences, or role-played simulations of a learning-teaching problem. Although the advocates for use of cases are increasing, some scholars are more cautious and are urging systematic study and analyses of how to facilitate students' knowledge growth and learning from cases.

One such systematic study was completed recently by Karen Stoiber at the University of Wisconsin-Madison who taught educational psychology to preservice teacher education majors using written and videotaped cases depicting dilemmas in classroom management. She assigned preservice teachers in educational psychology randomly to one of several approaches to teaching classroom management. At the beginning and end of the course, she assessed preservice teachers' knowledge, beliefs, and thinking using interviews and questionnaires. She found that the use of cases was particularly effective in the context of the learning and teaching of strategies aimed at reflective decision making. In this approach preservice teachers were encouraged to develop their own teaching schemata or representations for classroom management. Self-questions, inner-directed speech, and examples of reflective processes were provided to scaffold the teachers' development of their own representations of classroom management.

Cases were used in two ways. First, they were used in the context of decision making training. In this situation class members worked in pairs, and each pair member read a vignette about a classroom management situation that ended with a problem or dilemma. One member was instructed to act as a reflective decision maker who reported decision-making thought processes while the other acted as observer who critiqued her/his partner's reflective processing. Cases were also used by the instructor to lead discussions aimed at guiding participants to use specified reflective decision making processes to analyze a depicted teacher's handling of a classroom management event. In another approach (the technical skills approach), cases were used to teach and illustrate technical principles of classroom management derived from research by educational psychologists.

Stoiber's findings are provocative. Although teachers who experienced reflective decision making were not taught technical principles, they knew these principles of classroom management by the end of the course as well as did students in the technical principle group. Also, in contrast to students who learned the technical skills approach, students taught the reflective approach showed better understanding and processing of classroom situations when confronted with a videotaped case that posed a real classroom management dilemma. Stoiber concluded that the learning and teaching orientation in the reflective decision-making approach did more to facilitate sophisticated cognitive processing and thinking by the preservice teachers than did the orientation in the technical skills approach.

Although we have little research to go on, we are encouraged by Stoiber's research, by our own teaching experiences, and by the work of others to believe that cases may provide a meaningful context within which the student in educational psychology might learn and apply educational psychological knowledge. Cases provide a mechanism for shared thinking and construction knowledge in a group situation. Each student in educational psychology will see the same case differently because each brings different knowledge and beliefs to the experience. Thus, students in educational psychology, even when viewing or reading the same case, will construe the case or think about it in terms of their past and current teaching-learning experiences. Sharing of individuals' thinking about cases and arguing and justifying different interpretations may be particularly powerful ways of promoting thinking and reflection in prospective teachers. Moreover, individual cases might be selected and tailored to individual students of educational psychology. Although adaptation to the individual learner has long been advocated by educational psychologists, the development and use of educational psychological knowledge by students in teacher education may depend on educational psychologists listening to their own advice.

The Problem of Adaptation

Facilitation of transfer is often a reason for adapting content and methods of educational psychology to the individual learner. If the content and methods of educational psychology were adapted completely to the needs of the individual student in teacher education, the student would have little work to do to transfer or transform the information and content of educational psychology in order to learn and apply educational psychology to teaching. A relevant question becomes, "To what extent should the content and methods of educational psychology differ significantly for the elementary teacher who is going to teach first graders compared to the high school teacher who is going to teach mathematics to ninth graders?" As we have seen, cognitive research has demonstrated that specific subject matter knowledge plays an important role in learning and thinking. Thus, for the ninth grade mathematics teacher, at least part of the content and methods of educational psychology needs to focus on learning and teaching of mathematics in ninth grade. However, the ninth-grade math teacher also needs to understand more general issues of learning and development.

In teaching educational psychology, educational psychologists are faced with a fundamental dilemma: whether to offer an educational psychology that is primarily concerned with prospective teachers' own learning and development, or one that is primarily concerned with the learning and development of school children. Prospective teachers are adult learners and should be taught as adults. But they need to learn and know theories of learning and development relevant to the children and youth they will teach. A teacher-as-adult-learner approach to educational psychology would have educational psychologists teach in ways consistent with the learning and teaching processes that beginning teachers themselves should use in their classrooms. Possibly, even if teaching and learning are situated or domain-specific, teachers will deduce some principles from their adult learning experiences and will apply these principles to the actual situation in which they would teach.

Many constructivist approaches to working with teachers begin by having the inservice or preservice teachers work on learning tasks or solve problems themselves. Out of these experiences and insights into their own thinking and learning, teachers develop beliefs and understandings about cognition that may carry over to the way they think about the knowledge and understanding of their children as they teach. Alternatively, a psychology-of-young-learners approach suggests that students of educational psychology should study content and methods dealing primarily with specific children and school situations to be later encountered on the job. This second approach runs the risk of missing the mark when teachers find themselves working with students and in situations that differ in important ways from those they experienced during teacher preparation.

In sum, the problem of transfer and adaptation to the individual learner and teaching situation remains a fundamental dilemma that faculty need to consider as they conceptualize educational psychology in the new teacher preparation programs. We suggest that one possible technique that might be considered is the use of cases as described above. As faculty begin to design and use new techniques and methods, such as the case method, we hope that they also conduct research and collect data on the learning of teachers in these new, innovative educational psychology courses.

Issues and Challenges

Theory and research suggest that meaningful learning and application of educational psychology might be facilitated by closer collaboration between educational psychologists, teacher educators, and subject matter researchers. But the reward structure for faculty in research universities will need to change both to promote closer collaboration between these educators and researchers and also to encourage faculty to spend time and effort on working to design innovative approaches to teaching educational psychology in the context of teacher education within real classrooms and schools.

If we are to advance in our knowledge of the learning of educational psychology as a discipline, then we need to apply methods similar to those used to study childrens' knowledge and cognition to the study of learning by students in teacher education. Researchers might determine, for example, "What knowledge of and beliefs about learning and development do learners hold when they begin their study of educational psychology?" Certainly, by the time students in teacher education reach college, they have developed their own informal notions and theories of learning as a result of having been learners themselves for a number of years. In addition, researchers might ask, "How are teachers' general and subject-matter-embedded theories of learning related to their meaningful understanding and application of knowledge in educational psychology?" "How do teachers' knowledge and theories change through a course of study of educational psychology?" and "How is teachers' psychological knowledge—subject-matter-specific and general—related to their classroom practice and teaching?" As educators of learners, as well as researchers on learners, we may face the same dilemma noted by Monk, Stimpson, and Lampert. Like the teachers in their studies, we as teachers may find it difficult to focus on understanding our teacher education students' conceptions and informal knowledge, rather than on alleviating their misconceptions and on teaching formal knowledge related to educational psychology, even though as researchers, we are able to assume the stance of diagnosing and understanding teacher education students' knowledge and conceptions.

A new metaphor or metaphors are needed for the learning and teaching of educational psychology in teacher education. The metaphors need to convey the way that psychological knowledge is viewed and the way in which psychological knowledge can be connected to teaching. For example, the metaphor might convey the view that knowledge of basic facts and general principles of learning and their application to the problems of teaching are interactive and interdependent and that meaningful learning depends on relating the new knowledge from educational psychology with the teacher's already existing knowledge. Attention must be paid to the conceptualization of both the knowledge that the teacher education student brings to the learning situation and to the changes expected in the teacher's knowledge as a result of studying and learning educational psychology. A *web*, *network*, a *dialogue*, and a *lens* all are possible metaphors to consider in thinking about the learning and teaching of educational psychology.

References

Bloom, B. et.al., (1956). *Taxonomy of Educational Objectives: The Classification of Educational Goals, Handbook I: Cognitive Domain*, New York: Longmans.

Gagné, R. M. (1975). *Essentials of Learning for Instruction,* Hillsdale, Ill.: Dryden Press.

Resnick, L. B. (1987). *Education and Learning to Think,* Washington, D.C.: National Academy Press.

Slavin, R. E. (1988). *Educational Psychology: Theory into Practice.* Englewood Cliffs, N.J.: Prentice-Hall.

3

Practical Applications of Educational Psychology

The practical application of psychology to the problems of the schools is relatively recent. It is only within the last threequarters of a century that anything approaching a coherent science of Child Study has begun to develop, and the foundations of a scientific psychology of education are more recent still. Nevertheless, the conception of Child Guidance as a service of expert advice to parents, teachers and children themselves in the best ways of directing or re-directing the child's mental development has been a feature of educational writing for many centuries. In the works of Plato, Castiglione, Ascham, Comenius, Rousseau, Pestalozzi and Froebel, to name but a few, will be found explicitly stated the notions of education and educational method as constructive processes of guidance aimed to help each child achieve the fullest possible expansion of his personality and the fullest realization of his potentialities. Though the current jargon is not used, "Child Guidance", "Preventive Mental Hygiene" and a great many other ideas which underlie our modern attempts to apply educational psychology to the improvement of the education of the individual child, preceded, sometimes by centuries, the development of the scientific knowledge necessary to implement them.

Scientific child study, the parent of educational psychology, is a science which owes little to that "general psychology" which was the offspring of philosophy or to the physiological psychologists led by Wundt who concentrated upon a man as a neurological mechanism. Its origins are to be found in the work of the evolutionary biologists of the latter half of the nineteenth century. In 1877, Darwin published in *Mind* his "Biographical Sketch of an Infant", a work based upon careful and objective observation, which was hailed by Taine as "pointing the way to a new field of science". Similar studies followed: by Perez, Compayre and Queval in France, and by Preyer in Germany.

On the continent, the work of Herbert Spencer had an even greater influence than in Britain. Taine's book on *Intelligence,* avowedly an attempt to state the Spencerian point of view, was the starting point for the later work of Binet. These studies emphasing as they did the biological nature of man gave the beginnings of an empirical foundation to the view points expressed both by Bain and by Spencer twenty years earlier.

In 1884, Francis Galton opened his anthropometric laboratory and laid the foundations of the mental testing movement and of much else beside. Galton advocated the study of the individual child with a view to practical recommendations about his treatment at home, at school, and as an aid to subsequent vocational guidance. He stressed and began to investigate the differences, genetic and environmental, between individuals; and his laboratory, finally established at University College, London, may be regarded as the earliest psychological service or Child Guidance Centre, antedating by ten years the first similar organization (that of Witmer) across the Atlantic and by more than thirty years the first so-called Child Guidance Clinics.

The notion that psychological differences between children could be scientifically measured and made the basis of practical predictions and recommendations, was enthusiastically taken up by teachers themselves, notably by Dr. Sophie Bryant, a biol-ogist and headmistress of the Camden High School for Girls, London. Towards the end of the century, Sully, Professor of Mind and Logic at University College, London, opened the first psychological laboratory in Great Britain. It was there that William McDougall, his Assistant and Director of the Laboratory, began systematic observation and experiments with individual children. Courses were conducted that were attended by school inspectors like Winch, Kimmins and Ballard, the pioneers of those steady attempts at the reform of English education to make it more child-centred, which took place in the first decades of the twentieth century.

As a result of this and much other activity led principally by Galton and Sully, the *British Child Study Association* was founded in 1893 with the support of London teachers, inspectors and education officials. One of its primary objects was "to study the normal as well as the abnormal, paying special attention to the investigation of the commoner cases of minor deviations among normal children, as well as to the diagnosis of the rarer abnormal or pathological types". Sully contended that "medical science is more familiar with the rare but striking cases of mental disease and defect; mental science, on the other hand, though it has learned much from the suggestive analogies that may be drawn, has already shown that during childhood at least, the vast majority of cases consist of deviations *within* the normal range rather than aberrations *from* the normal. "Hence", he added "we need a new kind of specialist—a psychological specialist in fact" who should have a gift of sympathetic insight and a specific psychological training based upon a knowledge of general psychology and methodical practice in the application of the scientific methods of psychology to the study of individual children.

The foundation of the Child Study Association in London was followed by the establishment of branches elsewhere and by the inclusion of courses in "Child Psychology", "Individual Psychology" and the like in the syllabuses of University departments of Education and Philosophy. A centre like that of Galton was begun under McDougall's influence at Oxford and later Burt, a pupil of McDougall, started similar work in Liverpool with the co-operation and support of the education authority and the courts. Six years later on the initiative of school inspectors and of the Child Study Association, the London County Council set up within its Education Department the first official psychologists' office, and Cyril Burt was appointed as psychologist to the Education Authority.

From the commencement of his work in Liverpool, Burt devoted his attention to research into all the practical problems of the schools and especially to an exploration of the psychology of individual differences so important for the adaptation of education to the rhythms of child growth. As early as 1903, he was devising measures of higher cognitive processes through tests of Opposites, Analogies, Syllogistic reasoning and the like — types of test which still hold the field as the best measures of verbal intelligence. In 1911 he advocated the combination of such tests into a group test of general intelligence. He thus carried Galton's work further and laid the foundation of the mental measurement movement as applied to education. From the date of his appointment to the London County Council, his "Reports of the Psychologist to the London Council" begin to cover all the practical aspects of a functioning service as we now come to know them. He devised individual and group tests of educational attainment, and investigated the distribution and relations of educational abilities among school children, concerning himself with educational and vocational guidance; and began his classical studies of backward children and of young delinquents. From the early twenties, the influence of his empirical studies and still more of his capacity at once to develop a theoretical basis for child study and to express this in practical educational terms, began to influence the official publications of the Board of Education.

Burt's various contributions to the development of psychological services in England are difficult to overestimate. Perhaps in the long run his broad methodological contribution will prove to be the most valuable. From the outset he combined the observational case study method with group studies firmly based in an experimental and statistical framework. He set the abnormal individual against a background of normal growth and development; and his two great works on the *Backward Child* and the *Young Delinquent* are a masterly demonstration of the value of control groups in any investigation of human psychological characteristics. The service which he created set a pattern of close co-operation with the schools, of investigation by rigorous scientific methods of the practical problems of education, of the treatment of individual cases and of the integration under the guidance and inspiration of the Psychologist's office of the many special educational facilities of a large authority—a pattern which still dominates the best services in England.

Burt's work, first in Liverpool and then in London, was so successful that similar methods were adopted in many other areas both in England (Leicester and Stafford) and in Scotland (Edinburgh, Glasgow and Aberdeen). It was not until after the first world war, seven years after Burt's appointment to the L.C.C. and thirteen years after he had begun his work in Liverpool, that Crichton Miller established the Institute of Medical Psychology, subsequently renamed the Tavistock Clinic. Later still, the Jewish Health Organization started the East London Clinic under Dr. Emmanuel Miller. Both of these, lacking the close integration with the schools and their problems and the research orientation, at once practical and yet rigorously experimental, which Burt had given to the L.C.C. service, remained essentially psychiatric and preoccupied with the abnormal.

Very similar developments had been taking place in Europe, and especially in France. In 1894, the *"Societe libre pour VEtude de I'Enfant"* was formed in Paris; and shortly afterwards, impressed by the ideas of Galton, Binet published his series of papers on *La Psychologie individuelle.* In 1905, in conjunction with Vaney, he established a *"Pedagogical Laboratory",* and proposed to the Minister of Public Instruction a comprehensive scheme for the examination of subnormal children which included physical, medical, educational and psychological examinations with a report on social conditions. In 1904, he established the first version of his famous intelligence scale. In Germany, Meumann, Stern and Bobertag were also doing much to provide the theoretical background of child psychology and guild guidance. The three volumes of Meumann's lectures on experimental pedagogy (published in 1904) had a profound influence on English work, as well as on work elsewhere. Later Stern's Institute of Applied Psychology and his journal attracted great interest. But practical applications remained at first sporadic and tentative and were in many European countries almost entirely neglected.

In Italy, however, as early as 1899, Sante de Sanctis, recognizing that psychiatry was not the only, or even the most important, discipline involved in the guidance of abnormal children, initiated a cross disciplinary approach. In his *Asili Scuola per Anormali Psichici* he instituted a consultation based upon a team which included, as well as the psychiatrist, a specialised teacher, a psychologist and a social worker. Thus by nearly a quarter of a century de Sanctis anticipated the concept of teamwork in the diagnosis and treatment of severely abnormal cases put forward by the proponents of Child Guidance Clinics in the United States. His initiative, however, remained, in spite of the efforts of Montesano, Yidoni, Montessori, Banissoni and Cacchione, without sequel in Italy.

In Switzerland, a more propitious start was made. In 1900, Claparede interested himself, at the demand of a young teacher, in the educational problems of a class of subnormal children. In 1904, in the *Signal de Geneve* he published a series of articles on "La Psychologie de l'enfant et la Pedagogie experimentale" —the first sketch of his book of the same title which appeared in 1916. In 1906, he began his *"Seminaire de Psychologie pedagogique"* which was ambitiously planned to cover practical educational psychology, physiology, the health of the school child, and the pathology of childhood. At first it was accepted as part of the course of teacher training but after a year had to be abandoned, to the great regret of the practising teachers of Geneva, because of opposition from the Faculties of Arts, Science and Medicine.

However, undaunted, Claparede in conjunction with Bouvier, Milliourd and Pierre Bovet opened in 1912 the "Ecole des Sciences de l'Education", later the "Institut des Sciences de l'Education" at Geneva. Space does not permit full justice being done to the immense contribution of the Institut to the development of experimental education and child study. To it however we owe much of the dynamic of educational reform in the first decades of the century and, through the International Bureau of Education its later offshoot, many contemporary concepts of international technical co-operation in the field of education. From the outset, Claparede and his remarkable collaborators foresaw that the basis of the sciences of education was child study in all its aspects, and that training must go hand in hand with functioning services and continuing research. Consequently the years from 1912 onwards saw the training of teachers, psychologists, social workers and specialised educators of many kinds grow alongside a programme of basic research in most of the aspects of child psychology, educational psychology and scientific pedagogy. Particularly of interest in the present context were the *consultation midico-pedagogique* and the *Cabinet d'orientation professionnelle.* The latter, inspired by developments in'Belgium, concentrated upon the twin aspects—that of a psycho-social case study of the individual child and that of the detailed psychological study of each vocation. The former, established in 1913, was preoccupied from the outset with all those problems of a child's growth which might interfere with his educational progress. Quite early in its existence, it experimented with parent education, an initiative subsequently developed by the Ecole du Mail, and, from 1916 onwards, had associated with it, special remedial classes for retarded children.

Clapardde's initiatives were not without official sequels. In 1920, Hegg established in Berne under the Department of Education of the city, *La consultation pedagogique de la ville de Berne.* Eight years later, a school psychological service which included in its functions problems of delinquency and of vocational guidance, as well as a considerable task of public education, was begun in Basle—roughly contemporary with the

Laboratoire de pedagogic et de psychologie de Venfant at Angleur in Belgium.

In America, Stanley Hall, recently returned from Wundt's laboratory at Leipzig, founded in 1891 the *Pedagogical Seminary,* the first journal devoted to educational psychology and child study. In 1904, he published his great work on *Adolescence* which is remarkable for the number of empirical studies on which it is based and for its insistence on the genetic, biological approach. J. M. Cattell, who had studied in England under.

Galton, encouraged his pupil Witmer in 1896 to open a "Psychological clinic" at Pennsylvania University. Meanwhile another of Cattell's pupils, E. L. Thorndike, published his *Educational Psychology* for long a standard text book. Baldwin in 1921 published the first of the University of Iowa studies in Child Welfare on "The Physical Growth of Children from Birth to Maturity". In the main, however, the American psychologists, under the influence of Titchener and Watson, remained strongly attached to the intellectualistic and associationist standpoint, ignoring or explicitly rejecting the emphasis on the child's emotional life, upon education, and upon the influence of unconscious motives. It is not surprising therefore that in the earlier American clinics, the function of the pychologist came to be identified almost entirely with the application of intellectual and educational tests. It was the leading psychiatrist of his day, Adolf Meyer, who, incorporating much of the thinking of the British biological school, and of the views of Janet and Freud, termed his field of work "psychobiology". In 1909, a year after Burt had begun his studies of adolescent delinquents in Liverpool, Healy, a pupil of J. M. Cattell and William James, and a follower of Meyer, began his study of delinquents in Illinois. In the same year, Beers founded the *National Committee for Mental Hygiene.* This latter in the early nineteen-twenties turned its attention from conditions in mental hospitals to the psychiatric study of delinquent and difficult children and with financial support from the Commonwealth Fund set up a number of "Child Guidance Clinics" to combat delinquency.

It was not until 1928 that, financed by the Commonwealth Fund, the first so-called "Child Guidance Clinic" was set up outside the United States—in England. Originally, at the suggestion of Burt and Nunn, this was intended to provide the widest form of psychological service to schools, parents, teachers and children and not merely to concentrate upon the treatment and prevention of delinquency or upon "problem children". It thus represented a step forward on the original American conception; it bore an interesting resemblance to Claparede's consultation in Geneva, and embodied the fruits of the experience already gained by Burt under the L.C.C. Early in 1932 however this demonstration clinic became a separate entity from the Child Guidance Council and developed a narrower pattern in which a sharp distinction was made between the functions of psychiatrist and psychologist, a movement away from the European conception towards the then current American one. As the Director, Dr. W. Moodie, stated it, psychology was considered to consist of knowledge of the "structure and operation of intelligence" and psychiatry claimed to consist of "knowledge of the essential mechanisms involved in all forms of behaviour, normal as well as abnormal". This led to an attempt to limit the psychologist's functions to the application of intelligence and educational tests together with the coaching of children experiencing difficulty in any school subject. The study of the affective and conational aspects—that is of the emotional life, the evaluation of behaviour and the study of personality as a whole—was held by Dr. Moodie to be the province of the psychiatrist.

It need perhaps hardly be said that no leading psychologist in England ever accepted this view. But the fact that it could be and still is put forward in Europe and elsewhere, illustrates one of the major points of disagreement within the guidance movement itself in most countries, a difference of view which has given rise to different conceptions of work, to differently stated objectives, to differences of structure and staffing as well as to certain interprofessional tensions. The more moderate views put forward by most of the writers taking part in the recent symposium in the British Journal of Educational Psychology, by the Committee on Clinical Psychology of the Group for the Advancement of Psychiatry of the American Psychiatric Association, and by the Conference on Graduate Education in Clinical Psychology held at Boulder, Colorado, 1949, have done much to smooth the passage towards effective collaboration. Moreover, as the various professions concerned, become themselves better trained, gain greater insight into the complexity of the problems involved and into the nature of each others' competencies, and learn by experience of working together, relationships at the personal and local levels have improved markedly.

Trends of Development

There still remain however fundamental differences of emphasis, on both the practical and theoretical levels, and it is probable that the future lies with a combination of types of service or with a service which is genuinely polyvalent. After somewhat more than a half century of research, we still lack adequate surveys of the needs of communities, of schools, of children and of their parents; our knowledge of child development, of the psychology of the educational process, and of the nature and causes of maladjustment is incomplete and for a large part unsystematised. This accounts both for some of the heat which is generated in discussions as to the functions of various services, and for the variety of types of guidance service and their experimental nature.

Most services have grown up in response to a felt need; and the demands have arisen independently in a variety of circumstances. Historically the first and in many ways the most extensive needs are those experienced by the schools. The teacher confronts, daily, problems of intellectual and other differences among his pupils, the difficulties of the dull or abnormal child, the failure of a child who is backward in one subject or technique, aberrations of behaviour towards the too aggressive or the too submissive extremes.

As educational systems provide more opportunities of choice, the guidance of pupils becomes more and more necessary; and at the end of full time schooling, there are the problems of vocational guidance and integration into working life. In daily and prolonged contact with a considerable sample of children, the teacher is well placed to carry out guidance, and to detect what is "abnormal" in the sense of unusual. His preoccupation is at once with the development of the individual and with the growth of the whole group emotionally and socially, as well as educationally.

It is not surprising therefore that the educator insists primarily upon the guidance of the normal child, upon the psychology of the educative process and upon the positive use of the school, its methods and its atmosphere to maximize the potentialities of each pupil. The teacher too, by the very nature of his experience, tends to recognize how wide are the confines of the "normal". It will be remembered that the pioneers of child study, in England, France and Switzerland, and elsewhere, early insisted that aberrations within the normal range are more important numerically and practically than aberrations from the normal. Without unduly minimizing the contribution of psychopathology, it can with some reason be contended that the principal contributions both to the fundamental concepts of guidance, conceived of as implicit in a sound education and in the practice of aiding children to adjust and adapt to their environment, have come from the educators themselves.

Most of the basic research and many of the experimental services, have come from professors of education who were psychologists like Nunn'and Valentine, from practising teachers and school inspectors like Ballard, Sophie Bryant, Cousinet, Ferriere and Freinet, and from the pioneers of scientific child study and the techniques of psychological case work, measurement and research like Binet, Burt, Claparede, Susan Isaacs, Meumann, Piaget, Stern and Wallon.

A second line of approach is more specific and starts from the education of the mentally subnormal. Claparede recalls that it was a demand for help from a teacher of very dull children which set him off on the line of thought which culminated in his courses in educational psychology for teachers. Binet in France, Decroly in Belgium and Montessori in Italy began in much the same way.

Medical men had long been interested in children whose intelligence was either so impaired by physical or physiological defect or injury or for some genetic reason so markedly below normal that they could not develop like others. Fairly early the severe cases (idiots and imbeciles) and some of the less severe were segregated in institutions for physical treatment and care; and in many countries this tradition of segregation and of exclusively physical treatment persists.

It is only comparatively recently that research with mental tests and the results of specialised education have drawn increasing attention to the fact that *pathologically defective* children are relatively rare and that the vast majority of children who experience severe difficulty in ordinary schools are subnormal in their intellectual functioning rather than defective. They represent deviations within a range of continuously varying differences in intellectual ability which includes the highly intelligent at the other extreme. They are not a group apart. Moreover careful investigation has revealed the existence of a relatively larger group—about 10 per cent of children of school age—whose ability demands a modified curriculum and whose greatest need is for careful educational guidance, without which many develop into emotionally and socially malajusted individuals or even into delinquents.

From the preoccupation with mental subnormality has arisen in most European countries a service of special institutions for markedly subnormal, often outside the educational system; and in some—as in France, Holland, the United Kingdom and Switzerland—a system of special schools and classes for the educable subnormal. The practical educational work of Decroly in Belgium, of Descoedres in Switzerland, of Seguin and Itard in France, and the more recent activity of Heilpadagogik, a form of remedial education, under Professor Moor of Zurich, have all contributed to give a considerable impetus to this work and to wider problems of educational method and educational guidance. This, in its most advanced form, is seen in the differentiation of provision which is a growing feature of many educational systems which now tend to include special classes for the dull, for those with educational difficulties of a kind which respond to a brief period of special teaching (classes de rattrapage, opportunity groups, remedial education, and the special classes for those with reading difficulties in the United Kingdom, in Denmark and in Sweden). It should not be forgotten either, that general educational method has gained as much from practices developed first in schools and classes for the subnormal as it has from pioneer work in the nursery, kindergarten and infant schools.

Thus the guidance of the mentally subnormal child, beginning mainly as a means of excluding the "ineducable" from school, on the basis of a medical examination only, based often on so called "stigmata" is becoming less an affair of exclusion, and more a process of global assessment—physical, social, psychological and educational—and of the selection of the appropriate form of educational treatment. Further, though in most countries, practice and administrative provision lag well behind actual knowledge, there is an increasing tendency to see that a complexity of causes underlies the whole problem of educational maladjustment, and that a great flexibility both in guidance concepts and in provision is necessary.

A similar trend is to be observed in relation to delinquency. More and more in most European countries the courts have tended in the last few decades to seek information on the intellectual, emotional and social circumstances of children and adolescents brought before them and to develop, either under the Home Office (Ministry of the Interior) or under the Ministry of Justice a system of social and remedial services, centres of observation and the like. Earlier conceptions of "moral deficiency" of the "born criminal" marked out like the defective by stigmata have ceded to a less over-simplified theory of multiple causation, of prevention by social, educational and psychological means. The work of Burt in Liverpool and London, begun in 1907, of Healy at the Juvenile Court of Cook County, Illinois, begun in 1909, began to draw attention to the existence not only of psychiatric causes—psychosis, severe neurosis, psychopathic temperament and the like—but to causes related to environment, parental discipline, minor emotional disturbance, educational and vocational failure; and to point out that delinquency was a legal conception which did not correspond to a distinguishable psychological entity. The fact that an adolescent or a child committed what the law regarded as a crime has come slowly to be regarded as an indication that something is wrong with the individual's adjustment. American Child Guidance as embodied in the demonstration clinics, opened in St. Louis and Norfolk in 1923 by the National Committee on Mental Hygiene, and supported by the Commonwealth Fund, was originally essentially aimed at "the psychiatric study of difficult, pre-delinquent and delinquent children in schools and juvenile courts; to develop sound methods of treatment based on such study; and to provide courses of training along sound lines for those qualified and desiring to work in this field". This original idea of a "delinquency clinic" with psychotherapy as its only or main method of cure rapidly enlarged in America but was in fact never fully accepted in England or indeed in Europe generally where from the outset stress was laid upon environmental, developmental, educational and social factors in causation and consequently in remedy. We may just briefly indicate another trend of development, which is the outgrowth from adult psychiatric practice and particularly from the out-patient departments of psychiatric hospitals. Here the influence of the psychobiologic and$_t$ dynamic schools of psychology and psychiatry has had the effect of turning attention to the importance of experiences in childhood and adolescence in the causation of mental disease, adult psychosis and psychoneurosis. Consequently many such departments began to interest themselves in childhood problems and in not a few cases, in the late twenties and early thirties, established rudimentary services of "child guidance" as a part of their function.

Types of Services

These trends which have not fully converged in Europe, the impulse given to the more psychiatric type of service by the Commonwealth Fund and by the American training received by a number of European psychiatrists, accounts for the variety of concepts, organization, administration and finance that one finds in the whole field of guidance. Fundamental differences of view and preoccupation between the medical and educational professions, problems of jurisdiction between ministries of education, health and social welfare, and the like tend to perpetuate separate and sometimes partial services. In the different European countries some one or two of the kinds of service described below and, in some few, all kinds, exist; and in general where there are adjacent services, functional cooperation is good. Not infrequently however, while in practice differently conceived and staffed services work together, behind the scenes administrative and interprofessional struggles hinder the fullest development of genuinely comprehensive guidance for all children.

That which comes nearest to serving the needs of all children at least during school age is the system of the *school psychologist* which is found in some European countries. Under this method of organization, the psychologist, usually an experienced teacher with a considerable further training in educational psychology, has his office in one large school or group of schools to which his attention is exclusively devoted. He acts as adviser to his colleagues and to the Head or Director of the school on all matters which affect the development and progress of the pupils, individually or collectively. Frequently he works alone; in certain countries or circumstances he may have, in addition to his psychological duties, responsibility for a class. Sometimes he has a trained assistant as a secretary-tester. Where there are also school social workers, attendance officers, or welfare officers, they may be integrated into or closely associated with his services. In some cases, the psychologist can count on the services of a school medical officer as well as those of a social worker in his team.

As might be expected from his close association with the schools, and from the relatively small population with which he has to do, the school psychologist has as a primary aim the improvement of the atmosphere of the school, the improvement of methods of teaching, and the guidance and adjustment of the ordinary child. Thus school record cards where they exist are either established and maintained by him or completed under his supervision. Not infrequently educational guidance fades imperceptibly into vocational guidance under this system and the school psychologist conducts the group tests and where necessary the individual tests, on the basis of which he acts as the psychological member of the vocational guidance team. He is also concerned with subnormal, failing, maladjusted, or delinquent children and may undertake individual or group remedial work of various kinds, though usually, at any rate for serious cases, he would call upon outside help. It is he also generally who maintains contacts with the outside agencies who become involved with individual children—with the juvenile courts, the social welfare agencies, psychiatric units and the like—and with the parents. In many ways, notably in the numbers of staff involved if the service is extended on the basis of one psychologist even to 1,000—1,500 pupils, this is a solution de luxe.

A second type of solution rather similar to this but more thinly spread is the psychologist's office or Child Guidance *Centre.* The psychologist is not attached to any school or group of schools under this system but provides a service for the educational system of a district. His responsibility administratively is to the Director of Education or other principal local administrator. In its most developed form, this type of service operating from a centre where examination of individual children and remedial work of various kinds can be undertaken, has access to all the educational services of the community. Within its orbit therefore fall not only the work of ameliorating the methods and atmosphere of the ordinary schools, the general guidance both educational and vocational of children of school age, and the examination and treatment of various types of problem children, but also a task of advice and psychological supervision undertaken in all types of special school and class.

It will be noted that the emphasis in this solution, as in that of the school psychologist, is placed upon *constructive* mental health through research into education at home and at school, through the dissemination of information and through preventive and remedial work with individual children undertaken at the earliest possible moment. The "therapy" employed is in general educational and environmental; much of it is undramatic work undertaken slowly to assist the teachers or parents to carry out their task in a more effective fashion, and based upon a relationship of confidence between teachers, parents and psychologist in which the latter is regarded as a friendly consultant rather than an authority from outside taking over a "case".

These solutions are essentially urban and depend for their effectiveness either upon the large school unit or upon a central laboratory or office readily accessible to schools, pupils and parents. In rural districts, in parts of Europe where populations are scattered and the schools small, travelling psychological services have been tried with success. These are based either directly and ad hoc on the school needing help, or operate from a number of part-time centres in different areas. Inevitably such services tend less to stress the needs and guidance of the ordinary child and to undertake more action of a diagnostic, advisory or remedial kind with individual problem children. Because of the large population served, such services can only indirectly undertake such activities as systematic school surveys, experiments with improved educational methods, and general teacher or parent counselling. Nevertheless because they work in the schools themselves, they bring skilled aid to places which would otherwise be inaccessible. Coupled with adequate provision for special boarding schools and hostels, they provide the most effective solutions for areas of scattered population.

In completing this sketch of types of organization and orientation which spring principally from an educational and psychological view-point, we should perhaps mention services with more restricted objectives which in fact undertake guidance in various countries. Many schools and school systems have begun to develop systems of school record cards intended as the basis for the educational guidance of school children. Such cards or cumulative records are not in universal use but will be found in schools in Austria, in parts of France, the United Kingdom, and elsewhere. Frequently they originate from a psychological service or are built on the basis of research in educational psychology, and are intended as an instrument by which the teacher himself may fulfil the many of the tasks of the guidance of his own pupils. A necessary complement is of course a serious effort to train teachers in the use of these and other methods of objective child study and observation.

In some countries, specific problems of school adaptation have been made the starting point either for a direct ad hoc action or as an essential part of existing psychological services. Special attention has for example been devoted to certain phases of school life where children, teachers and parents have most need of guidance. Thus in Austria, in Norway and in Sweden, great attention is devoted to determining by tests, observation and other means, each child's readiness to begin formal schooling. In the United Kingdom, particularly since the 1944 Education Act, there has been the tendency to attempt to make of the examination at eleven which comes at the end of the primary period, a means of guidance among alternative types of secondary education rather than an instrument of selection for a particular type. So, too, countries like Belgium, Holland, France, and Yugoslavia, which have highly developed systems of vocational guidance, have tended to push the guidance process further and further back into the child's school life and to recognize effectively that vocational guidance is a continuous process and stems from educational guidance. One of the more interesting examples of this type of thinking is *"Le service ^orientation scolaire et universitaire"* of the French University Statistical Bureau described on pages 58-59. In a somewhat similar way, in Belgium for example, comprehensive types of school psychological service have developed from services of vocational guidance which have come to realise that guidance of a child at one point of his career is dependent for its success on what has happened before and that those cases which give the most difficulty in adolescence are just those which might have been discovered (and remedied) earlier.

The types of organization so far described are mainly educa-tional in their inspiration and directed more or less broadly to the problems of the schools. Though the distinction is not a sharp one—and as time goes on and experience accumulates the view-points tend to meet and exert a mutual influence— there are also types of organization which are mainly psychiatric and medical in their origin. Such services tend, at least at the outset, to concentrate upon delinquent, difficult and maladjusted children and to aim at an intensive diagnosis and treatment of a relatively small number of cases. Few of them rest at this, unless other services are already undertaking broader tasks, and many have preventive programmes aimed at the dissemination of knowledge of child development, parent education, collaboration in the training of teachers and so on.

In most countries of Europe, frequently under the inspiration of the Child Guidance Clinics, are to be found *Centres midico-psychologiques, medico-pedagogiques,* or *midico-psycho-pedago-giques* as they are variously called. Many of these operate with the classical team of psychiatrist, psychologist and social worker, some with psychiatrist and social worker only, and are more or less strongly psychiatrically—and often strictly psycho-analytically—oriented. Sometimes they are attached to the outpatient departments of hospitals and, not infrequently, there is no psychologist and they are largely "neuropsychiatric clinics" or "mental health clinics"— with little interest or competence in the educational field. They may have a relatively restricted clientele, confined to more serious cases and they tend to serve a considerable area rather than to have close functional contacts with local services of various kinds for children. Where circumstances are favourable however—as they were for example in the Child Guidance Clinic at Hill End Hospital, St. Albans, U.K., or the Mental Health services in Amsterdam, Holland—the work undertaken overflows the psychiatric field and, either through collaboration with school psychological and medical services or through direct contact with the schools, devotes some at least, and with the most highly developed services, much of its time to preventive as well as diagnostic and therapeutic work.

In many countries, such clinics have been set up, out of private funds, by University Departments of Medicine, Psychology or Education, by Education Authorities, by Health Authorities or by Hospitals. In some countries—in France for example—the *Centres medico-psychologiques* depend upon a semi-voluntary body itself subventioned by the State and at the same time receive payments upon a case basis from Ministries of Health, Welfare or Education according to circumstances. In others, conventional Child Guidance Clinics exist side by side with School Psychological Services where these are organized; and the fact that each may depend upon a different administrative authority and be financed from a different budget does not necessarily lead either to a duplication of services or to a lack of functional relationship.

There is no need here to describe the aims and function of the typical Child Guidance Clinic with its threefold team, usually psychiatrically directed and adapted peculiarly to the diagnosis and treatment of severely maladjusted, neurotic and psychotic children. Many such descriptions exist. Europe however has seen some interesting and significant developments which, by adaptation to local circumstances and needs have, in spite of administrative and financial limitations, succeeded in providing a wider service. One of the pioneers of the formula in Europe, and a more ambitious and wider spreading example is that begun by Dr. Andre Repond in 1930 in the Canton of Valais, Switzerland.

Problems of School Psychology Services

These few examples indicate the variety of inspiration and objective which underlies European developments in the general field of guidance. The picture is somewhat obscure because almost nowhere has finance and staff been forthcoming to develop all aspects of any service, educational or medical, as seen by its creators. Thus many services which would like to emphasize their preventive role have been pressed into a kind of first-aid activity and are obliged to concentrate upon diagnosis and the treatment of a relatively small number of cases; whilst others recognizing the need for constructive work through schools and other community services have not had the funds or skilled personnel necessary to undertake the long-term research, the training and the propaganda which seem to be essential. Only too often, no matter what the point of departure, guidance organizations by the sheer weight of need in comparison with resources are thrust back into a task of a short-term though pressing kind and are unable to develop the longer-term aspects of what they conceive to be their main purpose.

Another great problem—perhaps the key to the whole matter—is that of finding suitable, and suitably trained, staff. Many of the partial realisations owe their one-sidedness as much to the limitations of the training of those who run them as to other factors. The skills and insights of the educational psychologist,—who, it is now coming to be agreed, must have both educational and psychological training and experience—demand a lengthy, carefully contrived and intensive training. There are relatively few centres in Europe where such a training may be obtained. Although many universities offer the necessary basic courses in psychology and education, few indeed as yet have been able to develop the post-graduate, practical and theoretical training through experience in an actual service which is clearly necessary.

Moreover, the combination of University studies, of teaching experience and of subsequent training and work under supervision, is one which puts a great financial burden on the student. Many women and more men hesitate to undertake such a training in countries where vocational outlets for psychologists may be limited to some kind of auxiliary status or be rendered insecure because no legal or administrative recognition has yet been granted to their profession. Child psychiatry too is a very recent development of psychiatry and medicine, and possibilities of training in Europe are similarly limited.

So far the specialized teachers, social workers, play therapists, psychotherapists, speech re-educators and the like necessary to a full service can be recruited only ad hoc from among those who shew interest and pick up a training here and there largely by their own talents and industry. Although almost everywhere some kind or kinds of services are beginning or extending their work, in fact the day of the brilliant amateur is by no means over.

Nevertheless for the educational psychologist, centres of training do exist and standards of qualification are growing up in Europe. It is now generally agreed, though by no means enforced without exception, that as well as a sound university training in psychology, the psychologist who is to work in contact with the schools should himself have had considerable experience of teaching. In the United Kingdom, the Committee of Professional Psychologists insists upon an honours degree in psychology, teacher training and at least one year's teaching or other equivalent experience with children and young people. It insists too upon a minimum age of twenty-five before the intending educational psychologist undertakes his one year course of practical training, and withholds recognition until the trainee has successfully passed a further year working under a more experienced psychologist in a service. There are of course exceptions made to this rule; moreover the standards adopted are recommendations only, and local education authorities and other bodies sometimes make appointments of those who do not have such minimum qualifications.

On the other hand, University training centres, such as that at University College, London or at the University of Birmingham, often set their standards higher and may require, in particular, a longer experience of teaching. In the Scottish Universities intending educational psychologists are drawn from the ranks of expe-rienced teachers who pursue studies at the post-graduate level for the degree of B. Ed.

In France, school psychologists are recruited from the ranks of primary and secondary teachers who have had at least five years of successful full-time teaching experience. They pursue a course spread over two years in the *Institut de Psychologie* of the University of Paris leading at least to the Diploma in Educational Psychology *(Diplome de psycho-pedagogie)* and in most cases to the Diploma in Applied Psychology as well *(Diplome de psychologie appliquee)*. Many have in addition other diplomas—as teachers of backward children, vocational guidance officers and the like.

Elsewhere in Europe (e.g. Austria, Denmark, Norway) similar standards of qualification and training are becoming established. University Centres such as the *Institut des Sciences de VEducation* (University of Geneva), the Departments of Education and Psychology at the University of Utrecht, the

Department of Psychology of the Free University of Berlin have set up services of demonstration and research in which the practical training of educational psychologists may be undertaken concurrently with theoretical studies. So too institutions exist, under the State or under Universities—such for example as the Erica Institute in Sweden—for the training of such specialised staff as play-therapists; and others, in most countries, to train teachers for handicapped, maladjusted, subnormal, retarded and other categories of children as well as to conduct courses for teachers interested in the general problems of the guidance of normal children and the identification of those for whom some form of special education or remedial treatment is necessary.

Educational Psychology Services in Europe

Many of the types of service and many of the trends of development so far discussed exist side by side in the various countries of Europe. Almost nowhere are services as fully developed as those well acquainted with the problems would wish and in few do they cover the whole country. The picture is one of experimentation and of fluctuation.

Some of this is due to the difficulty of estimating needs, and of bringing into relation with a service, all those individuals and organizations which have something to contribute; partly it is because needs and problems which have existed for years do not make themselves overtly felt until a new service has demonstrated its utility and won the confidence of teachers and parents. A common experience is for a small service rapidly to be overwhelmed with demands for assistance the moment it becomes known, and to be left with very little time or staff available for the necessary preventive and constructive tasks which alone will in the long run diminish the load of cases for diagnosis and treatment.

Conversely where the level of teacher training is high and where a service can collaborate in the training of specialised social workers, remedial teachers, educational and vocational guidance officers, many of the tasks which it may have to assume initially, can later be delegated effectively, allowing the psychological staff to fall into a consultative, coordinating and research role except for those cases requiring expert attention.

The essential nature of a good psychological service is its adaptability and sensitivity to needs; and it is just this that does not shew in official reports or in research papers; nor would an elaborate tabulation of case loads, staffing or other administrative data provide the answer. The following descriptions therefore of the services in certain countries must be regarded as illustrative of existing initiatives and concepts rather than as a series of evaluative studies.

Austria

In a great many ways, Austria presents the picture of a country where psychological services have a considerable history and where, since the end of the last war, educational reform has been accompanied by an extension and systematization of guidance services. Those concerned with the welfare of children have steadily become more and more aware of the complexity of the problems which have to be faced and solved. The classical fields of behaviour difficulty, emotional and intellectual abnormality, delinquency and the like continue of course to attract attention and help. Increased emphasis however is being put on various more subtle and less spectacular aspects of preventive and remedial work. In recent articles in the official publication of the Ministry of Education *(Pddagogische Mit-teilungen),* attention is drawn to the needs for educational and vocational guidance, to the problems of general and specific retardation, backwardncss and school failure, to the need for research into the age at which children should begin school, and into the difficulties which may be experienced by children transferred from one class or school to another.

Similarly a great effort has been made to increase the facilities for special educational treatment. The number of specialised teachers was estimated at some 800 in 1952—double the number that existed in 1945. Nearly 500 special classes for rather more than 8,000 subnormal children, six schools for some seven hundred deaf, eighty five special classes for 1,500 maladjusted children, four institutions for the blind, thirteen classes for partially sighted, and eleven for speech defectives, are now established and represent a considerable provision for exceptional children. Only the needs of the physically handicapped seem not to be adequately met and it is estimated that some 200 such children do not receive the necessary special educational help. The school psychological services, as well as other guidance organizations, have close connections with special schools in their area. In one province (Salzburg) special guidance services exist for the deaf and for the mentally subnormal.

Since 1922 the provision of an adequate form of cumulative school record card for use by teachers, the school medical service, and the services of educational and vocational guidance, has been recognized as a basic step. Immediately after the war the experimental forms used before the war in a few schools were modified and improved, and in 1949-50 the system was introduced into all State Schools and made compulsory by ministerial decree. This record form which systematises social, educational, physical and psychological data on each child, depends for its effectiveness upon the knowledge and skill particularly of the teachers. It is on this basis of growing preoccupation with all forms of guidance that school psychological services proper have developed in the postwar period in the capital and in some of the provinces.

In a report made in 1947-48 the Federal Ministry of Education estimated that some 750 specially trained teachers were employed on psychological work, in the ratio of one to 150-400 pupils between the age of 10 and 14. Their task was that of examining each pupil in these age groups once a year as the basis of educational and vocational guidance and of examining other pupils as necessary. Since then, cautiously, the services have been developed until their type may be illustrated by that of Vienna, directed by Dr. Schenk-Danzinger, and founded in 1948 under the auspices of the education authorities.

It is staffed by six psychologists, two social workers and a medical consultant and works in five rooms set aside in a school building. Its principal tasks are the discovery, examination and treatment of learning and behaviour difficulties in children, of maladjustments of all kinds, and advice to teachers, schools and the educational administration. The main means of remedy at the disposal of the service are the guidance of a child to a special class or school, aid to the teacher in handling the problem himself, referral of certain cases of marked social or family difficulty to welfare agencies, psychotherapy, remedial education on a part-time basis for children with specific difficulties, and a small continuing class for slow developing children *(Foider-klasse)* under a specialized teacher. In addition, the service conducts a weekly consultation for parents in three of its schools.

The important feature of this service is its close connection with the educational system generally including the special schools and classes of the City and its environs. The psychological and educational examination of each child referred is preceded by a detailed report from the teacher and supplemented by a careful family study. When the case study is completed, a report is sent to the teacher and to the school inspector responsible, along with recommendations for further action if required. An idea both of the caseload of the service (apart from and in addition to the more general and preventive work undertaken) and of the way in which demand has grown is given by the fact that in 1948-49, 180 cases were undertaken as compared with 1,280 in the year 1954-55, the large majority referred by the teachers themselves.

Most of the provincial services are not as fully developed and staffed. That however of Upper Austria, directed by Dr. Sparowitz, has many interesting features. Recognizing that much of the effectiveness of a psychological service depends on the level of understanding, training and cooperativeness of the teachers themselves, the psychological staff assist in the initial training of teachers; and, in 1951-52, they ran a thorough training course in Linz for selected, experienced teachers who become psychological counsellors to their schools and, in cooperation with the psychological service, undertake much of the first line discovery of problems, and remedial education. The service also provides a "parents' school" and, in conjunction with the vocational guidance servicc, ensures the continuous guidance of children from school entry to the beginning of the working life. It works closely with the special schools and classes which are well developed in Upper Austria. In addition, because perhaps of its markedly eclectic outlook and strongly educational orientation, the staff of the service is engaged in ongoing research into such important problems as school readiness, problems of adaptation to the Middle School, and problems of adjustment to working life.

In Vienna itself, the School Psychological Service is supplemented by the Guidance Service for Grammar Schools *(Be-ratungsstelle fur Mittelschiiler)* and by the service of guidance established for the technical schools by the Viennese education authorities in 1951. The first of these centres which works solely in the Grammar Schools (children and adolescents from 10-18 years of age) of the city was established at first as a private initiative in 1950, but now is subventioned by the education and social affairs authorities. Its principal preoccupations are the examination and treatment of difficult pupils referred mainly by the schools themselves. Its research and preventive work is limited and the tasks of advising teachers, of general pupil guidance and the like, do not rank among the major aims, though there is some parent education and guidance through a parents' club. It resembles the conventional child guidance clinic both in its field of operation and in its staffing which consists of a psychiatrist, two psychologists, and two specialized educators who undertake much of the remedial and therapeutic work.

The guidance service for technical schools is directed by a psychologist and has a staff of another psychologist, a social worker and a psychiatric consultant paid for by the Viennese Social Security authorities.

In addition to these in Vienna and in some of the provinces, there are Youth Bureaux *{Jugenddmter)* which also undertake guidance, the examination and the treatment of educational and behavioural difficulties.

Such general services of guidance and remedial education and therapy are completed by a country wide service of vocational guidance and information. In 1946, the Ministry of Education set up a Central Bureau of Vocational Guidance *(Referat "Schule und Beruf"),* and followed this by establishing in each region a vocational guidance officer or service *(Landes-referent fur "Schule und Beruf").*

The central office issues a series of pamphlets giving detailed information on jobs and professions, the conditions and possibilities of training and the like, copies of which go to every school in the country. The tasks of the regional officers are vocational guidance and preparation for the choice of work, the necessary educational and psychological guidance which may be the preliminary to this, and the training of teachers who in one way or another may be involved. The vocational guidance officers are usually themselves experienced teachers who have attended training courses organized by the Ministry. For the more specialized psychological work and especially where individual psychological examination is necessary, they are assisted by fully trained psychologists. In at least one province (Steiermark) a travelling service which will include remedial education and direct psychological advice to the schools is proposed. Vocational placement and guidance after the educational period, is dealt with by the Ministry of Social Affairs *(Bundesministeriwn fur soziale Verwaltung)* through its Labour Exchanges and Placement Officers. Considerable stress is laid upon the fullest co-operation between the school psychological services, the vocational guidance services, the placement services of the Social Affairs Ministry and the Youth Bureau *(Jugendamt).*

In the capital and in most of the provinces, services of the types described above exist, either singly or together, more or less thinly spread according to their state of development and to needs. In addition, in certain places, there are clinics, centres and travelling services provided by universities, by hospitals, or by private institutions.

Many of these are highly developed and provide a comprehensive system of advice, guidance, psychological examination, therapy and remedial education. For example, in the province of Karnten where no school psychological service exists, the work of the Youth Bureau and of the Vocational Guidance service is completed by the Neurological, Remedial Education and Educational Guidance service *(Nervenambulatorium und Heilpddagogische Beratungsstelle).* This organization has an observation centre and a travelling service which ensures regular examinations in all the schools of the province.

In addition, it undertakes the in-training of teachers and social workers, laying special emphasis on remedial education. In Salzburg (town and province) it is the Institute of Comparative Education which assures the psychological service *(Erziehimgsberatungsstelle am Institut fur vergleichende Erziehungswissenschaft).* In the Tyrol, as well as the schools psychological service, the Innsbruck Neurological Clinic *{Kinderstation der Nervenklinik,* Innsbruck) provides a service of psychiatric and educational diagnosis and guidance, and the Psychotherapeutic Institute undertakes guidance and therapy for children, adolescents and adults.

In Vienna itself the University Pediatric Clinic has a Remedial Education Centre *(Heil-pddagogische Abteilung der Universitats-Kinderklinik)* with a case load of some 3,000 each year for rapid diagnosis and three hundred under observation and treatment, whilst the Psychiatric Clinic has started a general psychiatric service for children and another for epileptics. In addition there is the *Institut fur Er-ziehungshilfe,* run on Adlerian principles and similar in conception to the conventional Child Guidance Clinic, which includes parent guidance among its more usual activities.

Educational thought in Austria is tending more and more to emphasize that the principal responsibility for the guidance of school children and their parents, for making of education a global and constructive process, rests upon the individual teacher, aided, it is true, by the psychological specialist and by such devices as the cumulative school record. Hence while psychology is being brought more and more into direct relationship with education and educational method and while a considerable further development of school psychological services may be expected, a major effort is being directed to the training of the teachers themselves in understanding children and their developmental problems.

Belgium

Belgium was early a pioneer of vocational guidance and of the psychometric methods which underlay its development in the early part of this century. Similarly the applications of child study to the improvement of education, at first through the work of pioneers like Decroly, and later in the ordinary work of the schools, have had a considerable history. It is not surprising therefore that one of the first school psychological services in Europe, the *"Laboratoire de pedagogie et de psychologie de Fen/ant"*, should have been set up in 1928 at Angleur, for five primary schools in an industrial suburb of Liege. Its particular tasks were defined with great foresight. Under the direction of an educational psychologist, it conducts systematic surveys of the school population (physical and mental status, educational methods and material used), undertakes research in the improvement of education, especially through the supervision of experimental classes, and, in conjunction with the school medical service, ensures the sound development of all children. In addition it makes a special individual psychological study —and, if necessary, undertakes the remedial education—of all children who are difficult, refractory, failing in their work or absent from school for more than a fortnight. All children beginning school are examined with group and individual tests, and for each a record is prepared which brings together the psychological information along with medical, social and other data cumulatively gathered during the child's school career. On this basis, and on that of subsequent examinations, the staff of the Laboratoire aid parents and teachers in the guidance of children, especially towards the end of the primary school period. Through its experimental class and in other ways, the service contributes to the practical training of teachers in the new educational methods with which it is experimenting or has developed.

A rather similar service is that set up on a voluntary basis by the *Ecole Normale Charles Buls* in Brussels for the 800 pupils of five schools. The basis of the work done is the individual cumulative record for each child which contains medical, social, psychological and educational data. From 1945 to 1951 the service developed a number of specialised sections—such as medical gymnastics, a holiday home in the country, research activities concerned with the interaction of emotional and educational factors in personality disturbance, psychological guidance and a special educational service for subnormal children.

Since the war a number of larger communes have instituted services—like those of Liege and Forest-les-Bruxelles —covering primary and secondary schools. The work undertaken is less intensive than that of Angleur or the Ecole Normale Charles Buls, largely because each centre deals with a school population of several thousand. It consists mainly in the group testing of pupils at first entry to primary and secondary school, and at school leaving; and, at the request of parents, more detailed psychological examination of individual children for educational or vocational guidance and, in some cases, of children with difficulties of social or educational adaptation.

Certain large technical schools have organized their own guidance services. That of the Universite du Travail at Charleroi, for example, conducts entrance tests for the selection of students, works with the teaching staff in the progressive vocational guidance of pupils, and helps to standardise the examinations used by the school. Individual cases of failure are examined and the service has at its disposal services of remedial gymnastics, and social welfare as well as holiday homes.

In 1947, as an experiment, the Ministry of Education set up a number of *centres psychomedicosociaux,* and at present, there are fifteen such centres in the country. In general, these are set up inside a Lycee or Athenee and serve a school population of boys and girls in primary and secondary classes varying in number between 1,500 and 4,500 pupils. In general there is a psychologist responsible to the head of the school, assisted by a social worker and by the school medical officer; sometimes, in addition, there is a junior psychologist to conduct and score group tests. The principal emphasis of these services is upon progressive educational and vocational guidance and upon day to day collaboration with the teaching staff in the solution of the problems and difficulties of individual children, as well as upon cooperative research in educational method.

As in other countries, numerous services directly and indirectly concerned with the psychological care of children exist outside the educational system and a certain number of publicly or privately financed clinics of the child guidance type have been set up'under hospital or university auspices and by religious bodies. In certain cases, these have realised a close functional and administrative liaison with the educational services. A striking example is that of the *Dispensaire d'Hygiene Mentale* at La Louviere which has integrated its activity into the educational system of the commune and works closely with the administrative authorities, the school inspectors and the teachers. Among other achievements, this combined service instituted a system of standardised examinations at the end of each school year on the basis of which those children who are weakest educationally are screened out for careful individual study. According to their mental level they are then guided to B or C classes the function of which is an education designed so far as possible to remedy their weakness. In addition a class has been set up for the subnormal, and a short term hostel for those who need to be reeducated away from their family is projected.

Denmark

Since 1924 a Commission for Educational Psychological Research has existed in Denmark, consisting of representatives of teachers' organisations, pedagogical associations and research psychologists. With limited financial means, this Commission carried out invaluable work in the field of educational psychology and pedagogics, until it was superseded recently by the Danish Pedagogical Institute founded by the State and led by three psychologists.

Psychological services began to develop actively in the mid 1930's, when work was commenced by the municipal authorities in Copenhagen. Since then developments have been gradual and sure, and at the time of writing, nearly all Denmark is covered by some form of school psychological service. The nature of these is illustrated by that which serves Frederiksberg, a sector of Copenhagen, and an urban municipality of some 115,000 inhabitants, with 12,000 children in the 13 municipal schools. Under the aegis of the educational authorities, there is a school psychological office in the town hall, staffed by 10 psychologists, all of whom possess a university qualification in psychology.

This office is primarily diagnostic and advisory in function and its work is based on collaboration with the school and the home. Referrals are voluntary, although the past years have seen a steady increase in the amount of work, and have shown that the advice tendered by the educational psychologists as to the treatment and instruction of the children is nearly always followed. An idea of the scope of the service is given by the fact that about 500 new cases are investigated each year, which means that some 20-22 % of the pupils attending the public schools in the municipality come into contact with the office at some time.

If a pupil finds it difficult to maintain his place in his class or has any other difficulty of adjustment, his teacher may refer him, with the consent of his parents, to the school psychological office. The teacher completes a report form, describing the child's educational level, general behaviour, etc. The school physician in turn informs the office as to the child's physical development, vision, hearing, etc. The parents are then invited to the office with their child. The psychologist first discusses the problem with the parents in an attempt to elucidate the domestic background for the child's difficulties. A case study of the child himself is then undertaken by means of tests and interview, sometimes within a period of one or two hours, and sometimes through a series of sessions spread over several days.

The usual types of tests are employed, such as the common performance tests (Healy Picture Completion, form-boards, etc.) and the Danish revision of the Binet-Simon scale. In addition, standardised attainment, projective and personality tests are used whenever necessary.

When the study of the child and his circumstances has been completed, the matter is discussed with the parents and with the school, and a written report including the results of the study of the child and the conclusions based upon it is forwarded to the teachers. The interest and cooperation of the parents is indicated by the fact that a quarter of the cases referred to the Frederiksberg office in 1954-55 came on the initiative of the parents themselves. Sometimes it is possible to solve the problem simply by means of parent counselling and advice to the school. Should the child however prove to be mildly mentally subnormal or backward, he may be transferred to a "special aid" school, on the recommendation of his teacher and the head of the receiving school, and, if necessary, without the consent of his parents. Pupils in such schools usually have an I.Q. of between 70 and 90, and total roughly 1.5 % of the municipality's children of compulsory school age. In other municipalities, the figure sometimes reaches 3 %. There are never more than 15 children in a class in the special aid schools. Stress is laid on individual instruction, and special teaching materials have been devised, with financial support from the State. The teachers in charge have at least training as primary school teachers, and most have completed further special courses. Moderately and severely subnormal children (with I.Q. under 70) do not attend these schools but are usually reported to a special board, which then removes the children from the normal school organisation and places them either in a residential institution or, as is becoming more usual, in a special day school.

A far larger group of cases is composed of pupils with reading and spelling difficulties. In Frederiksberg, almost 6 % of the children of compulsory school age and of normal or super-normal ability receive some form of special instruction. In very serious cases, this may be given in a reading class, where there are never more than 16 children, under a specially trained teacher. Where the difficulties are less pronounced, an attempt is made to keep the child in his ordinary class, and special reading tuition is provided for 15 minutes daily, in private, at school, during school hours. The educational psychologist follows the pupil's development by means of regular control tests, and together with the teacher decides when ordinary school work may be recommenced. Special tuition in arithmetic is only rarely provided.

The provision for maladjusted children is more difficult to describe since maladjustment may cover many different things, and the advice that can be given and the procedures adopted will naturally vary considerably. Where the main problem is conflict between the child and its school or between home and school, transfer to another class or school is sometimes recommended. More recently there has been a tendency for the educational psychologists to add to their normal diagnostic and advisory tasks a limited amount of remedial work, especially play therapy. This can, of course, only be carried out with the full cooperation of the home and school.

Frederiksberg municipality also has a special residential school open all the year round where difficult boys may be placed for shorter or longer periods, and where the principal means of treatment is a radical change in environment. Such residential schools may prove excellent for children whose difficulties arise mainly from their home circumstances and many improve considerably after a period in one of them, where they are free, and treated with understanding and friendliness. But as most difficult children come from environments which have at least contributed to their difficulties, problems arise again when they return home. Hence the educational psychologist concerned, in conjunction with the head of the school (himself a trained psychologist), undertakes the re-education of the parents so that they adopt a positive attitude towards the child, an essential if the child's return is to be a success. Sometimes conditions are so difficult, that it is necessary to remove the child permanently from his home; but this is a matter for the child welfare authorities. The Central Copenhagen municipality has several such schools for girls and boys, as well as a number of observation classes. The latter are of two types: those concerned with difficult children, and those for children who, in spite of normal or supernormal intelligence, are failing in one or more school subjects.

Prior to sending a child to an observation centre or residential school, and sometimes even before play therapy is commenced, the psychological office asks for a psychiatric consultation. Normally the waiting list for diagnosis and advice is not long, but if some form of therapy is decided upon, the child may have to wait a long time, and many cases that really ought to receive treatment must be disregarded. A few cases may be referred to Copenhagen University Child Guidance Clinic, but the waiting list here is full for a year ahead. This clinic, directed by a psychologist, has a staff comprising psychologists, social workers, a psychiatrist and a pediatrician. The clinic, established originally with aid from the Rockefeller Foundation and now maintained by the State, carries out scientific as well as clinical work, and trains psychologists, who have graduated from the university, in child therapy.

Cases demanding psychiatric treatment are referred to the child psychiatric departments of the Copenhagen municipal hospitals or to the University hospital. Here again the waiting lists are long, and the places available too few to satisfy present needs.

Another feature of the Frederiksberg psychological service is that one of its psychologists is attached to the infant welfare centre, where parents may bring their children for medical examination between the ages of I and 7 years. If the physician considers it necessary, or if the parents so wish, they are referred for interview to the psychologist. He may in turn refer them to the school psychological office for a full study. Similarly the office cooperates with private medical practioners, institutes for the "word-blind", etc. and with the municipal child welfare board over cases referred by the board, or in supplying information concerning children who have been examined, and later for some reason are reported to the board.

The office also carries out tests for determining educational maturity. Hitherto these have most frequently been individual, since no suitable group tests are available in Denmark. However the office is at present conducting experiments in the hope of developing an adequate group test. A certain amount of public education in educational and psychological matters, particularly as concerns special educational provision is also undertaken. The psychologists take part too in courses for teachers arranged by the educational authorities and in meetings of parents held at the individual schools.

The aims and organization of the service in Frederiksberg are with certain modifications similar to other school psychological offices in Denmark. Many of those in the larger towns, however, are either completely unable to undertake play therapy, or can only do so to a very restricted extent, and there are only a few observation centres. In some towns, school readiness tests are more generally applied than is the case in Frederiksberg, and in one town there are kindergarten classes which function as a transition between kindergarten and school. The school psychological office of the municipality of Central Copenhagen, the largest in Denmark, caters for a school population of 97,000 pupils and employs 26 university-trained psychologists, some of whom are only part-time, which is equivalent to a full-time staff of twenty psychologists.

School psychological work in country districts presents greater difficulties. There is still even in the market towns a considerable need for the extension of services, but there are good reasons to suppose that this need will eventually be satisfied. At present each county has at least a consultant in special education, who may be called upon by the teachers for advice as to how they may best cater for the various categories of pupils within the limits set by the facilities available at the school concerned. The consultants test the children and demonstrate various types of teaching materials. About half the consultants have a university training in psychology, the remainder being elementary school teachers who have received more or less extensive supplementary training. The lack of uniformity in this respect is unsatisfactory. Professional opinion holds that consultants without a full university training do not have the requisite background to enable them to carry out the testing connected with their work, and they cannot administer personality tests. It is to be expected that all such consultantships will in time be filled by fully trained psychologists.

Normally the psychological offices do not concern themselves with psychotechnical investigations nor with vocational guidance, except in a few cases in connection with children already attending for other reasons. Parents who desire vocational guidance for their children go to the central employment bureau, if they are resident in Greater Copenhagen. A psychological investigation may then be recommended, which is carried out at the Copenhagen Municipal Psychotechnical Institute. This latter has a university-trained psychologist as its chief, and there are several trained psychologists on its staff. Vocational counsellors are often teachers. An Act has recently been passed to ensure that all Danish children may receive vocational guidance, and is being put into practice at the time of writing.

The school psychological offices in the larger municipalities are on the whole large enough not to need any considerable extension in order to carry out current research projects in addition to their ordinary advisory functions. Such research as has been undertaken so far has however usually been confined to enquiries suggested by the schools themselves; thus reading problems have been well studied, but not those one meets in arithmetic. Moreover whilst the work of diagnosis and advice has gradually been extended within the framework of the public elementary schools, the senior secondary schools and private schools, attended by a relatively small proportion of children, have not to any great extent been drawn into it. Similarly much more time could be profitably devoted to treatment, particularly as the need for this appears to be increasing.

The only recognised training for psychological work in Denmark is that given at the University of Copenhagen. Just after the war, courses were commenced with the specific aim of preparing school psychologists. Until then, the degree in psychology was mainly directed to a preparation for research work. This older degree was retained, while the new degree of

Candidatus Psychologiae was designed for more practical work and much of the strictly professional training is provided after the degree has been obtained. The main subjects covered by the degree are: general psychology, child psychology, and the psychology of the various school subjects, as well as their pathology. So far some 250 students have obtained the degree of candidatus psychologiae of whom approximately 80 are concerned with work in the schools. Since an increasing proportion of those who qualify go on, not to work with the schools but to clinical work, work with delinquents, to child welfare posts and to employment in the armed services, the course of study no longer fully satisfies all current needs. The curriculum therefore will soon be revised, to include among other things, a certain number of optional specialisations and some practical professional training prior to the degree. The length of the course will then become a minimum of 5 years.

At present, those who wish to be clinical psychologists receive their practical training after graduation at hospital clinics or at the University Child Guidance Clinic. The Danish Psychological Association also to some extent aids its members in their further training by means of special courses, for example in the use of the Rorschach test, and by shorter courses of a more general nature.

Prior to studying psychology all educational psychologists have completed a training as elementary school teachers and have had at least five years of practical teaching experience. Furthermore as part of their professional duties and to ensure a real and continuing contact with the work of the schools, they are required to teach twelve hours a week in an elementary school, with the exception of senior psychologists who may teach only six hours. Salaries are comparable to those of teachers, senior psychologists being paid as headmasters of schools and assistant psychologists as assistant heads of schools.

The Scandinavian psychological associations cooperate with each other, and hold an inter-Scandinavian congress every third year, as well as publishing a joint Scandinavian psychological journal.

France

In France the science of child psychology has a long history though its full application to the day to day problems of the schools is relatively recent, and by no means complete. Mainly as a result of the work of Binet and Simon, each area has a medico-educational commission which consists of medical specialists, teachers specialised in the education of the subnormal and, where they are available, of psychologists. These commissions have the specific task of finding those children who cannot follow the normal courses in the primary schools—usually the mentally subnormal or educationally retarded. In addition there are the social workers who, among their many tasks, have that of the detection of abnormal family conditions, of aiding where they can and of referring the more serious cases to specialised services. Under the Ministries of Education, Health and Justice, as well as under private auspices are organized various services of special schools and classes for blind, deaf, partially sighted, hard of hearing, delicate, physically handicapped, mentally subnormal, maladjusted, delinquent and homeless children. For example, for mentally subnormal children there are some 1,300 special day classes annexed to ordinary schools or independently constituted, with a total attendance of about 20,000. One thousand feeble minded children are catered for in day centres which combine educational or vocational training with medical care, and a further 10,000 are cared for in residential custodial establishments and psychiatric hospitals, and 7,000 in *Centres medico-pedagogiques* or residential schools. Provision on a similar scale exists for other officially recognized groups; and in one or two places attempts have been made to develop special opportunities for the highly gifted and for intelligent maladjusted children. The Ministry of Education has also instituted full time (six months) training courses for teachers, already experienced in ordinary schools, who wish to specialise in the teaching of physically handicapped or mentally subnormal children.

The *classes nouvelles* represent a considerable effort in another direction, that of the improvement of education and educational method by making it more child-centred, more active, and with more emphasis upon a thorough psycho-social and educational study of the pupil. All of these classes officially have been situated in the secondary schools under the care of specially trained teachers who volunteered for the task; but similar experiments have been tried in primary schools; and in a few cases whole schools, primary and secondary, devote themselves entirely to pilot projects in the newer methods, often in close association with psychological services or research institutions of various kinds. One of the most important aspects of the classes nouvelles from the present viewpoint is their experimental use of a cumulative school record card for each pupil which in addition to medical and social data contains a considerable section devoted to a continuous study and recording of the child's educational and psychological development, where possible by means of standardized educational and psychological tests as well as by systematised observations. This is made the basis of careful educational and subsequently vocational guidance giving reality and substance to the corresponding organization of the six years of secondary studies into a *"cycle d'orientation"* (the first three years) and a *"cycle de determination"* (the second three years).

It is against this background of partial but progressive and experimental educational reform, that the special services must be viewed. As in other countries, these services are incomplete, financed from different ministries and relatively unintegrated on a national level, though, locally, official and ad hoc collaboration between them ensures as full a coverage as possible. As elsewhere, too, informed opinion considers the existing services inadequate to meet the real needs and there are marked divergencies from place to place in the capacity of local services to meet all the demands made upon them.

The only service which is fully organized throughout France is that of vocational guidance for those children who leave school for work at the end of the period of compulsory schooling. In every department there is at least one vocational guidance service staffed by an officer who has been trained essentially in psychometric methods. A projected reform suggests that the training of these staff should be widened so that they may extend their field of operation beyond the immediate task of vocational testing and the giving of information on jobs.

Complementary to this service is the *"Service d'Orientation scolaire et universitaire"* organized by the Bureau Universitaire de Statistique (University Bureau of Statistics), a public service provided by the Ministry of Education. This service was founded in 1937 originally as a research project to devise methods of psychological investigation suitable for the academic secondary schools, and for the Universities and higher education generally; but it rapidly developed into a full service of guidance for the secondary schools, the Universities and the institutions of University status.

A study is made of all pupils entering the first year of their secondary course in the cooperating schools. This *"dossier scolaire"* is based upon a report made by the child's teachers in the previous classes, a questionnaire addressed to the families, a questionnaire completed by the pupils themselves, a series of standardized group tests of attainment, capacity and personality and is completed by an analysis of the cause of deficiencies and a psychological analysis of all the data. Where it seems justified, where the school requests it, or at the wish of a parent, the service undertakes individual examinations as a result of which it may advise parents or the school, suggest a more detailed medical or psychological examination or recommend a change of course or school in the hope of finding something better adapted to the child's tastes and capacities. A similar service is offered not only throughout the six or more years of the secondary academic course but also for the guidance of intending University students or those who, having begun a course of study, wish for help or to make a change.

The service is staffed mainly by psychologists who hold both the Diploma of Vocational Guidance *(Dipldme d'orientation professionnelle,* a state diploma) and the diploma of educational psychology and of applied psychology *(Diplomes de psycho-pidagogie et de psychologie appliquee,* awarded by the Institut de Psychologie, University of Paris); but has as consultants specialist teachers in the Lycees and Universities, and medical specialists of various kinds. It does not undertake remedial work or therapy but works in liaison with school medical and psychological services, vocational guidance services and psychiatric departments of hospitals or clinics to which it sends appropriate cases. In conjunction with its parent organization, the University Statistical Bureau, it undertakes a considerable body of research work concentrated mainly upon the classes preparing pupils for higher technical education, and university entrance, and upon the factors making for vocational success or failure in the liberal professions.

In contrast to this service, in France, as elsewhere in Europe, there exists a great number of services of varying structure, finance and objectives engaged mainly in the diagnosis and treatment of educationally, socially and emotionally maladjusted children and of delinquents. Some of these are privately financed and managed, others are of a public or semi-public nature, most receive state aid in one form or another, either through subventions or on the basis of payments from the Social Insurance, Public Assistance, the Ministry of Health or the Ministry of Education on a case basis. Most of these organi-zations in France are members of regional branches of *l' 'Union Nationale des Associations regionales pour la Sauvegarde de VEnfance et de V Adolescence,* a group of bodies recognized and financed by the State, which organizes technical conferences, sponsors local initiatives, and publishes a journal carrying research and other papers written by its members.

A considerable proportion of these services are psychiatric and medical in their direction—Consultations, Bureaux, Dis-pensaires d'Hygiene Mentale, Neuropsychiatric Clinics, Centres Medico-Psychologiques—and are concerned mainly with the examination of subnormal children, and the discovery and diagnosis of maladjustment. Many of them have only a psychiatrist and social worker as their staff, though some have a psychologist, a specialised teacher, lay psychotherapists, speech reeducators and others as well. Largely because of staffing difficulties, rather fewer than half undertake remedial work, psychotherapy, or the more general educative and preventive tasks of informing teachers, parents and others, and the conduct of research work. In some cases the psychological and psychiatric work is directly integrated with the school health service; in others with the public health service; in some cases a service operates from a University or a hospital clinic; in others it takes the form of a child guidance clinic working outside the educational system but serving school children and their parents over a considerable area. Apart from official services, or services provided by lay bodies, there are those financed by religious and especially Catholic groups.

In a number of regions, religious bodies, private societies, and official bodies, some affiliated to the *Association pour la Sauvegarde de VEnfance et de VAdolescence,* run observation centres. As their name suggests, these are centres which board children for a short or long period during which a diagnosis of difficulties may be made on the basis of their behaviour; they tend however more and more to combine with this the function of short-term remedial and therapeutic institutions rather like residential schools for maladjusted children. Similarly there are reeducation centres whose primary purpose is that of helping retarded and maladjusted children but which also take on some diagnostic functions. In general the case loads of these Observation Centres are between ioo and 150 children yearly, the number tending to decrease in proportion as the Centre undertakes treatment. The *Consultations d'hygiene mentale,* the *Centres medico-psychologiques* and similar services—many of which are not full-time—tend to have annual case loads of between 100 and 200 new cases for diagnosis, though some are much above this figure. It seems also that the Observation Centres receive the majority of their cases from the courts, the *Consultations d'hygiene mentale,* and the Social Services, whereas, for the other types of service which do not provide boarding accomodation, the source of referral in something like a third of their cases is the social services while another quarter come from the schools. Referrals from the school health services, and from private medical practitioners are relatively few. Among the more interesting initiatives of the *Sauvegarde de VEnfance* to bring psychology and psychiatry more fully and closely into relation with the life of the school and through this, with the out of school lives of children is the *Centre psycho-pedagogique du Lycee Claude Bernard* at Paris. This Centre represents a developed concept of the Child Guidance Clinic as put forward in the United States and financed in Europe for a time by the Commonwealth Fund. It is situated within one of the large lycees and is under joint educational and psychiatric direction; and, through a considerable part-time and full-time staff of specialised educators, speech therapists, psychiatrists, social workers and psychologists, provides a very full range of diagnostic, therapeutic and remedial services. Although research is not one of its main functions, it has conducted some enquiries particularly into the emotional, intellectual and educational problems of children at the stage of secondary education. It accepts cases referred by parents, by secondary schools, private doctors, school psychologists and the social services. Closely associated with it is the *"Ecole des Parents et des Maitres",* an organization which, in conjunction with the Faculty of Medecine of the University of the Sorbonne, undertakes parent education through a series of public lectures, a monthly journal, a series of pamphlets and through marriage guidance counselling, small parent discussion groups and individual consultations.

In the field of delinquency, the French Ministry of Justice through the *Direction de VEducation Surveiilee* has instituted a psychological service which though still experimental is of considerable interest. Specially chosen and trained psychologists, either employed in one of the three residential Observation Centres established by the Ministry of Justice or in one of the two non-resident services attached respectively to the Children's Court of the Seine, and the Children's Court at Lyons, are charged with the full study of delinquents before their appearance in court, including a social case history, measurement of psycho-motor, intellectual and educational development, and an emotional and personality diagnosis. On the basis of this thorough examination, the psychologist makes a report to the judge both as to an explanation of the delinquency and as to future treatment. It is hoped that the service will be extended beyond the diagnostic function to include specialised reeducation and psychotherapy both in the institutions for delinquents and in the probation service. Perhaps the most interesting aspect of this scheme is that the psychologists employed by the Ministry of Justice are carefully selected for this work and in addition to their university theoretical and practical training, undergo a further practical course of six months to one year organized by the *Direction de VEducation Surveiilee* itself.

In many ways the most interesting and well integrated of the French post war initiatives is the experiment of school psychologists. At the suggestion of the *Laboratoire de psychologic de Venfant* of the *Institut de Psychologie* of the Sorbonne, University of Paris, and of the Director of the Educational services of the Seine, sixteen posts as school psychologists in primary schools were established in 1946. Two years later the Director of Secondary Education established 24 posts for the lycees in Paris. At the same time the experiment was extended to Grenoble and Lyons (for primary schools) and to Orleans (for secondary schools).

The important features of the experiment are that the school psychologist administratively and functionally belongs to the school or the group of schools in which he works. His task is to aid in the better adaptation of the pupil to the school and of the school to the pupil; and since this is regarded as a differentiation or specialisation of one of the functions of education, the school psychologist is the collaborator of the teacher and is indeed a teacher with specialist competence in the field of psychology applied to education. Much of this work consists in the continued study of the development of individual pupils, as well of the whole climate and atmosphere of the school. Nevertheless the improvement of educational method and the adaptation of the school to the pupil imply coordinated research. Hence, in the Paris region, and, to some extent, elsewhere, the university training centre assumes a responsibility for directing and coordinating the research work undertaken by the school psychologists and acts as a specialist service to which individual cases can be referred for a second opinion or more thorough examination.

Some idea of the scope of the services given is indicated by the figures published concerning the number and nature of the group and individual examinations undertaken in the schools. In the year 1952-53 for example the 14 psychologists working in primary schools examined over twelve thousand children of whom some 5,000 were seen individually. The bulk of these individual examinations (46.4 %) was undertaken to develop for each child a systematic psychological and educational record by which his progress through school could be followed and guided and a further quarter were concerned either with the specific educational guidance of individual children or with difficulties such as educational failure or retardation. Theessential integration of the service with the schools is shown by the fact that 75 % of the requests for individual examinations came from teachers, head teachers and school inspectors.

The extension of such a service—-which is based upon one psychologist to 1,000-1,500 pupils—clearly depends upon a recognition by education authorities of the needs which it fulfils and not less upon the availability of suitable candidates and suitable centres of training. Development is hindered in France as elsewhere by a lack of established and officially recognised standards of qualification and of a legally and administratively defined status for school psychologists. However certain universities, in the provinces as well as in Paris, have organized training not merely of a theoretical kind but also at a postgraduate professional level. The convention is beginning to grow up that the school psychologist, in addition to a basic university qualification in psychology, needs to have at least five years of successful teaching experience before entering upon a practical professional training in child development and applied educational psychology, at least part of which will take place in a functioning service. It is unlikely however that more than a few devoted pioneers will be attracted to a profession requiring so considerable a preparation unless, whilst retaining their status as members of the teaching profession, school psychologists are employed and paid as a special service.

Italy

In Italy, in spite of the early initiative of de Sanctis, and in spite of a considerable extension of health services, including the school medical service, little was undertaken before the outbreak of the last great war to develop services of psychology for the schools and children generally. There were individual initiatives, of course; but in general the educational authorities themselves were opposed, and indeed still remain cautious in their attitude. After the war, largely through the initiative of Carlo de Sanctis, Porta, Bollea, Busnelli and Bernini and through the visits of Bovet, Heuyer, Piaget, Rey and others to Italy, the question was reopened; and since 1946 there has been a considerable growth accompanied by the establishment of schools of social work, of faculties of psychology in the universities, and of psychiatric and pediatric clinics and hospitals. In the more strictly educational field, *Centri Didattici Nazionali* have been established to carry out studies and research work, in educational psychology, educational method and the like usually in connection with a particular branch or level of education; some of these have established demonstration services inside schools similar to those provided by the French school psychologists. Finally there are a number of national organizations for child and adult welfare, of local services depending upon provincial and communal authorities, and of university centres and clinics, which provide diagnostic, psychological services and in some cases undertake treatment.

Special educational provision is well developed in some aspects whilst much is still to be done in others. The first school for subnormal children in Italy was founded in 1898 but it was not until 1928 that official regulations were framed to set up special classes for backward children *(classi differenziati)—of* which there are now some 325 for 7,500 pupils and a waiting list of nearly 5,000—and training colleges—of which there are seven plus four other recognized courses—for teachers of the subnormal *(Scuole Magistrate Ortofrenice).* Five years later, with the passing of the administration of the school system from the local authorities to the state, special schools, day and boarding, were established. The special classes are attached to ordinary primary schools and take those children whose backwardness seems to be due mainly to environmental causes, and who therefore after two or three years may be expected to return to the ordinary school. The special schools are established for those children whose difficulties, intellectual, physiological, emotional or social, are more marked, and who therefore may be in need throughout their school lives of a specially adapted remedial education. Where it is possible to work with the family the school is a day boarding school *(scuola autonoma),* of which there are twenty-two; for those children who have no family or have to be separated from their parents, there are some twenty boarding schools *(institute medico-pedagogicd).*

In addition there are eight other special institutions subven-tioned or maintained by the State. Most of these specialise, but some of them accept children with a wide range of difficulties in addition to, or other than, inferior intelligence—severely maladjusted, delinquent, epileptic, psychotic and the like. Other types of State special schools—for physically handicapped, blind, deaf, and delicate children—exist, mainly in the big towns. An idea of the balance of provision can be given by the figures for the city of Milan (population 1953: 2,559,201). Here, there is one large school (31 classes, 45 teachers, 371 pupils) for subnormal, markedly backward, pathologically maladjusted and delinquent children; there is a school for physically handicapped; one school for tuberculous (5 classes, 5 teachers, 80 pupils); one for epileptic (12 classes, 16 teachers, 111 pupils): two schools for delicate children (45 classes, 57 teachers, 1,311 pupils in all); a school (17 classes, 17 teachers, 200 pupils) for the blind and partially sighted, and another for the deaf and hard of hearing. In addition to the provision made by the Ministry of Education, or receiving a State subvention, there are certain classes and schools maintained by private funds.

The teachers in the State schools, as well as a basic teaching qualification, possess a specialised diploma awarded after a one-year course in one of the *Scuole Magistrali Ortofrenice* or its recognised equivalent. These training colleges have been responsible, through their demonstration classes, for much research into teaching method and other problems, as have such institutions and organizations as the *Opera Nazionale Anormali Psichici Orfani di Guerra,* the *Instituti medico-pedagogi,* and particularly, the national association for medico-psycho-pedagogic assistance to the handicapped *(Societa Italiana per I'Assistenza medico-psico-pedagogica ai Minorati deWEta Evo-lutiva* (S.I.A.M.E.) which, as its name suggests, groups men and women from all the disciplines involved—medecine, psychology, education, social work, and law—and directs its attention to research, practical educational problems, and to the improvement of law and administration in the field.

It is against this background of the development of special education, of the immense problems left behind by the war, of the attempt since 1946 by various bodies to tackle some at least of the more urgent problems, and of the thorough enquiry into the structure and effectiveness of Italian education made by the Ministry of Education, that the pattern of psychological services must be seen—tentative, experimental and expanding only cautiously in step with experiment, experience, and, in particular, with the availability of qualified staff.

Most of the work which is done ressembles the child guidance or psychiatric clinic in conception and is the offshot of services of child- welfare or maternal and child health. For example the *End Nazionale per la Protezione Morale del Fanciullo* has provincial commissions in every province which provide child and family welfare services, including a service of school social workers. Through the activity of these services, cases of difficult children are discovered and referred to the *Cetitri e Consultori Medico Psico Pedagogici* (CMPP) which exist in twenty-seven of the provinces. Most of these CMPP are situated in a school though some have independent buildings, and are staffed, typically, by a neuro-psychiatrist (part-time—three sessions weekly each of three hours), a psychologist and a social worker (full time). Their main task is diagnostic; in addition to special school placement, treatment is undertaken, for some ten per cent of cases (where staff and time permit). An idea of the case load is given by the fact that in 1953 twenty-two centres diagnosed rather more than three thousand new cases and saw nearly three thousand for the second or third time. Nearly half the children referred are sent by the school social service, and a further 12 or 13 per cent by the social services of the region. In certain districts, the CMPP undertake psychological examinations for the children's courts.

The *Opera Nazionale per la Maternita e Vlnfanzia,* in addition to its maternal and child health services, has set up four psychological clinics in big towns and proposes to add seven more; certain others of its provincial branches have partial psychological services as part of their pediatric clinics.

Apart from these national bodies, some provincial administrations have Mental Health Dispensaries, some communal authorities (Milan, Reggio Emilia, Novara) have set up clinics and centres of child guidance, and two centres exist, one in the Institute of Psychology and one in the Pediatric Clinic of the University of Rome.

The services so far described are in the main under psychiatric direction and concerned principally with children who stand in need of direct psychological help. Though some of them undertake a small activity of educational guidance or collaborate with vocational guidance centres, few are staffed adequately to carry out the broader guidance tasks of a school psychological service or to undertake the fundamental research in child development and educational psychology which is necessary.

It is with this larger conception that the *Centra Didattico Nazionale per la Scuola Secondaria* is cautiously experimenting. Basing its concept generally upon a multidisciplinary approach, the centre has set up in some twenty-four secondary schools, differing types of service ranging from the complete team of psychiatrist, psychologist, social worker and specialised teacher to that of a school psychologist aided when necessary by the school medical officer and school social worker. Its aim is to try out which of the various types of organization most effectively meets the needs of the schools. In addition, for all the schools in Rome, it conducts a diagnostic and advisory service for children referred because of school failure. Under its direction a group of five psychologists has undertaken a coordinated research in Rome and Milan to make a detailed psychological and educational study of some

1,500 pupils in sixty classes. This is regarded as the first step in a programme of basic research necessary to develop an applied science of educational psychology as the background to the study of individual cases.

Of potentially equal importance is the Centre's contribution to the development of a concept of the tasks of the educational psychologist. In the course of the *"Giornate nazionale della Scuole Secondaria"* the Centre called together a group of psychologists to discuss this problem. The main suggestions made were: that the psychologist is excellently placed to aid the teacher in his task and to make the link with school medical and social services; he should undertake systematic research to determine the psychological bases of educational method; he should make the first diagnostic study of problem children referred to him by the school, and, where appropriate, carry out individual or group remedial work calling upon more specialised diagnostic or remedial services, if necessary; finally he should collaborate with the teacher in the task of educational and vocational guidance. These suggestions were complemented by an insistence upon the need for a better preparation of teachers themselves in child development and in applied social and educational psychology.

Spain

In recent years, and particularly in Madrid and other large cities, the Spanish authorities have considerably developed their maternal and child health services. Within these, a very considerable effort has been made to raise the general level of parental care, especially of young children; and nurses and others have been trained to give advice and guidance to parents not only in matters of physical health but also in general child development. As early as 1929 moreover services of vocational guidance were organized and have steadily developed. The National Institute of Psychotechnics in Madrid *(Institute National de Psicotecnia),* the Psychotechnic Institute of Barcelona, and vocational guidance offices in the principal provincial capitals provide between them, at least for the children in the towns, a service of guidance particularly in choice of work. They work mainly with technical and other vocational schools. In addition there are vocational guidance services maintained by local authorities (for example at Valencia) or by private organizations (e.g. the Altos Hornos of Bilbao). These services are staffed in each case usually by a teacher, a medical practitioner and a psychologist.

Certain children's courts (Barcelona, Madrid, Bilbao, Seville, etc.) have their own psychologists' office concerned with the examination of delinquents, and other cases which come before the tribunals. Finally we may mention the National School for Abnormal Children *(Escuela National de anormales)* and other publicly and privately maintained schools for mentally and physically handicapped children.

Official opinion sees that these services are inadequate for the needs, particularly for those of parent education, the discovery and treatment of problem children and the development of vocational guidance in such a way as to link it with a sound system of educational guidance. The department of psychology of the University of Madrid has begun to train educational psychologists, with the specific intention of developing the personnel necessary to a school psychological service. The Ministry of Education projects a law setting up a national organization of educational and vocational guidance based upon local, provincial and national centres, and with the task of making a psychological study of children as early as possible in their school life as the basis either of special education or subsequent educational and vocational guidance. Until however the University has trained sufficient psychological staff at an adequate level, it is not considered wise to attempt to set up so ambitious an organization.

Sweden

Since the recent war, Sweden has initiated a comprehensive educational reform, the technical basis of which was a thorough psychological study of nearly the entire school population, mainly by means of group tests. Apart from the questions of method and organization raised by this enquiry, by the school reform projects and by the recent educational acts, such matters as teacher training, special educational provision, educational and vocational guidance and the development of school psychological services have been the subject of study either by the Royal Board of Education or by various official committees. What follows therefore is an account of a transitional and developing situation.

Sweden is relatively well provided with special schools and classes for blind, deaf, physically handicapped, mentally subnormal and dull children. In addition, with considerable local variation, there exist classes for children with reading and writing difficulties, for maladjusted children, for children who have reached school age but not school maturity, for the hard of hearing and for speech defectives. Classes for the partially sighted are contemplated. For teachers of almost all these groups, and especially for the blind, deaf and mentally subnormal, special training courses of one year or two years full time study exist, mainly organized by or under the direct supervision of the Board of Education. Almost all the teachers trained in these courses, or in the shorter ones organized for those who wish to teach the dull, or to take charge of remedial groups for those with special difficulty in reading and writing, have all the basic qualifications necessary to teach in primary schools and in most cases have a number of years teaching experience before they undertake further training.

In some districts preventive and advisory services are established. In certain places, for example, specially trained elementary school teachers administer school maturity tests which bear mainly on the intellectual development of school entrants and which allow the detection of children who may need help for a short period, placement in a special class or for whom school entry should be delayed.

Vocational guidance services in secondary schools are assured by vocational guidance officers from the Youth Employment Service (Royal Labour Board) in collaboration with teachers. The responsible authorities, in their instructions, stress the importance of close cooperation between teachers and vocational guidance officers—for example in discussing the pupil's school performance, his abilities, interests and prospects outside school. In the experimental comprehensive school *(enhetsskolan)* which will be found in some fifty of the 800 school districts, specially trained teachers are responsible for guidance during the last two years of the course and the children have the opportunity whilst still at school to gain experience of different jobs. Both nationally and locally, parent-teacher cooperation is organized with the participation of psychologists and psychiatrists, who, in addition are active in arranging lectures, courses, study groups and the like both for the benefit of parents and teachers and as part of the training of doctors, teachers, nurses and other similar key professions.

There is thus a considerable background activity and, in particular, the ordinary teacher in Sweden has a good general training in educational psychology and child development.

It is in this context that current provision for special services must be viewed. The bulk of these are of the Child Guidance type and exist in

Stockholm, Gothenburg and in six of the twenty-four county districts. An idea of their size is given by the fact that between them they employ 30 psychiatrists and doctors, 21 psychologists and assistant psychologists, 29 social workers, 13 psychotherapists, and 15 specialised teachers. In addition there are three private child guidance clinics. School psychological services are less extensive, employing three psychiatrists and twelve psychologists only two of whom are full time, the rest having teaching duties. In addition to these specifically children's services financed either by the county councils, communes and larger cities, there are of course the psychiatric departments of the hospitals, and of the University Faculties of Medecine (Stockholm, Uppsala, Lund). Special mention should be made too of the Erica Medico-pedagogical Institute, which, as part of the practical training given to psychotherapists, maintains a guidance and treatment department for some 150-200 children yearly.

Some of the difficulties in the way of increasing and extending these services, and in particular of developing an effective school psychological service, are due to the fact that there is no organized training of psychologists in Sweden. Many of those at work are teachers who, to their basic qualifications, have added one or other of the specialised courses for teachers of handicapped children and in some cases have attended advanced university courses in psychology. A committee established by the Royal Board of Education to study the whole problem of the establishment of services and the training of psychologists has just made its report. Among other things, it recommends that a complete psychological training should take six years. Three of these are intended for fundamental university studies in psychology, pedagogy and sociology; then follows a year of practice and two further years mainly devoted to scientific methodical training under the guidance of working school psychologists or in a centre engaged in practical and research work. Teacher training and teaching experience are considered to be desirable preliminary qualifications.

Meanwhile the needs are known to exist: in 1952 for example it was estimated that to implement the regulation of 1945 establishing a psychological advisory centre in each county district, some 60-70 child psychiatrists would be needed; to develop and extend school psychological services with a minimum diagnostic and treatment task, it seems that some 70 chief psychologists and a considerable number of assistants are required. If the demands of the schools are to be met, this however is a minimum.

An enquiry made by questionnaire to all schools and school authorities in the country in 1953 revealed that the problems of the differentiation of method and curricula, and of the adaptation of the school to the child are in the forefront of the teachers' preoccupations, and this demands research in educational psychology within which the more immediately pressing needs expressed by the teachers—for help with the difficult and failing children, for educational guidance at entry to school, at transfer to secondary school, and in choice of studies or of employment—take their appropriate place with some chance of a satisfactory solution.

Switzerland

Because of its federal organization and the independence of each of its twenty-two cantons, Switzerland presents a picture of great variety and unevenness. Yet with a total of 52 services of various kinds (1953) working in the main city centres but extending their activities into the smaller towns and the countryside, it is one of the countries in Europe having the fullest development. It was also, as will be recalled from earlier remarks, one of the pioneers of psychological services, with the initiatives of Claparede in Geneva in 1912 and of Hegg in Bcrnc in 1920. Nevertheless it is calculated that for example in the Valais (population 160,000) which is one of the best provided cantons having already a service staffed by one full-time and two part-time psychiatrists, three to four non-medical psychotherapeutic staff and a social worker, a further fifteen psychologists and psychotherapists would be necessary to operate a full service for school children. For Zurich some thirty psychological staff would be necessary by the same criteria.

A similar picture presents itself in the field of special education. Throughout the country, residential schools and institutions exist for physically and mentally handicapped children, for the maladjusted, and for speech defectives. There is also a considerable activity of remedial education *(heilpadagogik)* not only for the dull and subnormal but for the retarded and educationally backward. Nevertheless it is calculated that provision should be made for some 4-6 % of the population of school age, i.e. for about 18-28,000 children—whereas, currently, provision is made for 6,274 children, or for only about one third of those held to need special education.

Certain towns, for example Bale (6.04 %) and Geneva (3-95 %) are, of course, well above the national average and within measurable distance of having a fully sufficient provision. All these special institutions are grouped in the Swiss Association "Pro Infirmis" though many of them depend upon the *Societe suisse d'utilite publique* or upon cantonal, educational or health authorities.

To complete this background it may be remarked that the basic training of many Swiss primary and secondary school teachers contains a considerable element of child study and educational psychology and that many of the University centres notably Geneva, Zurich and Bale, have advanced courses for experienced teachers who wish to specialise in educational psychology, for those who wish to teach the subnormal, and for those who wish to become educational psychologists. As a research centre in child study, first under the leadership of Claparede, and subsequently under that of Piaget, the Institut des Sciences de l'Education of the University of Geneva is too well known to need mention.

The psychological services of the country are of three main types: those which form part of adult psychiatric services *{consultations de psychiatrie infantile);* services inspired by the Child Guidance formula *{services medico-pedagogiques);* and school psychological services of various complete or partial forms *{Consultations de pedagogie curative, Services d'obser-vation des ecoles, Services psychologiques scolaires,* etc.).

Of the first we may cite as an example the *Consultation de psychiatrie infantile* of the *polyclinique universitaire de Zurich.* This service which also serves university training purposes, is staffed by a director, two to three psychiatrists, a psychologist and a social worker. One of its medical staff is at the same time director of an observation home in Zurich for maladjusted children. The service is essentially occupied with children having severe problems of behaviour or development, and does not normally work with the schools. The town of Zurich however possesses a school psychological service integrated with the school medical service and a *Consultation de pedagogie curative {Heilpaddgogik)* attached also to the University.

Of the services which base themselves upon the child guidance clinic formula, that is upon a team of psychologist, psychiatrist and social worker, the most highly developed is that founded in 1930 by Dr. Andre Repond in the Canton du Valais. Based on psychoanalytic principles including a considerable activity of psychotherapy with children, the service operates from the Maison de Sante de Malevoz and has travelling consultations in most of the canton, reaching even the more remote villages. Its objectives are mainly the discovery and treatment of abnormal children, the prevention of maladjustment and the arousing of interest in such problems. Where necessary, it works with schools but it does not, except incidentally, undertake direct preventive or constructive work through the educational guidance of normal children or through the application of mental health principles to common problems of the classroom or of educational methods. Similar services exist elsewhere in Switzerland, particularly in the French and Italian speaking areas, e.g. the cantons of Vaud, Neuchatel, Tessin.

The school psychological services are very varied in their structure and more or less complete in the services which they are able to offer. The *Consultation pedagogique de la ville de Berne,* for example, directed by Dr. Hegg, the educational psychologist who founded it in 1920, is an autonomous part of the school medical service: its principal tasks are those of psychological adviser to the schools, the discovery, examination, and treatment—by psychotherapy, remedial education and other means—of difficult or retarded children and the general psychological supervision of the special classes of the town. Its action is limited by the smallness of its staff (one psychologist as director, one assistant psychologist and a social worker), but nevertheless includes a good deal of in-training of teachers, general educational and vocational guidance and parent education. In the canton of Berne, in each educational district, a specialized teacher with a university training undertakes a service of educational psychology for the schools. A rather similar formula is that of Lucerne where the Professor of Education at the training college (Dr. Simmen) has gathered together and trained a group of 18 primary school teachers to undertake the discovery and examination of problem children and to provide a service of educational guidance in the schools.

The education authorities of the city of Geneva, inspired in part by the work of the Institut des Sciences d'education, set up in 1930 a *"Service d'observation des ecoles"* which in many ways seems to meet most of the needs of the schools. It is directed by a psychologist who is at the same time inspector of special schools and classes. He is assisted by a part-time (10 hours a week) psychiatrist, a full-time assistant psychologist, a social worker and a speech therapist. The service provides educational and vocational guidance, arranges for remedial education or other forms of treatment, the discovery and examination of problem children, especially at the nursery school stage and acts as psychological and educational adviser to the special schools and classes. As well as with the schools, it works closely with the child welfare services of the city and with the children's courts.

Finally we may mention a form of organization which has proved successful in districts of scattered population—the travelling school psychological service. With similar objectives to the services described above, the school psychological service of St. Gall, for example, works mainly in the schools of the canton and serves a school population of some 50,000 children. Originally (1939) staffed with one psychologist only, it now has two full-time psychologists and a social worker. Essentially it is an advisory service to the teachers and to the education authorities, with whom the decision as to the action to be taken rests; and its activity though widespread, is limited especially, on the remedial side, by the smallness of its staff.

Almost all the types of services described undertake functions of a wider kind than that of examining and treating children with difficulties of one kind or another. Most of them carry on a considerable activity of public education in the principles of mental hygiene; many run short training courses for teachers; some, for example, the *Service medico-pedagogique Valaisan,* provide a full practical training for child psychiatrists, psychologists, psychotherapists and social workers; others, apart from parent guidance in connection with specific children, undertake the general education of parents; and most collaborate as occasion demands with other services concerned with the welfare of children. Since the end of the last war, there has been a steady increase in services and a widening of their scope to include more preventive and constructive activity both through the schools and in the training of teachers. The French concept of an *Ecole des Parents* has found an echo in Geneva and Lausanne where, in addition to lectures and discussion groups, parents can obtain consultative services; and in one or two other centres—for example Winterthur—attempts have been made to associate the psychological education of young mothers with physical health services.

The existing services however remain, according to informed opinion, insufficient in extent and—quite rightly—experimental in their development, depending largely for their direction and preoccupations upon local needs and conceptions and upon the skill and insight of their staff.

The United Kingdom

From the outset, British educational psychology emphasised social factors, no doubt because the Industrial Revolution had left behind it great social problems and because public spirited people like Charles Booth, the Webbs and others realized the significance of social handicaps and their effects upon school children. McDougall among others was greatly influenced by this movement, and his most widely read work was entitled "*Social Psychology*"'. As a consequence of this and of the general English educational tradition, a peculiarity of psychological work in England from the start has been the emphasis on remedial training rather than on treatment—an approach via the science of educational and social psychology rather than via medical psychology. Even those psychologists favourable to psycho-analytic concepts placed more emphasis upon reeducation than was usual elsewhere.

Since the turn of the century the education departments of the Universities, as well as undertaking the training and further training, particularly, of secondary school teachers, have increasingly interested themselves in educational research, educational psychology and the science of child development.

Much indeed of the research, basic to practical services of child guidance and educational guidance, has been the work of professors of education and their postgraduate students. Similarly, following the example of the early pioneers, certain University Departments of Education and of Psychology between the two wars, set up demonstration educational and and psychological services and clinics as part of their practical training programmes. After the second world war, many English Universities brought about an even closer association between practising teachers, local education authorities, teacher training colleges and the Universities. In some cases, through the creation of Institutes of Education in which all those concerned with education in a considerable area participate, this has led to a considerable expansion of research facilities to the development of post-graduate training courses for specialised teachers and for educational psychologists, and to the establishment of further experimental psychological services of different types. It is thus fair to say that a minimum knowledge of child development and of the psychology of education is well spread among teachers in the United Kingdom; in addition, a considerable proportion of teachers and educational administrators, through short courses run by University extra-mural departments and through the opportunities offered for part-time and full-time study for higher degrees in Education, have received a theoretical and practical training in applied psychology and research. The British Psychological Society, founded early in the century, now has a membership of more than two thousand among whom the largest group is directly or indirectly concerned with education, and outside the Society there are many teachers, administrators and training college staff whose knowledge of psychology is considerable though not complete.

The *British Journal of Educational Psychology,* jointly sponsored by the British Psychological Society and by the Association of Teachers in Colleges and Departments of Education has a circulation of over two thousand copies inside the United Kingdom. In addition there are two national research institutions concerned with enquiries into the psychological aspects of education—the Scottish Council for Research in Education and the National Foundation for Educational Research in England and Wales—each of which involves practising teachers in ongoing research work and publishes the results either in the form of monographs or through the professional journals.

Parallel with this interest in psychology applied to practical problems of education, there has been a marked trend, since before the first world war, towards an increasing differentiation of educational provision. This has been expressed on the one hand in the development of different kinds of secondary education in England especially since the English Education Act of 1944, and in a diversified system of special schools and classes for children with physical, mental, or social handicaps, such that their needs cannot adequately be met in the ordinary school.

This diversification of provision has, not unexpectedly, accentuated the need for adequate guidance of normal children and adolescents, between schools, classes or courses, and within the schools themselves. As one of the means of aiding teachers and others in this task, cumulative school record cards containing details of the educational progress, interests, character and personality traits of each child have been developed. Their use is by no means universal; the cards themselves are not of a standard pattern; and their value is directly dependent upon the knowledge, insight and skill of the teachers using them. Nevertheless, some Local Education Authorities have made them obligatory at least in their primary schools and, through a vigorous programme of research on the one hand and of the in-training of their teachers on the other, have developed them as an integral part of a system of effective guidance.

The crucial general problem of guidance in the English educational system however has always been that of the choice of secondary studies, particularly of those able to profit from an academic education. This problem became acute with the Education Act of 1944 which made all education after the age of eleven free in the state maintained schools. Owing to the greater prestige of the Secondary "Grammar" Schools which cater for the abler pupils and prepare for entry to the Universities and to the professions and to a shortage of accommodation in them as compared with the modern and technical schools, this allocation at eleven took on, and still bears, more the appearance of selection than of guidance. Much effort has been devoted to developing a system which shall be valid in prognosticating success; which shall be fair in that a child shall get a chance of academic education if he is suitable for it, irrespective of his social or educational history; and which shall be acceptable to parents. The system adopted by most local education authorities in England is to apply to all children between the ages of ten and eleven a series of standardized tests of educable capacity, of English and of Arithmetic, on the results of which they are allotted to the Grammar, Secondary Technical or Secondary Modern schools according to the numbers of places available. The examination is thus competitive—in some places heavily so—and while many of the major and minor sources of error have been eliminated by improvements in the technique of examining, few educationists are fully satisfied that the present system is more than making the best of a difficult job. Many education authorities are experimenting with variations on this basic method, including the use of individual psychological examinations for children on the borderlines, interviews, and the use of cumulative school record cards as an additional criterion or even as a substitute for the examination.

As elsewhere in Europe, the earliest provision for handicapped children goes back to the turn of the century or before and was made by independent benevolent bodies for the blind, the deaf, the grossly physically handicapped and the markedly mentally subnormal. Between the two wars and especially since 1945, there has been a marked expansion within the state system both of the number of places available as well as a formal recognition of new categories. The English Education Act of 1944 confers on parents the right to ask for the examination of any of their children aged two or more to see if they require special educational treatment. The Education Authority is bound to have this examisnation carried out and if the child requires special educational treatment, even before compulsory school age, this must be provided if the parent so wishes. However most children who need special treatment are discovered after they have begun school (5 years) and then usually through the observations of their teachers. The school medical and psychological services carry out the necessary examinations, and advise the Local Education Authority which has the power to enforce attendance at a special school or class if necessary.

This statutory duty to discover all children needing special help, and the increasing emphasis upon the need for careful examination and guidance which began well before the second world war, led to the recognition of several broad classes of children in need of an adapted education and to the growth of a considerable number of different kinds of school, some of them directly maintained by Local Education Authorities, some of them financed by voluntary bodies with direct or indirect state assistance. In 1945, the English Ministry of Education recognized ten broad classifications of handicapped children; the blind, the partially sighted, the deaf, the partially deaf, the delicate, the educationnally subnormal, the epileptic, the maladjusted, the physically handicapped and those with speech defects. It was not intended that all the children falling into any one of these categories should attend a special school; nor that the schools or classes developed should rigidly correspond to any particular category. This may be illustrated by the category of the "educationally subnormal". It is estimated that some ten per cent of children fall into this category, the criterion for inclusion in which is that the child, for whatever reason, is retarded *educationally.* This retardation may be due to intellec-tual subnormality, irregular school attendance, specific difficulties in reading or in arithmetic, social or personal maladjustment or to other causes. Whether the child attends a special school for children of subnormal intelligence, whether he attends a special class in an ordinary school, or whether he receives some form of individual help, will depend upon local facilities and upon a careful study of his case during the process of his education.

The category of "maladjusted children" is also a wide and inclusive one covering many kinds and types of emotional, personal, or social difficulties. For such children, day and boarding schools are provided, some specialised in a particular kind of maladjustment; there are, too, hostels from which the children go to ordinary schools, special remedial groups in child guidance centres or in ordinary schools, and so on. In the education of physically handicapped there have been several recent developments, notably the provision of specially conceived schools for cerebrally palsied children; day and boarding schools for children with multiple handicaps and schools which cater for different specific types of physical and mental handicaps.

The expansion of these special educational services has been hindered by the evident financial cost of provision and by the lack of suitably trained teachers. No one would say that all needs are satisfied and, while the large towns are fairly well served, there are parts of the country which are not reached. Training facilities for specialised teachers are inadequate. The blind are relatively well served by the courses conducted by the College of Teachers of the Blind, and the Department for the Education of the Deaf at the University of Manchester has been training specialist teachers of the deaf since well before the last war. One year courses for teachers of the educationally subnormal now exist in certain University teacher training departments; and the courses in Child Development and Remedial Education conducted by some of the Institutes of Education for experienced teachers provide a sound basis of professional knowledge and skill for those who wish to teach maladjusted children. The Ministry of Education itself and many local education authori-ties conduct short courses for teachers to increase the level of knowledge and understanding in the general field of special educational provision. It is likely too that in the near future as the result of a ministerial advisory committee there may be an improvement in the supply and training of teachers for handicapped pupils in England.

An idea of the extent of the special educational provision currently made is given by the fact that in Scotland in 1953[s] for a population of some 830,000 children of school age some 10,000 children were being educated in special schools and classes. This does not include those for whom special arrangements are made in ordinary schools without these constituting a special class; nor does it include the population of schools for delinquent children. In England and Wales, with a school population somewhat above six million, provision is made in 680 special schools alone (maintained and voluntary) for rather more than 54,000 children. Official estimates of the proportions of children needing some form of special educational treatment —not necessarily in special schools or classes—vary between about 10 per cent to as much as 15-16 per cent of the school population. From these estimates the numbers of the delinquent are omitted. It will be seen that, even allowing for the fact that, for example, many of the largest group of all, the educationally subnormal, will be accomodated in ordinary schools with a specially adapted curriculum, there is still a considerable gap between what is considered desirable and what has so far been possible. In England it is estimated that some 20,500 children are awaiting places in special schools.

It is into the pattern rather summarily described above, and with local and national differences, that the various services of child guidance fit. Here it should be remarked that, although there are somewhere between two and three hundred child guidance clinics, child guidance centres, services of remedial education, child psychiatric clinics and the like in England and rather more than thirty in Scotland, such services are in many cases incomplete in one or other respect. Moreover many of the tasks of educational guidance for ordinary children, research into child development and its applications to the improvement of education, parent education, constructive and preventive mental health work in the schools are either not carried out at all or are frequently undertaken independently of the official services. In part this is because the basic concepts and emphasis of these services are not yet fully worked out; in part because, administratively, similar services may depend either upon the health or upon the education services; and in part it is because of a considerable cleavage of opinion between those who see psychological services as having a primarily psychiatric direction with emphasis upon the treatment of the abnormal and those who conceive of them as a broader service of psychological help to the school system with an emphasis upon remedial education rather than principally upon the examinatike play-therapy.

In addition, those clinics, which give a direct service to the education authorities or do much work with children of school age, usually employ one or more full-time educational psychologists who, apart from the psychological and educational examination of children which is part of the normal routine, may undertake remedial education, play therapy, act as consultants to special schools, and generally maintain the contacts with the schools and the education authorities. Not infrequently where the psychiatrically oriented clinic has no full-time psychologist, it is the educational psychologist employed by the local education authority who undertakes the necessary work.

Child Guidance clinics and Child psychiatric clinics partly or wholly maintained by the Local Education authorities are frequently under the nominal or actual direction of the school medical officer, or of a full-time or, more usually, a part-time psychiatrist employed by the Health Service. In these cases effective direction is usually in the hands of the senior educational psychologist, and the staff is completed by one or more social workers, sometimes by non-medical psycho-therapists and by specially trained remedial teachers. Such clinics, because they are administratively more closely linked with the educational system and because the psychologist is in effective charge, have much closer, more frequent and more fruitful contacts with the schools than would be expected of hospital or other clinics outside the educational service.

Some education authorities in England and Wales and many in Scotland where Child Guidance has been from its inception an educational service, believe that what before all else is necessary is a service of a preventive, advisory and remedial kind for the schools. They have therefore tended to establish, under the direction of an educational psychologist, a school psychological service or a Child Guidance Centre the main preoccupation of which is not with serious maladjustment but with the far greater numbers of children who experience difficulties of personal, social and educational adjustment. This point of view has been strongly endorsed by the Association of Education Committees' Sub-committee on Child Guidance and as strongly attacked by various psychiatric professional bodies.

These school psychological services, Child Guidance centres, or Educational centres, as they are variously called, are usually wholly maintained by the local education authority. Their full-time staff consists, according to their size, of one or more educational psychologists, one or more social workers, remedial teachers, speech reeducators and the like. Among their tasks is that of the ascertainment of children in need of special educational treatment, including the educationally subnormal and the emotionally maladjusted, consultative work with the special schools and classes set up by the education authorities, general educational, and sometimes, vocational guidance, work with parents individually or through parent-teacher associations, and advisory work with teachers in the ordinary schools. Such services or centres invariably have access to the school medical service and can obtain any necessary psychiatric help either on a consultant basis or through psychiatric clinics attached to the Health Service.

Sometimes they contain or are closely associated with a system of remedial teachers or remedial classes.

Next perhaps to the expansion of all kinds of services for maladjusted children, the development of remedial education has been the most striking feature since the war. Among the groups of children needing special educational treatment, the educationally subnormal were recognized officially to be the most numerous. Furthermore many local education authorities became alarmed at the results of age group surveys by means of standardized tests of attainment and ability which indicated a considerable proportion of educational backwardness even among children of normal or superior innate ability, and a number of children who though not technically backward, were in fact retarded as compared with their capacity. Some of this was due to the disturbance of education during 1939-45, but it was, and still is, felt that here is a problem which though reduced by a return to more normal conditions, is likely to remain.

Much research into the general problems had been undertaken between the wars on the basis of which the University of Birmingham Institute of Education, immediately after the end of the war, began a study of educational retardation which developed into its Remedial Education Centre opened officially in 1948. This centre provided the practical basis for a one year course for experienced teachers in child development with, however, special reference to remedial education for bright children experiencing educational difficulties.

Experienced teachers trained by the University Institute in 1946, 1947 and later, found employment with local education authorities as specialist advisers some of them setting up remedial education centres or services. In 1952 a survey of 116 local education authorities revealed that 32 of them had special identification procedures (usually by means of school record cards, or periodic age-group testing), 53 gave assistance by means of educational guidance services, in the form of specialists who visit the schools, 23 provided remedial teaching in schools or child guidance centres, 7 provided special remedial centres, and 29 made provision for bright retarded children in their classes for the backward. The survey also revealed that the expansion of the service was greatly hindered by the lack of suitably-trained staff.

In addition to the above services, many local education authorities, especially the larger ones, employ a chief educational psychologist in a mainly coordinating and advisory role. As well as some work in a Child Guidance Clinic or Centre, supervision of remedial education, consultant work in the special schools or classes, advice on the use of mental tests for school survey purposes or for eleven plus selection, he has the general task of advising the chief education officer on all psychological matters relating to the schools, arranging for or taking part in the short in-service training courses for teachers which many authorities arrange and a considerable variety of other work.

It is coming to be agreed in England that while the classic conception of the child guidance clinic with its threefold team of psychologist, psychiatrist and social worker should be preserved, it is not sufficient alone to meet all the problems of the schools in the most economical manner. This team is peculiarly adapted to the diagnosis and treatment of severe maladjustment and psychosis in children; but, while there are theoretical and professional disagreements as to what constitutes maladjustment demanding psychiatric diagnosis and treatment, there is at least tacit accord that many school problems—and those from the teachers' point of view the most urgent—fall into the province of remedial education and educational psychology. Hence while Child Guidance Clinics and especially Child Guidance Centres have increased markedly in numbers since 1930, progressive education authorities have tended more and more to supplement their work with a variety of special psychological and educational staff. Sometimes these staff are formally integrated with the Child Guidance Clinic or Centre into a thoroughly comprehensive service; sometimes they exist side by side with more or less of cooperation according to personalities and local circumstances. The Committee of Professional Psychologists (Mental Health) of the British Psychological Society advocated that a complete psychological service for schools should include a Child Guidance Centre, and should provide advisory services to Children's Departments, to parents, to Welfare Clinics, as well as to ordinary and special schools; it should also be responsible for services of educational and vocational guidance and of remedial education, as well as having close contact with hostels and schools for maladjusted children and a Child Psychiatric or Child Guidance Clinic. It considered that a chief educational psychologist should be responsible for the preventive and guidance services and that in the special educational field, including the treatment of maladjusted children, he should collaborate with the school health service and through that have access to outside specialist medical services as these may be necessary. This is the pattern which predominates in Scotland, and is exceptionally well embodied in the services provided by the Corporation of Glasgow, Education Department, and the City of Aberdeen. Similar organizations are to be found in Barrow-in-Furness, Birmingham, Coventry, Leeds, Leicester, Middlesborough, Sheffield, the West Riding of Yorkshire and elsewhere in England. A special Committee set up by the Ministry of Education to consider the future development of services for maladjusted children has cautiously recommended an extension of this formula as did the Advisory Council on Education in Scotland.

Little has so far been said of vocational guidance, apart from the work which is incidental to some psychological services, child guidance centres or clinics. Administratively every local education authority has the right to develop a juvenile employment service; if it does not choose to exercise this right, the task is undertaken by the local organization of the Ministry of Labour. Each area in England has a Juvenile Advisory Committee concerned with youth matters and a Juvenile Employment Committee representing the authorities, the schools and the employers, the trade unions and welfare organizations. This latter committee helps and advises the Youth Employment Officers who are available in most areas for the guidance of school leavers. A very considerable range of pamphlets has been prepared giving details of careers in industry, commerce and the professions with particulars of the educational levels, and personal qualities required, the kind of training available and so on. Not infrequently the youth employment officers visit the schools, speak to the school leavers and their parents and hold with the staff, parents, and children a "choice of employment conference". Little general attempt is made at a systematic use of standardized tests for vocational guidance, although a number of experimental schemes have been set up and have given striking results. The National Institute of Industrial Psychology (N.I.I.P.) which has pioneered scientific vocational guidance in England since its vocational guidance department was organized by Burt in 1923, has done much to prepare for the considerable postwar development and to foster the growth of official as well as voluntary services. In the secondary grammar schools and in the public schools, Careers Masters or Mistresses—many of them trained in short courses conducted by the N.I.LP.—make themselves responsible for continuous guidance and information towards the end of the school career and for cooperation with the Youth Employment Service on the basis of a carefully compiled and cumulative school record card.

In the country there are, in addition to the general services described above, a number of unique institutions, publicly maintained or privately endowed, which have either a special scientific point of view or a particular function. Mention has already been made of the *Remedial Education Centre* at the University of Birmingham Institute of Education and of the *National Institute of Industrial Psychology*. The *Institute for the Scientific Study and Treatment of Delinquency* should also be recorded. As its name implies, it is concerned with the prevention of delinquency through child and parent guidance and with the treatment and care of delinquents.

Even more widely known in Europe is the *Tavistock Clinic* which as well as undertaking the diagnosis and treatment of severe maladjustment in children and adolescents through its "Department for Children and Parents", has a considerable training and research function. The *Maudsley Hospital* as well as having a Children's Department has a psychological and psychiatric research centre forming part of the Institute of Psychiatry, University of London, and provides training for clinical psychologists and child psychiatrists leading to the award of a University Diploma. Similar research centres exist elsewhere notably at the Crichton Royal Hospital, Dumfries, Scotland. The Hampstead Child Therapy Clinic, a private organization, directed by Anna Freud, is one of the two centres for the training of play therapists (the other is the Tavistock Clinic).

We may in conclusion briefly indicate the nature of the training of educational psychologists in the United Kingdom. The Committee of Professional Psychologists (Mental Health), an organ of the British Psychological Society, has a membership of rather more than three hundred and fifty psychologists. It has laid down certain minimum standards of qualification for those educational psychologists to whom it grants recognition and membership. These are (a) In England: a University education in Psychology to the level of a good first degree or its equivalent, training as a teacher, and two years experience either of teaching or some other work with normal children, and a special practical professional training of one year in clinical and educational diagnostic and remedial work. Recognition is not normally granted until the candidate has worked, after qualification, for at least one year as assistant to a fully qualified educational psychologist, (b) In Scotland—the post-graduate University degree of B. Ed.

in educational psychology constitutes the basis of recognition by the educational authorities and much of the practical training is given on the job by functioning services. The Committee of Professional Psychologists grants recognition only to candidates who in addition to this basic training and experience have satisfactorily completed two years practical work under the supervision of a principal psychologist.

Training facilities, in England at all events, are insufficient and only 20-30 educational psychologists are trained each year. The training with the longest history is that given by the Department of Psychology. University College, London, which is recognized by a University Diploma. The National Association for Mental Health (which incorporates the Child Guidance Training Council) gives grants to students for training either at the Child Guidance Training Centre, London, The Tavistock Clinic, or Guy's hospital Department of Psychiatric Medicine.

The Department of Education, the University of Birmingham, has since 1948 instituted (at the Remedial Education Centre) a training course for educational psychologists, students pursuing which are recognized by the Ministry of Education as eligible for substantial training grants.

Yugoslavia

Psychological services of any kind are for the most part recent and tentative developments in Yugoslavia. The earliest established, as elsewhere in Europe, were vocational guidance offices, the first of which was established in 1931 by the Chamber of Commerce and Industry in Zagreb. It ceased to function in 1948 and was reopened in 1952 under the administrative and financial direction of the people's committee of the town. In Belgrade a similar organization exists under the control of the education authorities. The third centre at Ljubljana is part of the Central Hygiene Institute of the town.

Each of these centres is staffed by psychologists who to a university training in psychology have added practical courses and experience in vocational guidance. Medical services are assured either by a full-time staff or through the school medical service. As would be expected, the major clientele of these offices consists of children at the age of school leaving (14-15 years); however a number of university students and others following higher training courses come for advice from time to time. For the most part, children and adolescents come on their own initiative, though sometimes they are sent by their parents, by their schools, or by the workshops in which they are employed. The centres work closely with the employment offices, especially in Zagreb, and consequently there are frequent cross-referrals.

Relationships between the centres and University departments of psychology, medicine and neurology are close. For example, the head of the Institute of Psychology at the University of Zagreb is also head of the vocational guidance centre, and practical and theoretical training courses are organized in common between the two departments for students who wish to become vocational guidance officers. In Belgrade, the chief psychologist of the neuropsychiatric clinic of the medical school collaborates closely in certain cases.

An idea of the work undertaken by these centres is given in the following figures: Zagreb, the largest, has an average case load of 2,500-3,200, many of whom are children who come for simple information and advice and are not psychologically examined. Ljubljana has an annual load of about 500, but tested a further 1,200 pupils in secondary schools as basis for standardizing certain measures. The Belgrade centre in 1953 saw 660 children of whom 220 were psychologically examined, and at the same time tested many more for research purposes.

Because of the needs which exist, the centres frequently have to undertake tasks not strictly within their province. For example the Zagreb centre, as well as the vocational guidance of school leavers, gives a service to university students and even to adults seeking change of employment. It also undertakes vocational selection for industry. Moreover it fulfils certain psychological functions of guidance for children who are failing in school, for the subnormal, and for children with personality and behaviour problems. As other psychological services develop, it is expected that these marginal activities of the vocational guidance services will diminish.

In the Republic of Slovenia, at Maribor and at Ljubljana, there are two centres of educational guidance. These centres, the first of which has existed for several years and the second just been set up, are concerned particularly with the problems of abandoned and predelinquent adolescents.

In Zagreb there is a service concerned with mentally subnormal children of pre-school age and in 1950 the city set up a mental health unit concerned originally mainly with the prevention and treatment of alcoholism.

This unit has recently developed a special service for children which fulfils many of the functions of a child guidance clinic and which treats some six to eight children daily, referred by schools, the school health and social services or by the parents themselves. The service collaborates closely with the vocational guidance service, the children's homes and the schools. In addition, it organizes public lectures, and courses for teachers and parents on mental hygiene topics. It has begun also to issue a journal. A similar centre is projected for Belgrade under the health authorities.

A beginning has also been made with a school psychological service by the appointment to the schools of Belgrade of an educational psychologist. His first task is the detection and diagnosis of mentally subnormal children for placement in special classes and a check upon placements already made. The recently formed Societies of Psychologists which are to be found in some at least of the republics are studying carefully both the structure of future services and the training and qualifications of psychologists. The current idea is that, as well as full-time educational psychologists who would form part of the Educational Council of the town, there should be specially trained teachers in each school who, whilst they would continue to do some teaching, could undertake the wider tasks of guidance of their own and their colleagues' pupils.

The difficulty in Yugoslavia, as elsewhere, resides in the lack of adequately standardized psychological instruments and techniques for the examination and guidance of school children. This in turn reflects the need for research workers in the psychological and educational fields, and of fully trained psychologists. Psychology for nearly thirty years has been an independent university discipline; but, outside the academic world, there have been few chances of employment in the vocational guidance centres. Hence trained and experienced psychologists are lacking to man the services or to develop the practical training which will meet the needs now very clearly seen.

References

Alexander, W. P., (1943). *The Child Guidance Service in Principle and in Fact.* Sheffield, Education Committee.

Blacker, C. P., (1946). *Neurosis and the Mental Health Services.* Oxford. Oxford University Press.

Clark, K., (1954). "The APA Study of Psychologists" *Amer. Psychology*, 9, 3, Mar, 117-120.

CWS, N. E., (1955). (Ed.) *School Psychologists at Mid-Century.* Washington.

Daniel, R. S., Louttit, C. M., (1953). *Professional Problems in Psychology*. New-York Prentice-Hall.

Erickson, C. E. & Smith, G. E., (1941). *Organisation and Administration of Guidance Services*. New York and London, McGraw-Hill Book Company.

Schonell, F. J. & Wall, W. D., (1949). "The Remedial Education Centre", *Educational Review*, Vol. II, no. I.

Wall, W. D., (1955). "Psychological Services for Children in Europe", *Yearbook of Education*, London, Evans Bros.

Wjtmer, H. L., (1940). *Psychiatric Clinics for Children*. Oxford, Oxford University Press.

4

Psychological Services at Various Stages of Education

Compulsory education has brought into the school, children from all types of social background and of all varieties and levels of ability. Thus the teacher is faced with the problem of individual differences in its most acute form. Our increasing knowledge of human psychological growth emphasizes not merely the uniqueness of each child, but a hitherto unsuspected range of interrelationships between a child's capacity to learn, the effects upon him of his experiences inside and outside the classroom and in his earlier life, and the pressures to which he is subjected by his whole social environment.

On the other hand the school has the social function, delegated to it by society, of preparing each child to participate in and contribute to his society as fully as his innate endowment permits. The core problem is that of reconciling this essential, normative preparation with the needs and rate of growth of the individual. Moreover this reconciliation has, in practice, to be made within the framework of the relatively large class, the group of thirty, forty or even more children under the care of one teacher.

As the child grows older, while there is a process of assimilation brought about by the greater uniformity of school experience, there is also an increasing differentiation of capacities, aptitudes, tastes and interests which in fact widens the range of differences between individuals. This is recognized in educational organization by offering an increasing choice between alternative studies within any school and by the choice between schools of different types. Later still, the complex economic and industrial organization of society itself opens an even wider variety of occupations each with its particular satisfactions and each making its special demands.

Thus the school is faced with two main and closely interlocking methodological tasks, fundamental to its principal objects of aiding each child to develop fully and at the same time to become dynamically adapted to society. The first of these is to individualize methods and curricula so as to make the maximum allowance for differential rates and kinds of development among its pupils. The second is that of helping each child to choose from among the many alternatives offered, those which offer him the best chance of full personal growth.

These are not new problems; but before the turn of the present century at least, the choice of studies, of schools and of jobs was more restricted and society had evolved rough and ready methods of guidance between such alternatives as existed. For the contemporary school the problem is acute: social changes, changes in our educational philosophy and theory and an increasing awareness of difficulties, dictate an organized attempt to bring a solution by all the means at our disposal.

Such an attempt, which must inevitably rely on new specializations of function, carries with it the danger that the traditional responsibilities of the teacher, of the family, and of society itself, may be in some sort undermined; or at least, that they may be shelved and thrown solely on to the expert. Such a tendency is already manifesting itself in other fields, particularly that of social welfare. Thus while underlining the need for skilled guidance for all children, this committee is of the opinion that the dangers inherent in such guidance should be recognized and guarded against. Nevertheless the legitimate responsibilities of parents and teachers are not protected by a refusal to use to the full the insights provided by the science of child psychology or by a rejection of the whole idea of experimentation cautiously undertaken.

The problem to be solved is that of bringing school, parents and psychologist into effective partnership. This in turn will depend largely upon the tact and skill of the expert himself, his respect for the parents and the teachers, his professional knowledge and above all upon his being trained to put his insight freely at the disposal of others.

Guidance

Guidance between educational alternatives cannot however be left to rule of thumb. Because of its implications for the whole future of a child, it demands the fullest use of the techniques and knowledge provided by the developing science of educational psychology, and implies the close, continuous and objective study of each pupil as a complete individual in an environment or series of environments. Not merely must an attempt be made to assess intellectual potentialities, special abilities, physical and physiological capacities, but we must gain a picture of the development of the child's personality, emotional life, attitudes and interests. In turn this must be related to and in part explained by, his developmental history, the pressures of his immediate family environment and of the larger milieux of his town and the streets, of the school, of his whole status in the human groups of which he forms part. Only by recognizing that each child is the centre of a series of groups each influencing him in interrelated ways and by basing our study upon his individual psychology as well as upon his social roles can we aid him to make the choices which, by the organization of the school and later of society, we offer him.

Educational Methodology

Such guidance, however soundly based upon the close study of the child, will fail if the school exacts a rhythm of development to which the individual cannot respond. In many countries certain arbitrary standards of attainment are set by the schools; methods have been evolved from the intuition of the adult or from his conception of how children should learn rather than from any close study of the ways in which children do in fact learn. Syllabuses are, frequently, consecrated more by tradition or inertia than by a carefully objective assessment of their educational effectiveness. The result is that school systems present the picture of a proportion at least of children struggling along but falling ever more in arrear of the levels expected of them by teachers and administrators.

Complementary, therefore, to the concept of guidance, is the need to adapt the necessary demands made by the school to the rhythms of growth of its pupils. The individualization of materials, the study of group influences on children, the development of methods more in accordance with what is known and comes to be known of the ways in which children learn, are all necessary if human material is not to be wasted and if individual human beings are not to be warped or destroyed by their education. The administration, organization, methods and curricula of our schools are not ideal. They are based largely upon assumptions which have never been tested in the light of our knowledge of child development or upon pseudo-psychological conceptions of mental faculties, mental discipline and the transfer of training which are known to be fallacious. Thus while children should be helped to adapt happily to things as they are, psychological and educational research should be directed to an amelioration of those conditions, often outside the control of the individual teacher or school, which frequently are the true causes of children's difficulties.

Exceptional Children

A third main problem is posed by the considerable group of children who, because of physical handicap, mental subnormal-ity, sensory defect, severe emotional or personality deviation or disturbance and the like, cannot satisfactorily be educated in the ordinary class without some form of special provision. It is important to note that for the most part such children do not form a separate group presenting clearly distinguishable characteristics implying markedly different educational needs and methods; they are, rather, pupils who have in a more marked form, difficulties similar to those which arise (and pass away) in the personal and educational development of most children at some stage of their career.

The more adequately the school is organized to cater for individual differences, the smaller becomes the proportion of children to whom it cannot adapt itself. Nevertheless however organized, and certainly with classes of thirty or more children, the ordinary primary or secondary school cannot, in justice to its more normal pupils, accept any great proportion of those who diverge markedly from the norm.

Severely handicapped children are usually detected early and easily; the milder cases of sensory defect, of mental subnormality, of specific disability, of emotional disturbance or personality deviation only too frequently pass unnoticed until the child's whole educational and psychological growth has been jeopardized. Early detection of such difficulties not only prevents wastage and maladjustment, but enables positive measures to be taken if necessary, either within the class or by some form of individual provision, to enable the exceptional child to develop as satisfactorily as possible. Moreover if such children are early discovered and carefully supervised it will be found that many are not inevitably inferior or handicapped, but can after a period of special help be reintegrated into the normal class.

The Teacher and The Psychologist

These three tasks, of guidance, of research into the adaptation of methods and curricula, and of the discovery and, if need be, of the special remedial education of exceptional children, cannot normally be discharged by the teacher unaided. Neither by his training nor by his preoccupations is he equipped to stand aside from the child and from the educational process as a detached observer. Normally he does not have the knowledge of the techniques of child study nor the necessary training in psychological research methods. Moreover his main task is to educate, to be himself identified emotionally with the process of which he constitutes an essential factor. Thus while the teacher at all stages is and should be closely involved, he needs the assistance of the specialist in psychology. He should be helped to see the problems of the class room and the broader problems of edu- cation through the eyes of psychology, drawing from the accumulating store of psychological knowledge and research, new insights into the children he teaches and the methods he employs without however relinquishing his ultimate responsibility as a teacher.

Thus a primary function of the specialist in educational psychology is that of consultant to the teacher and to the school. Situations arise however, where the teacher or school staff are unable to accept a full responsibility for an individual problem child without injustice to the rest of the class; or, for example, a retarded pupil may need a more intensive examination, more attention or special remedial training, than the teacher is able to give. Hence specialist remedial and psychological services should be accessible to the schools, either to give expert assistance, or, in a minority of instances, temporarily to take over responsibility.

Applied Educational Psychology

It is clear that if psychology is to be of service to the schools in the ways outlined above, it must begin from the problems as they are met, not in the laboratory or in the clinic, but in the classroom and the whole life of the school. Effectively to do this however the psychologist must himself have profound insight into the life of the schools, into the educational process, and into the preoccupations, difficulties and professional skills of the teacher. Only on the basis of such a common professional understanding can an effective relationship be built up between teachers and psychologists so that each may, without usurping the function of the other, jointly study a particular child or a specific classroom difficulty. Without such a common understanding, the teacher is likely to reject the suggestions of the psychologist as impractical or, alternatively, to find his professional responsibilities undermined.

This is not proposed as an invariable rule. The crucial thing however is that whoever works with the teachers should have a sufficient practical insight into school conditions for effective co-operation. On the other hand, the committee wishes to underline the importance of the study of educational psychology and child development both in the basic professional courses for intending teachers and in further training for those who have already had classroom experience. Only on such a basis will the team work between teacher and psychologist, between schools and the psychological services develop and the disciplines of education and psychology become integrated for the benefit of all children.

Contact with the Home

In recent years it has come to be more and more clearly realized that a child's progress in school is intimately affected by his family life. In a stable society where family and school represent much the same values, and where their complementary functions rest upon an undisturbed basis of custom, there is probably little need for consultation. Contemporary society is in a stage of rapid change; and many parents are uncertain in their handling of their children and unguided by a healthy tradition. Moreover, universal education brings into the same classroom children from very different family environments. Thus there is a great and increasing need for home and school to co-operate in the education of children; and in a great number of cases parents need guidance and even skilled aid in the upbringing of children.

A recognition of this need has resulted in the development of various forms of parent-teacher co-operation, of parent education and the like, as well as of more specific attempts at consultative or advisory services to parents when particular decisions as to the child's future have to be made. Periodic general meetings of parents, working groups concerned with matters which touch the school at some point, visits to parents who do not attend such meetings, are all likely to facilitate contact and to bring home and school to a common understanding.

Such contact with the parents is of great value to teachers themselves, giving them often both a greater knowledge of children and a deeper insight into particular pupils and their needs. Extreme specialisation, common at the secondary stage renders it difficult however for teachers to make genuine contacts either with individual children or their parents: the teacher who has hundreds of pupils may not even know them all by name, still less exercise a personal influence over them or have any knowledge of their family circumstances. Hence at least the head of the school, the form master or mistress or counsellor must maintain some form of personal contact with parents and be accessible to those who wish to discuss with him particular problems of their child's education.

To such co-operation the psychologist has a general contribution to make from his knowledge of child development. Particular situations involving individual children demand something more than this. Whenever a child is shewing signs of educational, social, or personal maladjustment, a detailed study of his home circumstances becomes essential. It often happens that the principal remedial measure to be taken is one, not of directly helping the child, but of changing the attitudes of the family towards him. Similarly the improvement shewn by a disturbed child during his period at a residential school may disappear when he has returned to the milieu which was a basic or contributory cause of his difficulties.

In such cases, contact with the home is a delicate matter requiring skills and insight which usually come only from a specialized training. Parents are likely to resent or reject enquiries from teachers with whom their children are in daily contact; still less is the school able to undertake the continuous help and advice to parents that may be necessary in certain cases. Recourse to some outside service then becomes essential. If the school psychological service is adequately staffed, it normally would undertake such work or, where the mal-adjustment is severe, refer the case to a psychiatric clinic. It is necessary to insist here upon an essential difference in function between the psychologist or social worker on the one hand and the member of a school teaching staff who co-operates generally with parents or gives help in the case of a particular child. By his training the teacher is an educator involved professionally in the success or failure of his pupils and should be the adviser on educational matters. The psychologist or social worker is trained to study objectively both the home and the school environments of the child and to interpret the one to the other. In many cases he will be called upon tactfully to help both to change in their methods and attitudes towards a particular child.

Psychological Services at Pre- and Primary Schools

It is clear from the foregoing that the contribution of psychology to education is likely to be most effective if it is pervasive and integrated in the life and atmosphere of the schools, enabling the educator to attain his aims in harmony with the growth needs of each pupil. This is largely to be achieved through encouraging among all who have to do with children, an increasing sensitivity to the importance of good personal relationships. Nevertheless differentiation of function between the teacher and the psychologist is often essential. We may therefore briefly discuss those particular problems and situations in education for which some kind of specialized service is necessary.

Pre-school institutions (Nursery schools and classes, kindergartens, Ecoles maternelles, Jardins d'Enfants) and Primary schools, in fulfilling their general task of socializing children assuring their emotional and personal growth and helping them to develop certain fundamental intellectual techniques, are brought face to face with difficulties inherent either in the rhythms of child development or in educational organization; or, as is more usual, in the combination of both. These may be summarily listed as follows:

a) *Problems of Transition:* Most educational systems impose an age at which the child must begin school. Hence the general task of helping young children to achieve a satisfactory adaptation to a new environment is complicated by different levels of intellectual and emotional maturity which will be found in any miscellaneous group of five, six or seven year olds. Transition from home to school poses specific problems of the emotional 'weaning' and socialization of children. Later, transitions from class to class and from school to school, though effected without obvious difficulty by most children, give considerable trouble to some.

b) *Curricula and Method:* In the primary stage, the question of guidance between alternative studies hardly arises except towards the end. All children however have to acquire certain basic intellectual techniques and a certain minimum knowledge. While this is achieved more or less effectively by the majority, there is a more considerable proportion than is usually thought —it may be as high as one in four or five children— who experience undue difficulty and for whom temporary or permanent modification of method is essential, coupled frequently with some direct assistance to the home.

c) *Home-School Co-operation:* Apart from general, continuous and informal co-operation between teacher and parent, there are specific occasions on which contact must be as close as possible and where the family may need skilled outside help. Such are, for example, the early months of a child's school career, the time at which choice of secondary education is to be considered and whenever the child experiences continuing difficulty of educational or personal adjustment.

d) *The Discovery, Examination and Special Education of Children with Intellectual, Social, Emotional or Physical Handicaps:* The early discovery of children who are in any way handicapped, and the accurate evaluation of their needs and possibilities is an essential step towards helping them to make the most of their capacities. Individual remedial or therapeutic work, special educational methods, grouping in appropriate schools or classes is a task outside the competence of the teacher unless he has been specially trained for it.

Thus a specialized service might be expected to undertake the following tasks:

(i) Close collaboration with the teacher in the study and recording of the development of all children, and in particular in the systematic observation of individuals or of groups betraying difficulties of adjustment;

(ii) the discovery and detailed psychological and educational examination of children with physical or mental handicaps, and the suggestion and undertaking of appropriate measures, remedial or therapeutic, as seems necessary;

(iii) close collaboration with the families of problem children, with special schools or classes, or with outside services which may undertake treatment;

(iv) the propagation, in practical form, of notions of child development among teachers and parents;

(v) collaboration, through advice, through the initiation of research or through direct research assistance to teachers, in the improvement of curricula and methods, both generally and for special groups of children.

(vi) collaboration with the school medical service especially as concerns physically and mentally handicapped and problem children.

Psychological Services at Secondary Stage

Special Needs of the Period

Two general considerations justify the provision of psychological services designed to help children at school during their pre-adolescent and adolescent years.

In the first place, in the more developed countries where primary schooling leads to some form of secondary education for all children, the proportion who fail in their school work is very large, and roughly the same in different countries. But, since school attendance has become obligatory beyond the early primary level, it can no longer be said only that the child should adapt himself to the exigencies of the school; the school also should be adjusted to its pupils.

In the second place, certain aspects of contemporary social and economic development, which are likely to give rise to emotional tensions and so produce maladjustments, affect the child more particularly during the period of adolescence: the decrease in the economic and social importance of the family and the fact that it is not so closely knit a unit as in the past, tend to increase the number of difficulties between children and their parents; the growing complexity of society makes the achievement of economic independence more difficult; and these disturbing influences are magnified in the industrial, urban communities which are becoming ever commoner. The school cannot dissociate itself from these emotional problems because they are one of the important reasons why so many children fail to benefit from the education it provides; and the economic and social progress of society depends on the success with which the oncoming generation is educated.

The problem of Guidance

When primary education is finished, the range of possibilities for pupils is considerably widened and diversified so that the problem of educational guidance arises in an acute form. Secondary education demands of the child mental activities of a somewhat different type from those required in the primary school, in particular when he begins to learn the abstract subjects. Moreover, he comes into contact with teachers who know him much less intimately, spend less time with him, and leave more responsibility to him for the organisation of his own work.

Neither success in the primary school nor objective testing at entry have, in themselves, sufficient prognostic value to serve as the sole basis for later guidance. This committee strongly recommends therefore that the early years of secondary education should be planned to allow continuous and progressive guidance of the pupils. At this stage curricula might include as well as the revision of the basic primary school subjects, an initial and active experience of a range of subjects which would permit the pupils' tastes and aptitudes to manifest themselves: some verbal and abstract studies such as a more systematic study of the mother tongue and the first steps in algebra; some essentially practical and creative courses, like manual work, craftwork, geometrical or technical drawing; some artistic activities; and some involving other forms of self-expression. These introductory classes should be small in order to permit an easy transition from the primary school atmosphere and the teachers should be chosen for those teaching abilities and psychological traits which are particularly necessary for this special task.

It would seem desirable to continue such a period of orientation at least until such time as the diversity of interests is abundantly clear—that is, up to 14 or 15 years of age. In any case, at least the first post-primary year should be the same in content, though not necessarily in level of difficulty, for all pupils. Thereafter, curricula should be specialized only gradually and progressively so that those pupils whose special aptitudes appear late may transfer from one type of course to another if necessary.

The problem of orientation is not however entirely resolved by these more flexible arrangements. The capacities which become dominant during adolescence are differentiating factors each of which may emerge and develop at a different time; moreover, the emotional effects of enlarged social experience at this age are another factor making for temporary or permanent variation in interests. And the progressive specialisation in secondary education will necessitate fresh groupings almost every year.

Clearly throughout this period of orientation and progressive specialisation, the psychological service should follow the development and progress of the children, aiding teacher, child and parent to come to decisions which are realistically based on a full appraisal of all the factors involved. It is only by continuous, skilled and *unobtrusive* supervision throughout his secondary education that little by little the pupil will find the most suitable course with the fewest of those frustrations and disappointments likely to interfere with the development of a well-balanced personality.

Personal Problems

In many contemporary schools, teachers are concerned primarily with the quality and results of their own teaching. They do not consider themselves called upon to understand and allow for the out-of-school lives and the emotional development of their pupils. This lack of interest in wider questions has sometimes been explained by the pressure of work; it is doubtful, however, whether merely lightening the teaching programme would suffice in itself to change the traditional attitude.

Psychological services thus may fulfil a double function: that of screening out, examining, and if necessary treating maladjusted children; and that of contributing through case discussion and other means, to a change in teachers' attitudes and to helping them to increase their insight into the relation between a child's emotional life and his school work. Experience demonstrates that, where a good relationship between teacher and psychologist is developed, the school can not only become a happier place for most children but make a contribution to the prevention of maladjustment and delinquency. Once the problems have been discovered, the school psychologist himself may undertake remedial measures or in cases requiring prolonged examination or treatment, may call in the Child Psychiatric Clinic or some other specialized service. The school psychological service however must not lose contact with the child.

Psychological Services in Technical and Pre-vocational Education

In technical, pre-vocational and multilateral schools there is an even greater necessity for continuous guidance between educa- tional alternatives and for skilled handling of personal difficulties and problems. In the schools with a more markedly occupational bias, however, educational and vocational guidance should be earlier and more intimately associated. Moreover, in guiding pupils who will ultimately be integrated in commerce or in industry, physical factors and aptitudes and medical contraindications may be of more importance than they are for those whose education is preparing them for an academic career. In most countries a considerable democratization of education has taken place; but it remains true that the academic secondary course preponderantly attracts those whose socio-economic circumstances are good.

Technical, trade, and vocational schools on the contrary, tend to have a higher proportion of pupils from relatively unfavourable socio-economic milieux. Consequently contact with and help to the families as well as aid to individual adolescents assume an even greater importance. There rests a further series of problems peculiar to the size of many such schools and their tendency to offer a larger and larger variety of courses. The big multilateral school may have many parallel classes corresponding in part to differences in ability of the pupils and in part to differences in choice of options. In any one grade, there may be as many as ten or more class units.

The distribution of pupils among these so that individual needs are not neglected and at the same time so that the range of ability in any one class is not too wide, can only be based upon an objective study of the capacities, aptitudes and interests of the pupils. Examinations too, whether for promotion from class to class or at the end of studies, raise the problems of objectivity, prognostic value, and equivalence. The educational psychologist trained in research methods and well aware of the limitations and possibilities of tests and measures is an essential collaborator with the teacher in this field.

Psychological Services and Vocational Guidance

It is necessary in this connection to clear up an ambiguity which may arise in the use of the word guidance (orientation) in two connections, an ambiguity which sometimes leads to regrettable confusions.

A *vocational guidance* service is concerned with the choice of employment, may not have responsibility for putting into practice the advice it gives, and uses the results of psychological testing along with other types of data such as job analysis and information as to the state of the labour market.

A *school psychological service* can be fully effective only to the extent to which it is integrated with the school; the guidance it offers depends on psychological information of very various kinds and it is concerned with helping children whose development it follows closely.

Guidance a Continuous Process

Clearly vocational guidance cannot be effective if it takes the form of a snapshot intervention at the end of the child's school career and on the threshold of working life. To a considerable degree educational guidance, particularly at the secondary stage, is itself a form of vocational guidance by the implications which the choice of studies has for a subsequent widening or narrowing of the field of vocational choice. The expert committee would not wish to suggest that educational guidance should be based upon vocational considerations; the main preoccupation should be that of guiding the child's general personal and educational development. However, in the later stages of compulsory schooling or in the final years of the secondary school the choice of a career becomes increasingly important psychologically to young people and the school psychological service must enter into a closer functional relationship with vocational guidance services. Ideally, there should be a convergence between the services giving educational guidance, and those concerned with the vocational field.

How this is to be brought about will depend upon factors peculiar to the educational systems of different countries. A truly comprehensive service would—though with differences of personnel and of emphasis—follow a child from his entry to school until he is satisfactorily integrated into working life. Where, however, as is not unusual, school psychological services and vocational guidance services depend on different ministries and are financed from different sections of the budget, then means must be found, not merely to effect an interchange of information at a relatively late stage in the child's school career or even after it is over, but to bring about a continuous working co-operation throughout at least the second half of post-primary education.

Vocational guidance services can usefully be called in to tell pupils something about the chief local occupations and draw their attention to those which have vacancies or offer chances for advancement. On the other hand, the work of the vocational guidance services can be given a more secure basis by making use of some of the information available from the school psychological service, in particular that built up by the school staff and the psychologist and contained in the school record card. According to local circumstances, and in particular to the training and qualification of its staff, the one service or the other would carry out any necessary supplementary examination and study of the aptitudes, interests and personality of the adolescents concerned.

A more thorough understanding of each other's work and specialisation will enable the psychologist and vocational guidance officer to avoid duplication of effort. And, in the final phase when children and parents have to decide upon choice of occupation or of vocational training the two services should be present in conference, at least for the difficult cases. b) *Difficulties of entry to the Workshop:* Guidance as to choice of occupation is not however sufficient to ensure a smooth transition from school to working life. Statistical studies show for example that, especially among young workers who have not had the transitional experience of a vocational school or apprenticeship, a high proportion make many changes of job before they settle down more or less satisfactorily. Nevertheless, most young people are glad to leave school, moved by the hope of achieving greater independence or status, by the wish for the adventure of adult life, or sometimes simply by a dislike of school where they have been bored or disappointed.

Children are however apt to experience the change as unexpectedly abrupt and bewildering. Their school has essentially treated them as individuals whose welfare was a first consideration. The workshop, they find, is concerned with an impersonal and often abstract thing, production; they feel themselves to be merely cogs in the machine. Often they find little help from the adult workers or foremen, who are themselves in a similar situation. In short, especially among the least qualified, the impression that they are being used for secondary tasks which have no glamour, disappoints their hope of acquiring adult prestige rapidly. This is one at least of the sources of states of tension which show themselves either by manifestations of discouragement, or by a negativistic attitude—-blustering or waggish—or by indifference and lack of interest in work. And the search for noisy or narcotic distractions is often only a compensation for basic lack of satisfaction in work.

It can safely be said that nowhere as yet has a solution to these and similar problems of transition been satisfactorily found; nor indeed are we fully aware of all the factors, social, psychological and economic, which tend towards adjustment or maladjustment to work. Nevertheless, much could and should be done through apprenticeship centres, through factory welfare services, through part-time day release classes, technical colleges, and the like, and through interesting foremen and senior workers in the adolescent, to avoid the waste, frustration and even serious disturbance which result from a system of laissez-faire.

In such an effort, a comprehensive psychological service containing within itself or collaborating with services of vocational guidance and advice, and working in close co-operation with centres of extended eduation, apprenticeship schemes, community social services, trade unions and factory managements could play a dynamic role. This committee hopes that in the near future carefully planned experiments of various kinds will be undertaken by industry in co-operation with the available services and aimed not only at an empirical solution of the many problems that beset the young worker at the outset of his career but also at a clearer appreciation of the psychological and social pressures which may operate to produce a progressive dulling of the capacity actively to enjoy work and leisure.

Guidance and Counselling Services at University Level

The proportion of university students who experience severe psychological difficulty—either in the first year of their studies or later—seems to have increased to disquieting proportions. Apart from the toll of personal frustration and failure which this entails, it represents a grave loss to the community as a whole and is a sufficient justification for efforts to organize effective guidance services in institutions of higher education.

A word may be said as to the causes of this increased incidence of mental disturbance among university students. Since the early twenties at least there has been a steady increase in the number of students attending universities and other institutions of higher education. This has inevitably meant a democratization of recruitment.

Many, if not the majority, of students now come from families of modest means and suffer from the strain of feeling that they must, at all costs, succeed vocationally. At the same time they may receive little support and understanding from a family which, however well intentioned, has had no prior experience of what higher studies mean. Another factor of uncertainty lies in the inability of the student (a situation also found at the secondary level) to orient himself among the ever-increasing number of specialized courses at a time when he is still ignorant of the realities of the profession towards which his studies are leading him.

The growing complexity of technical, economic, social and administrative activity moreover makes satisfactory vocational guidance and entry into employment more difficult. In former times most students found entry to a profession relatively easy after completing their university courses. Nowadays the university qualification or even the technical diploma does not guarantee employment; and worry on this account may already be affecting the student during his course of study. Political insecurity and the uprooting of populations is another source of anxiety; in certain countries, gifted young people, in addition to the effort demanded by their studies and the misery of having had to leave their native country, have to earn their living. These factors lead to a kind of ambivalent attitude which is not always favourable to well-balanced intellectual development: the need for rapid success seems to demand narrow specialisation, but leaves unsatisfied the desire to profit from the cultural riches offered by University life.

Difficulties may have begun moreover before the end of the secondary school course, with the tension and often the overwork experienced by students in those countries where secondary studies end with external or internal examinations, on the results of which depend any chances of receiving higher education. Nor is the transition itself easy from the more or less regimented life of the school to the freer and more responsible atmosphere of the University. Certainly in the long run it may well be a very useful experience, conducive to personal development, for the student to have to organise his own life and develop a method of work. But at the cost of how many checks and wasted efforts is this experience acquired by those fortunate ones who succeed in passing the danger-points without serious accidents?

It is clearly important that schools and universities should find some solution to those problems and it seems at the present time that a number of convergent measures is better than any single method. These it is suggested should be as follows:

(i) Educational guidance must be continued up to the end of the secondary course, and into the first university year at least. Such guidance is greatly facilitated where school and university co-operate to provide, for example, visits in the final school year to special laboratories or institutions, lecture courses by specialists on the opportunities offered by Universities, what they lead to, and on other aspects of university life. A further valuable measure is the setting up of University Offices of information and documentation linked both with the schools and with employment services. Such centres, however, need the collaboration of the professions and adequate and up-to-date statistical services in order to give a real picture of the activities and current conditions in the possible professions to which the various courses may lead.

(ii) As at the beginning of the secondary school course, so at the outset of higher studies, a course of orientation should help the students to make the transition from secondary school to university. In certain countries the highest form in the secondary school is organised with this aim in view; the instruction, rather than attempting to cover an overloaded programme superficially, is concentrated on a thorough study of a few typical subjects, and a considerable part of the timetable is reserved for pupils to work up the material themselves. When economic conditions permit, it seems desirable that such a course of orientation should be given at the beginning of higher education, provided that University teachers do not, on the pretext of providing general culture, use the time at their disposal to extend their own courses. The objective would be to concentrate the attention of the pupils on the methods peculiar to the disciplines which they wish to follow so that they may see their way more clearly. At the same time, as well as contributing to general culture, such an orientation period would allow both an informed choice of later specialisation and an appraisal of the vocational field.

(iii) In many Universities there are supervisory services intended to help the students during their first years. Sometimes this is by the tutorial system whereby students are attached to a member of staff who acts as supervisor of studies and may, if he is humanly able to do so, act also as a guide, philosopher, and friend to his charges. Sometimes tutorial responsibility is exercised by university graduates in the town, who stand in *loco parentis* to a student coming from the same region or belonging to the same social class. More often, it is students in their later years who, at the request of their associations, take responsibility for younger students. This system often leads to the spontaneous organisation of discussion groups among the students, where personal problems are broached with more complete freedom.

(iv) There remains however a core of problems for which these solutions do not suffice, and which demand more skill and insight than can reasonably be expected of university teachers preoccupied with academic specialities. For these the most efficient solution is likely to be the provision of a complete student guidance service. Such a service which might co-operate with or even form a part of the student health service, would need one or more full time counsellors and should be able to draw upon the part-time assistance of colleagues with special qualifications in departments of psychology, medicine and social science. For those students who pursue courses in Education, Psychology, or other of the Social Sciences, much can be done also through their actual courses in Psychology, if some at least of these take as their point of departure, an examination of the personal problems actually arising in the life of the students. This however is desirable only if the teachers have themselves a sufficient practical training in psychology and can understand and control the emotions and anxieties which such a direct approach may unleash.

Teacher Training

A word should be said specially concerning the training and further training of teachers. Prospective teachers have the same needs as University students generally and the same considerations apply. There are however, in addition, three further roles which the science of educational psychology should increasingly fulfil, in part at least through applied services.

It is recognized that in the educational development of the children he teaches, the personality of the teacher plays a large part. In spite therefore of the shortage of candidates for training as teachers, many countries are experimenting with methods of selection which at least will exclude those who for various personality reasons, are unsuitable for the profession. Teacher training departments, University centres of research, and the psychological services, might well collaborate closely in research to define methods and criteria of selection and in their application and follow-up.

It will be obvious, from what has earlier been said, that a psychological service for schools cannot function adequately without the informed co-operation of the teachers. The foundation for this must be laid in the years of basic training when the student should not merely receive theoretical and practical instruction in educational psychology but should also, if possible, be brought into contact with a functioning service. This facilitates later co-operation and gives reality to courses which only too often students find dull and irrelevant. It is indeed probable that the psychologist in daily contact with problems of the social and educational development of children through participation in a school psychological service, is the person best situated to aid training institutions in giving the future teacher a sound insight into child development.

The third task in which the psychological services should co-operate is that of the further training of experienced teachers. We have already stressed the value of discussion between teacher and psychologist of particular problem children or of particular aspects of educational method. This is a continuing process of in-service training which will operate to the mutual advantage of teacher and psychologist.

There however remains the whole field of short courses and of more extended specialized training, especially for those teachers who will undertake remedial work or work in schools or classes dealing with mentally or physically handicapped children. Here again the psychological service from its intimate contact with the practicalities of education and with social and psychological factors outside the usual range of the class teacher's preoccupations, has a major part to play.

Specialities of School Psychological Services

In no country in Europe have services been developed to the point where all the needs, outlined in the first two sections of this report, are fully and adequately met.

The central problems of organization are those of seeing to it on the one hand that the technical help of psychology is at the daily service of the teacher without usurping his proper functions and on the other that specialized treatment of the appropriate kind is available when it is needed.

Hence a school psychological service has advisory, remedial and co-ordinating functions and should make the bridge between the schools and all the other services, social and medical, which directly or indirectly contribute to the healthy, personal, educational and social growth of children. It should also aim at ensuring that all the needs are covered adequately at all stages of growth from the pre-school period to integration into adult working life.

Size of the Population to be Served

A service so conceived will have need of different types of worker with different patterns of experience and qualification—but essential to it is the educational psychologist in intimate daily contact with the schools, and with children at all stages in their school career. The provision of enough fully trained and competent psychologists however is probably a dream for the future. Neither the supply of suitable candidates for the profession nor the present facilities for training is adequate to meet the foreseeable demands even of the most modest kind. The expert group moreover is firmly of the opinion that it is better to have too few psychologists of high quality than to multiply those whose lack of theoretical training or whose inadequate experience leads them into serious mistakes and undermines the effectiveness of the service given.

The educational guidance of the school child, which has been insisted upon earlier as a vital task, is not one that can be discharged by a snap judgement or even by a day or two of testing. It is a matter for continuous and careful observation supplemented, in those cases where the child has no declared aptitudes or where particular difficulties arise, by a more specialized study. As such, in addition to the services of a supervising psychologist, one class counsellor or specially trained teacher would be necessary for 400-500 children, and could work with a whole school staff. Where the school unit is a large one—say one to two thousand children—it is necessary to have a school psychologist and a social worker together with a teacher trained in the administration of group tests. Such a team can assure the tasks of counselling and guidance, and the more general functions of aiding the school staff to ameliorate the psychological atmosphere of the school; it can give assistance with more difficult individual cases, and screen out and undertake the treatment of those cases which require deeper, and more prolonged study.

Such a solution though desirable in many ways, is far from being generally realisable and alternative solutions have to be sought. The nature of these depends in part upon circumstances peculiar to each country and its school system and in part upon the actual type of population in question. For example, where the teachers, and especially the heads of schools, have themselves had a sound psychological training, and where an effective system of school record cards is in use, the task of guiding children between options can safely be left to the school staff, the psychological service giving its particular attention to difficult cases and generally trying to improve guidance methods for use by teachers. Similarly in rural areas where schools are small, it would be impossibly uneconomic to attempt to provide one psychologist for each school; in such circumstances the travelling psychological service operating from a number of part-time centres has been found effective.

The range and variety of services offered, the co-ordination made among the varied types of workers in one way or another entering into a psychological contact with children and with their families—district nurses, welfare workers, teachers, doctors, magistrates etc.—and the effectiveness with which the various kinds of more or less serious psychological problems met with among school populations can be tackled, does however directly depend upon the number, as well upon the quality of psychological staff available. And the number of staff required cannot be defined in terms of a case load, since the time required by an individual case may vary from an hour to as much as several days or even weeks.

Hence the only practical basis of estimate for the staffing of a school psychological service, in terms of all the functions it should fulfil, is continued experience; and this experience will be dependent upon such factors as density of population, accessibility of the service, the sociological nature of the population, and the richness of the services provided. The committee does not wish to lay down hard and fast standards but experience seems to indicate that a minimum service, in an urban area presenting no special difficulties of communication or of social composition, can be assured by not fewer than two psychologists for a school population of 12,000-15,000 children.

Such a minimum implies that the teaching staff of the school are sufficiently trained themselves to assure the effective educational guidance of the majority of children; that the facilities of a fully staffed child guidance centre are at their disposal; that adequate special school provision, remedial classes and the like are integrated with the service; and finally that close liaison is maintained with a sufficient service of vocational guidance. It is reemphasised, however, that this is a minimum, and not the ideal; and that, moreover, the suggestion made does not imply that it is more than an acceptable alternative to the psychologist operating within the large school unit.

Organisation of a Service

It is not possible at the present stage to lay down organisational details of a school psychological service which would be universally applicable; it is however possible to suggest certain principles which embodied in organization, administration and finance will allow the development of a service able to meet the needs described earlier in this report. These we believe to be as follows:

a) The service should be *comprehensive and flexible* both in organization and in staffing so that it may develop to meet the needs of the schools as they declare themselves and may be able to follow a case through to a successful conclusion;

b) *The contact with the schools should be close and intimate.* On the personal level this will come about through the training of the psychologist himself who would normally be recruited from the teaching profession. Organizationally however this contact is best secured by attaching the service directly to the education authority, national or local.

c) *The service itself should contain the necessary specialised units* for child guidance, remedial teaching, speech reeducation and the like and be closely associated with special schools or classes for various types of exceptional or handicapped children. It should also contain or be very closely associated with vocational guidance services and with student counselling work in higher education.

d) *It should co-operate especially over particular cases with, but not be subordinated to, the school medical service and through this have access to the specialised medical services as may be necessary.*

e) *Its responsibilities should not be limited to children of compulsory school age.* Thus it should be possible for the service to enter into co-operation with the maternal and child welfare clinics at the one end and with factory welfare schemes for the adolescent worker at the other.

f) A special word should be said on finance. *The finance provided must be adequate* to enable all aspects—the schools advisory service, the diagnostic and treatment services as well as the numerous special calls upon the skill and knowledge of the staff—to function as the needs make themselves felt and with shifts of emphasis as the work develops. In work of the kind proposed for the school psychological service, experience repeatedly shows that a ton of prevention costs less than an ounce of cure; and the financing of the service should be such that the preventive aspects of its work are not sacrificed to the need to maintain a given case load for examination and treatment in order to earn a grant. The commit-tee strongly recommends that a global grant be made from the education budget in a category distinct from that for other services; in this way the psychological service will be enabled to function as a unity rather than as a series of differently financed and more or less separate services.

Co-Ordination with Other Services

The educational psychologist, whether working in the school or from an external service, will normally not have the time to deal completely with all the individual difficulties which may present themselves among children. Many of the questions of method and of organization, for example, demand extensive research in which a number of classes or schools may be involved. Similarly, although the majority of difficulties arising in the course of the education of children can be solved by collaboration between psychologist, parent and teacher yet there is a core of problems which demand both more intensive study and more specialized treatment than the school psychologist may have time to give.

Severe cases of maladjustment arising from conditions internal to the pupil, or in his home life, for example, may demand special remedial action, psychotherapy or a radical change in the child's environment. The psychologist must be able to refer such cases to the specialist services of a child guidance centre, a psychiatric unit or medico-educational institute either for a more thorough study or for remedial action.

Many problems of retardation among children of all levels of ability also require special study and special remedial methods which may involve the removal, temporarily at all events, of the child from his normal class, and his placement in a remedial or coaching group. Similarly University departments of research or special research institutions should provide the facilities for the basic research in child development and educational method necessary for the progressive adaptation of the school to the child and the child to the school. Clearly too the psychologist should have access to the school medical service and to the welfare and social services of the community.

Most European countries are developing a considerable variety of special provision for children who cannot be educated in the ordinary schools though none has sufficient as yet. The blind, the deaf, the crippled, the partially sighted, the hard of hearing, children with speech defects, the mentally subnormal and the severely maladjusted or delinquent are more or less adequately provided for. Such schools or classes however should have a functional connection with the normal educational system and should have access to the school psychological services. In many instances it will be the psychologist himself who first recommends special schooling for a particular child; in others it will be the medical services; in the case of delinquents it may be the court or the probation service which recommends that children be seen by the psychological service so that appropriate educational advice can be given. In all instances, and particularly in those cases which are marginal, a close psychological supervision is necessary if the child is to profit from the special provision made for him and to be returned whenever feasible to the normal stream of education. Thus a complete service must envisage a number of specialized services with which the school psychologist should act as a link and which in the majority of cases he will co-ordinate, especially where for administrative reasons they are separately conducted and financed.

Because, however, of national or regional peculiarities of development or because of financial difficulties, the school psychological service may not contain within itself all the specialized diagnostic and treatment units which may be necessary. Moreover there are other services which from time to time are necessary and which, although they touch on the educational sphere, have their main preoccupations elsewhere.Not infrequently the services required to help any given child and his family are fragmented among a number of administrations and are financed from different budgets.

Where no co-ordination exists, wasteful overlapping is regrettably frequent. Workers from different services severally make contact with the family, give sometimes conflicting advice and make financial and administrative arrangements which may well be at variance. We may accept the rule that only one authority should be concerned principally at any one time and add that the overriding authority should be the service which takes the case in hand. In most cases which arise in school the educational psychologist is essentially at the service of the teacher. The power therefore to take action affecting the instruction and education of pupils, and the responsibility for such action, remains with the teacher and the school. If, however, the psychologist or the psychological service undertakes remedial work, then the responsibility for direction of the case must be in the hands of the service. If an outside unit—such for example as the medical service or child psychiatric clinic—is called into consultation merely, responsibility still remains with the psychological service or the school. If, however, a specialized unit undertakes treatment, then while the school psychological service will continue to maintain contact and to collaborate, direction and responsibility will pass to the specialized unit.

Even when based on such a principle, however, collaboration and integration between different services inevitably raises administrative and financial questions and problems of professional responsibility. Certain aspects of a truly comprehensive service—for example the guidance of parents of very young children—may perhaps fall within the scope of the maternal and child welfare service; others—for example that of vocational guidance and adjustment to work—may be considered as more in the field of those administrations concerned with labour problems.

The core of the services for the child of school age will clearly be in the province of the education authorities. It should not however be beyond the bounds of possibility to bring about, at the administrative level, a reasonable division of financial and organisational responsibility and at the functional level a close working relationship between the services provided. Similarly on the basis of a recognition of and respect for the different contributions which can be made by the specialisations of education, psychology, medicine and social work, it is possible for a team approach to be developed among individuals working together over particular problems.

The composition of such a team, its leadership and the responsibilities of each member should vary widely with the circumstances. It may range from the relatively simple collaboration of the teacher and psychologist, to more elaborate groups, such as the child guidance clinic team of psychologist, psychiatrist and psychiatric social worker, or specially constituted groups to consider the complex problems posed by cases in which particular physical or sensory difficulties enter. In such team work it is essential that each member should contribute from his own specialized viewpoint and that the group should reach a *joint* decision based upon all the contributions. Where the decision is truly joint, questions of leadership and of the responsible discipline do not arise; where there is a conflict of opinion then it must be resolved in the way outlined earlier. The committee is however concerned to state that no considerations of inter-professional or inter-administrative rivalry should be allowed to hinder the organic use of available services for the benefit of all children: and it is sometimes of value to set up a joint committee for continuous consultation among the authorities concerned, at least in the early stages of the development of a psychological service.

Staffing

Though the key worker in a psychological service for schools will be the educational psychologist himself, many other types of worker are required, all of whom should have some general insight into the work of the schools. Normally, for example, contact with the homes and much of the task of aiding parents will be discharged by the social worker or, in part, by the school welfare officer. Remedial education for individual failing child-ren or the special education necessary for some types of disturbed, mentally or physically handicapped children will be undertaken by teachers specially trained for the tasks. So too where teachers with a sufficient complement of psychological training are available, they may well be called upon to act as class counsellors, to aid with general educational guidance and in some instances to conduct the first examinations of children presenting problems of educational and personal development. In view of the high level of training and of professional responsibility required of the educational psychologist, efforts should be made to increase the number of those who can, under his supervision, undertake many of the time-consuming and more or less routine tasks which form the main load of a service, leaving him with time and energy free to concentrate upon these problems for which his training specially fits him.

The specialized services of vocational guidance, child guidance, educational and psychological research, have need of psychologists with an emphasis of training different from that required for direct contact with the schools and will call upon other specialities, such as psychiatry, pediatrics, statistics, industrial psychology and social work. The Committee however wishes to point out that, in so far as the staff of these services come into contact with children of school age or with educational problems they too need to have more adequate knowledge of schools than is simply derived from once having been educated.

In certain cases the school psychologist may be expected to work both in the school and in the specialized unit such as the child psychiatric clinic or vocational guidance team. In others he may be required to interpret to colleagues from other disciplines the educational considerations of which account has to be taken in dealing with individual children. Such co-operation is greatly facilitated where the psychologist himself through his training and his work is given an insight into the activities of other professions and where the training of the medical and social work personnel concerned includes a genuine study of education and psychology. It is to be hoped that in the not too distant future the training and further training of all those professions directly concerned with children and adolescents of school age, will contain certain common studies and will in part be undertaken conjointly. In this way the basis of team work will be laid and differentiation of function will not lead either to rivalry or to wasteful overlapping.

Research

The practical functioning service has its roots in and should draw its life blood from continuous association with Universities and with special institutes of educational and psychological research. There should be a constant interchange between the work in the field which throws up research problems and the laboratory or research team which commands the facilities for rigorous enquiry. In such a way the field psychologist and the research worker may both derive benefit and the daily service will not lag behind in the application of the findings of educational and psychological experiment. This general recommendation may be carried further. The committee holds the view that the professional training of the educational psychologist should be conducted in close association with active departments of educational and psychological research.

Moreover the psychological service should be so staffed and financed that the practising psychologist has the time and is encouraged to co-operate closely with a research institute in the scientific study of the problems posed by his daily practice, at least, if not to undertake individual research work himself. Only in this way, will the full and continuous growth of the service in its technical aspects be ensured and the results of fundamental research in the various aspects of child study and education rapidly be ploughed back into practice.

Attention is however drawn by the committee to the fact that in most countries, even those in which psychological work is relatively well developed, research in the field of child study and of the psychology of education is badly underfinanced and depends for the most part upon the good will and voluntary effort of a few psychologists in universities and in existing services. Adequate research into the psychological development of children, into methods of treatment and of special education and'into all the multitudinous problems which currently present themselves in the field of applied psychology, requires staff and money which organisations hard pressed by other demands cannot give. The committee urges upon the responsible authorities the need for a considerably expanded finance for research into this important field.

Basic and applied research should be complemented by a third type which in the present state of development of services is equally essential. In each country, at least one controlled pilot project of a full service should be carried out over a period of years, under research conditions and with the widest facilities for experiment in organisation, administration and staffing. Such experiments should be carefully planned to take place in typical areas presenting as many as possible of the problems to be faced. They should aim at a continuing evaluation of the effectiveness of different methods of bringing psychology into the service of the school, the value and limitations of different types of training, and of remedial methods, and should offer an ideal towards which other services elsewhere would move.

Role of Educational Psychologist

It has been stated earlier that the educational psychologist is the key to a successful school psychological service. Properly chosen and fully trained, working either within a particular school or group of schools or from an external service in close contact with the schools, he is the most effective channel whereby knowledge of child development may be brought directly into the service of education. He can advise the teacher over the minor difficulties presented by individual children, carry out more intensive and detailed case studies, assess levels of intellectual and personal development and suggest modifications of method or programme in the light of his observations. He too is well situated both to initiate experiments in educational methodology and to pass on to his colleagues the teachers the results of research.

Working in this way as the teacher's collaborator, he is in a particularly favourable position to influence the whole life of the school by bringing the insights of psychology to bear upon its daily problems. He does not make his colleagues into psychologists; he should however, by his way of looking at particular cases and situations, bring them to see their task in the light of the developmental psychology of childhood. Similarly the psychologist either working alone or collaborating with the teacher or with the school head, can greatly assist in establishing co-operation with parents and, in special cases, with the families of those children whose school difficulties are a reflection of disturbances at home. The success which he ultimately achieves in that task, however, depends directly upon his insight into and understanding of the teacher's problems; and such insight and understanding can only rarely be developed by the psychologist who has not himself been a teacher. Therefore most countries which have developed a school psychological service now insist upon considerable teaching experience as a necessary qualification for the practice of psychology in the educational field.

The committee here wishes to reemphasize the essential difference in function and aptitude between the teacher and the educational psychologist. The main responsibility of the teacher is to educate his pupils. In doing this, his own personality is part of the educational climate in which the child learns; he builds up an affective relationship, positive or negative with the children he teaches and is himself deeply involved in the process. The psychologist must be observant, able to evaluate and understand objectively all the factors in the child and in the educational situation, without becoming himself emotionally involved to the point where his judgment is affected. It is essential that he should be able not only to understand and use the methods and techniques of his profession but to understand the human problems posed by each individual case. The psychologist not infrequently finds it necessary to draw the attention of the school to the importance of the affective relationships between pupils and teacher which may be overlooked in too exclusive a preoccupation with method. On the other hand he must see to it that the teacher does not become too immersed in the multiplicity of human relationships and thus lose control of his class.

Thus while insisting that the educational psychologist should himself have been a teacher, the committee wishes to add certain cautions. The training, experience, and professional preoccupations of the teacher are essentially different from those required by a psychologist. Moreover the qualities of personality called into play are often not the same. Thus careful selection and a thorough supplementary training are necessary; the first to ensure that the personal qualities necessary to the profession of educational psychologist are present or can be developed; and the second as the basis for effective work.

The very newness of applied psychology, the relative uncertainty of many of its findings and techniques, and the wide and far reaching demands which are made upon its services, all mean that it should only be exercised by those who after a long and profound training are fully aware of its limitations. This is not to say that teachers with a complement of psychological knowledge short of the full training outlined later are not of value to the whole life of the school; it is however to insist that final responsibility for the applications of psychology to education and to individual children, should only be entrusted to those whose training is as complete as current knowledge can make it.

A word too should be said about the practice in some countries of having a psychologically trained teacher or even an educational psychologist in charge of a class and at the same time acting as adviser to his colleagues on psychological problems. The committee considers that, in view of the distinction between the teaching and psychological functions, they cannot normally be exercised simulta- neously and that it is inadvisable for one and the same person to be class teacher and psychologist to the same group of children.

It is not easy for all purposes and for all social and administrative situations, to define the appropriate functions of the school psychologist. These will in part depend upon the qualifications expected of those who exercise the psychological function in the schools, upon the availability of other specialists and auxiliaries, and upon the existence of specialized psychiatric and remedial services. Moreover it is in just those areas where teachers are not as well trained as they should be and where the various auxiliary services of special education, child guidance and the like do not exist that the remedial and advisory services of the educational psychologist are most necessary. Such areas, often rural districts with small schools widely spread, would find a full service difficult to institute and to finance and initially the activity of a psychologist may have to be confined to immediately urgent problems. Nevertheless, without setting priorities, the following minimal functions may be indicated as a first goal towards which any service should work.

(a) He will collaborate with the teachers in the general work of educational guidance, applying whatever standardized tests may be necessary and making thorough individual case studies of children as appropriate. The problem of guidance may be expected to arise not only at the beginning of the secondary school course but whenever a choice of studies must be made and whenever cases of children experiencing difficulty in any particular course are reconsidered;

(b) Naturally following from the above, he will be responsible for establishing in conjunction with his colleagues the teachers the cumulative individual record card for each pupil, for training teachers, if necessary, in its use, and for assisting them to maintain it as a principal document to be consulted when important decisions are to be made;

(c) He will work with teachers, heads of schools and the inspectorate to improve educational methods and the climate of the classroom, bringing to bear upon such problems the specialized knowledge derived from research. In this connection it is important that he should have sufficient time to take part in educational research in conjunction with his colleagues or with teachers.

(d) He will co-operate in, and if necessary, assume the major responsibility for, the examination of children with personal problems. According to the nature of the case, he will raise the question of remedial or other treatment in whatever quarter seems appropriate; with individual teachers, with the head of the school, with the social worker, school medical officer, or with outside services or organizations;

(e) He must be responsible for liaison between all those different services concerned with the educational progress and healthy mental and emotional development of the pupils;

(f) So far as is possible he will take part in school staff meetings, particularly when general problems of child development are to be discussed, or when individual children are considered.

Selection and Training of School Psychologists

Clearly even to discharge such minimal functions effectively and with a full sense of the responsibilities which he may have to assume, the school psychologist should be carefully selected and have a training of the highest quality both theoretical and practical. The following minima seem to meet with general agreement (though far from universally realized) in those countries where psychological services are effectively functioning.

(a) Basic Training and Qualifications

(i) A teaching diploma or other professional qualification as a teacher.

(ii) Educational experience. At least five years of teaching experience, preferably varied, should be required for those who wish to work in schools. A minimum of three years of work with normal children should be demanded of those who wish to work more particularly in the clinical field.

(b) Eelection for Professional Training

It may be agreed that there should be little or no selection (other than is customary for entry to other university schools) of those who wish to study psychology at the undergraduate level. It is however essential that a rigorous selection should subsequently be made of those who wish to become school psychologists. The committee agrees that the criteria should be at least as follows:

(i) In those countries where different levels or classes of university degree exist, a high level of academic attainment (1st. or 2nd. class honours for example) should be demanded of a candidate for professional training;

(ii) The candidate should satisfy the training institution that he has a good level of capacity and has achieved a good professional adjustment in teaching or any other acceptable type of work with children;

(iii) By means of a preliminary period of at least one month devoted to observation and information, the training institution should satisfy itself that the candidate possesses the personal qualities necessary to the profession of educational psychologist, and that he is well acquainted with its demands.

To the above general criteria, of selection, training and qualification one may envisage two types of exception, which will be handled according to local conditions. The first is for those already working in the profession before the establishment of conditions of admission. Clearly, subject to the necessary professional safeguards, such workers should be confirmed in their acquired right to practise. Secondly, there are candidates with something of value to contribute but whose previous training and experience are different from those outlined above. Such cases should be considered individually on their merits with the proviso that the preliminary qualifications demanded should be equivalent in value.

It is clear that, under the conditions outlined above, educational psychologists will in the main be recruited from among those who already have some seniority in teaching or another cognate profession. Hence this committee urges administrative authorities (and in particular Ministries of Education) to take measures, by the release of staff members for professional training, and in selected cases, for the basic training as well, on full salary or aided by bursaries, to ensure that suitable candidates come forward.

(c) Responsibility for Professional Training

The committee recommends that the professional training should be undertaken by a University or institution of higher learning of university status and should lead to a special diploma in Educational Psychology. The content and method of the training and the final examination however should be agreed between the training institution and the appropriate professional body.

(d) Length of Professional Training

This professional training should last for at least *two full years* and from the outset should be both practical and theoretical. It is desirable that theoretical training should predominate in the first year backed however by diversified practical experience (in schools, clinics, etc.). The second year should lay greater stress upon practical training, particularly upon work in a psychological service under the supervision of an experienced educational psychologist.

(e) Content and Method of Professional Training

It is inappropriate here to enter into details of training. The committee however suggests that this should be balanced between courses covering systematic theory, practical work, and continuous periods of supervised practice. The educational psychologist should come to understand the structure of groups as well as the psychology of individuals. He should be fully trained in child development, the psychology of subject matter, in observational techniques, in tests and measurements, in experimental and research design, and in remedial methods of all kinds, so that he may give educational guidance, conduct psychological examinations, undertake remedial work and cooperate in or carry out research.

Professional Responsibility

In few countries as yet have educational psychologists a legally protected professional status other than that conferred upon them by their teaching function. In many however the specialization has been administratively recognized and a de facto status acquired. This committee urges on the attention of responsible bodies (notably Ministries of Education) the need for establishing jointly with the profession, a professional code and an adequate register of those competent to practise. As an interim measure, pending legal sanction, a council of the profession itself should invite the participation of the teaching profession, the educational administration and possibly of allied professions working in closely related fields, in the setting up and control of training standards and the granting of professional recognition to newly trained psychologists.

One of the more important items in any professional code will be that related to professional discretion and confidence. The psychologist by the very nature of his function receives confidential information from parents, teachers and children. He will also through his professional investigation discover facts concerning individuals, their personality, background, capacities and the like which, while necessary to the formation of an adequate opinion, should not in their crude form be divulged to those not competent to interpret them. Thus only such information as is in the best interests of the child, should be passed on to colleagues in other professions, and this information should be transmitted in a form which is intelligible to them. Detailed case material, the results of psychological tests and the like should not be generally divulged. Only in this way can the psychologist observe a professional code of ethics and justify the confidence reposed in him by all concerned. Where the psychologist is acting primarily as consultant to the teacher he is naturally under a special obligation to inform his colleague of all that is directly relevant to the teacher's task and responsibility vis a vis the child, without of course abandoning his duty to observe the confidence reposed in him by the parents or by the child.

References

Alderblum, E., (1950). "Beginning School-Guidance early". Mental Hygiene, U.S.A., Vol. 34, no. 4, Oct.

Cassidy, R. & Kozman, H. CL., (1947). *Counsefing Girls in a Changing Society*, New York & London. McGraw-Hill Book Co.

Cleugh, M. F., (1951). *Psychology in the Service of the School.* London, Methuen.

Erickson, C. E. & Smith, G. E., (1947). *Organization and Administration of Guidance Services.* New York & London, McGraw-Hill Book Co.

Hamley et al., (1937). *The Educational Guidance of the School Child.* London, Evans Bros.

Little, W. & Chapman, A. L., (1953). *Developmental Guidance in Secondary School.* New York, Toronto &London, McGraw-Hill Book Co.

Strang, R., (1948). *Educational Guidance: Its Principles and Pratice.* New York, McMillan.

5

Constructivist Approaches to Teaching

One of the most important principles of educational psychology is that teachers cannot simply give students knowledge. Students must construct knowledge in their own minds. The teacher can facilitate this process by teaching in ways that make information meaningful and relevant to students, by giving students opportunities to discover or apply ideas themselves, and by teaching students to be aware of and consciously use their own strategies for learning. Teachers can give students ladders that lead to higher understanding, yet the students themselves must climb these ladders.

A revolution is taking place in educational psychology. This revolution goes by many names, but the name that is most frequently used is *Constructivist theories of learning*. The essence of constructivist theory is the idea that learners must individually discover and transform complex information if they are to make it their own.

Constructivist theory sees learners as constantly checking new information against old rules and then revising rules when they no longer work. This view has profound implications for teaching, as it suggests a far more active role for students in their own learning than is typical in many classrooms. Because of the emphasis on students as active learners, constructivist strategies are often called *student-centered instruction.* In a student-centered classroom the teacher becomes the "guide on the side" instead of the "sage on the stage," helping students to discover their own meaning instead of lecturing and controlling all classroom activities.

Historical Roots of Constructivism

The constructivist revolution has deep roots in the history of education. It draws heavily on the work of Piaget and Vygotsky, both of whom emphasized that cognitive change takes place only when previous conceptions go through a process of disequilibration in light of new information. Piaget and Vygotsky also emphasized the social nature of learning, and both suggested the use of mixed-ability learning groups to promote conceptual change.

Social Learning

Modern constructivist thought draws most heavily on Vygot-sky's theories, which have been used to support classroom instructional methods that emphasize cooperative learning, project-based learning, and discovery. Four key principles derived from Vygotsky's ideas have played an important role. First is his emphasis on the social nature of learning . Children learn, he proposed, through joint interactions with adults and more capable peers. On cooperative projects, like the one in Mr. Dunbar's class, children are exposed to their peers' thinking processes; this method not only makes the learning outcome available to all students, but also makes other students' thinking processes available to all. Vygotsky noted that successful problem solvers talk themselves through difficult problems. In cooperative groups, children can hear this inner speech out loud and can learn how successful problem solvers are thinking through their approaches.

Zone of Proximal Development

A second key concept is the idea that children learn best the concepts that are in their zone of proximal development. For example, if a child could not find the median of a set of numbers by himself but could do so with some assistance from his teacher, then finding medians is probably in his zone of proximal development. When children are working together, each child is likely to have a peer performing on a given task at a slightly higher cognitive level, exactly within the child's zone of proximal development.

Cognitive Apprenticeship

Another concept derived from Vygotsky's emphases both on the social nature of learning and on the zone of proximal development is *cognitive apprenticeshi*. This term refers to the process by which a learner gradually acquires expertise through interaction with an expert, either an adult or an older or more advanced peer. In many occupations, new workers learn their jobs through a process of apprenticeship, in which a new worker works closely with an expert, who provides a model, gives feedback to the less experienced worker, and gradually socializes the new worker into the norms and behaviors of the profession. Student teaching is a form of apprenticeship. Constructivist theorists suggest that teachers transfer this long-standing and highly effective model of teaching and learning to day-to-day activities in classrooms, both by engaging students in complex tasks and helping them through these tasks and by engaging students in heterogeneous, cooperative learning groups in which more advanced students help less advanced ones through complex tasks.

Mediated Learning

Finally, Vygotsky's emphasis on scaffolding, or mediated learning, is important in modern constructivist thought. Current interpretations of Vygotsky's ideas emphasize the idea that students should be given complex, difficult, realistic tasks and then be given enough help to achieve these tasks (rather than being taught little bits of knowledge that are expected someday to build up to complex tasks). This principle is used to support the classroom use of projects, simulations, explorations in the community, writing for real audiences, and other authentic tasks. The term situated learning is used to describe learning that takes place in real-life, authentic tasks.

Top-Down Processing

Constructivist approaches to teaching emphasize top-down rather than bottom-up instruction. The term *top-down* means that students begin with complex problems to solve and then work out or discover (with the teacher's guidance) the basic skills required. For example, students might be asked to write compositions and only later learn about spelling, grammar, and punctuation. This top-down processing approach is contrasted with the traditional bottom-up strategy, in which basic skills are gradually built into more complex skills. In top-down teaching, the tasks students begin with are complex, complete, and authentic, meaning that they are not parts or simplifications of the tasks that students are ultimately expected to perform but are the actual tasks. As one instance of a constructivist approach to mathematics teaching, consider an example from Lampert . The traditional, bottom-up approach to teaching the multiplication of two-digit numbers by one-digit numbers (e.g., 4 × 12 = 48) is to teach students a step-by-step procedure to get the right answer. Only after students have mastered this basic skill are they given simple application problems, such as "Sondra saw some pencils that cost 12 cents each. How much money would she need to buy four of them?"

The constructivist approach works in exactly the opposite order, beginning with problems (often proposed by the students themselves) and then helping students figure out how to do the operations.

Recall how the Master Minds bounced ideas off of each other, tried out and discarded false leads, and ultimately came up with a solution and a way to prove that their solution was correct. None of the students could have solved the problem alone, so the group work was helpful in arriving at a solution. More important, the experience of hearing others' ideas, trying out and receiving immediate feedback on proposed solutions, and arguing about different ways to proceed gave the Master Minds the cognitive scaffolding that Vygotsky, Bruner, and other constructivists hold to be essential to higher-order learning.

Cooperative Learning

Constructivist approaches to teaching typically make extensive use of cooperative learning, on the theory that students will more easily discover and comprehend difficult concepts if they can talk with each other about the problems. Again, the emphasis on the social nature of learning and the use of groups of peers to model appropriate ways of thinking and expose and challenge each other's misconceptions are key elements of Piaget's and Vygotsky's conceptions of cognitive change.

Discovery Learning

Discovery learning is an important component of modern constructivist approaches that has a long history in education innovation. In *discovery learning*, students are encouraged to learn largely on their own through active involvement with concepts and principles, and teachers encourage students to have experiences and conduct experiments that permit them to discover principles for themselves. Bruner, an advocate of discovery learning, put it this way: "We teach a subject not to produce little living libraries on that subject, but rather to get a student to think . . . for himself, to consider matters as an historian does, to take part in the process of knowledge-getting Knowing is a process, not a product".

Discovery learning has applications in many subjects. For example, some science museums have a series of cylinders of different sizes and weights, some hollow and some solid. Students are encouraged to race the cylinders down a ramp. By careful experimentation the students can discover the underlying principles that determine the cylinders' speed. Computer simulations can create environments in which students can discover scientific principles. After-school enrichment programs (Bergstrom & O'Brien, 2001) and innovative science programs are particularly likely to be based on principles of discovery learning.

Discovery learning has several advantages. It arouses students' curiosity, motivating them to continue to work until they find answers. Students also learn independent problem-solving and critical-thinking skills, because they must analyze and manipulate information.

Self-Regulated Learning

A key concept of constructivist theories of learning is a vision of the ideal studentas a self-regulated learner. *Selfregulated learners* are ones who have knowledge of effective learning strategies and how and when to use them . For example, they know how to break complex problems into simpler steps or to test out alternative solutions they know how and when to skim and how and when to read for deep understanding; and they know how to write to persuade and how to write to inform . Further, self-regulated learners are motivated by learning itself, not only by grades or others' approval, and they are able to stick to a long-term task until it is done. When students have both effective learning strategies and the motivation and persistence to apply these strategies until a job is done to their satisfaction, then they are likely to be effective learners and to have a lifelong motivation to learn .

Scaffolding

According to Vygotsky, higher mental functions, including the ability to direct memory and attention in a purposeful way and to think in symbols, are mediated behaviors. Mediated externally by culture, these and other behaviors become internalized in the learner's mind as psychological tools. In assisted learning, or *mediated learning*, the teacher is the cultural agent who guides instruction so that students will master and internalize the skills that permit higher. cognitive functioning. The ability to internalize cultural tools relates to the learner's age or stage of cognitive development. Once acquired, however, internal mediators allow greater self-mediated learning.

In practical terms, scaffolding might include giving students more structure at the beginning of a set of lessons and gradually turning responsibility over to them to operate on their own. For example, students can be taught to generate their own questions about material they are reading. Early on, the teacher might suggest the questions, modeling the kinds of questions students might ask, but students later take over the question-generating task.

Research has measured parents' use of scaffolding while helping fifth-graders with math homework. Researchers measured the degree to which adults shifted their level of intervention to fit the child's zone of proximal development. When the child is having difficulty, the adult who stays within this region increases his or her directiveness just enough to provide support but not so much as to take over the task, then reduces directiveness when the child begins to succeed. Findings revealed that make use of this principle predicted gains in children's learning of mathematics. Scaffolding is closely related to cognitive apprenticeship; experts working with apprentices typically engage them in complex tasks and then give them decreasing amounts of advice and guidance over time.

APA's Learner-Centered Psychological Principles

In 1992 the American Psychological Association's Task Force on Psychology in Education published a document called *Learner-Centered Psychological Principles: Guidelines for School Redesign and Reform* . Revised in 1997, this publication presents a consensus view of principles of learning and motivation among prominent educational psychologists primarily working within the constructivist tradition.

The Learner-Centered Psychological Principles paint a picture of the learner as actively seeking knowledge by (1) reinterpreting information and experience for himself or herself, (2) being self-motivated by the quest for knowledge (rather than being motivated by grades or other rewards), (3) working with others to socially construct meaning, and (4) being aware of his or her own learning strategies and capable of applying them to new problems or circumstances.

Constructivist Methods in the Content Areas

Constructivist and student-centered methods have come to dominate current thinking in all areas of curriculum. The following sections describe constructivist approaches in reading, mathematics, and science.

Reciprocal Teaching in Reading

One well-researched example of a constructivist approach based on principles of question generation is *reciprocal teaching*. This approach, designed primarily to help low achievers in elementary and middle schools learn reading comprehension, involves the teacher working with small groups of students. Initially, the teacher models questions students might ask as they read, but students are soon appointed to act as "teacher" to generate questions for each other. Note in the example how the teacher directs the conversation about crows at first but then turns the responsibility over to Jim (who is about to turn it over to another student as the example ends). The teacher is modeling the behaviors she wants the students to be able to do on their own and then changes her role to that of facilitator and organizer as the students begin to generate the actual questions. Research on reciprocal teaching has generally found this strategy to increase the achievement of low achievers.

Questioning the Author

Another constructivist approach for reading is Questioning the Author. In this method, children in grades 3–9 are taught to see the authors of factual material as real, fallible people and to then engage in simulated "dialogues" with the authors. As the students are reading a text, the teacher stops them from time to time to ask questions such as "What is the author trying to say, or what does she want us to know?" and then follows up with questions such as "How does that fit in with what she said before?" Ultimately, the students themselves take responsibility for formulating questions of the author's intent and meaning. A study of fifth- and sixth-graders found that students who experienced this technique recalled more from texts than did a comparison group, and were far more likely to describe the purpose of reading as *understanding* rather than just memorizing the text.

Constructivist Approaches to Mathematics Teaching in Primary Grades

Carpenter and colleagues described four approaches to early mathematics instruction for the early elementary grades. In all four, students work together in small groups; teachers pose problems and then circulate among groups to facilitate the discussion of strategies, join students in asking questions about strategies they have proposed, and occasionally offer alternative strategies when students appear to be stuck. In Supporting Ten-Structured Thinking, children use base-10 blocks to invent procedures for adding and subtracting large numbers. Conceptually Based Instruction (CBI) makes extensive use of physical, pictorial, verbal, and symbolic presentations of mathematical ideas and gives students opportunities to solve complex problems using these representations and to contrast different representations of the same concepts. Similarly, the Problem Centered Mathematics Project (PCMP) leads children through stages, from modeling with counters to solving more abstract problems without counters. Cognitively Guided Instruction (CGI), unlike STST and CBI, does not have a specific curriculum or recommended set of activities but provides extensive professional development for teachers of primary mathematics, focusing on principles similar to those used in the other programs. There is good evidence that this program increases student achievement not only on measures related to higher-level thinking in mathematics, which is the program's focus, but also on computational skills.

In these and other constructivist approaches to mathematics, the emphasis is on beginning with real problems for students to solve intuitively and letting students use their existing knowledge of the world to solve problems any way they can. Only at the end of the process, when students have achieved a firm conceptual understanding, are they taught formal, abstract representations of the mathematical processes they have been working with .

Constructivist Approaches in Science

Discovery, group work, and conceptual change have long been emphasized in science education, so it is not surprising that many elementary and secondary science educators have embraced constructivist ideas. In this subject, constructivism translates into an emphasis on hands-on, investigative laboratory activities.

Research on Constructivist Methods

Research comparing constructivist and traditional approaches to instruction is often difficult to interpret, because constructivist methods are themselves very diverse and are usually intended to produce outcomes that are qualitatively different from those of traditional methods. For example, many researchers argue that acquisition of skills and basic information must be balanced against constructivist approaches. But what is the appropriate balance, and for which objectives ? Also, much of the research on constructivist methods is descriptive rather than comparative. However, there are studies showing positive effects of constructivist approaches on traditional achievement measures in mathematics, science, reading, and writing. Furthermore, a study by Knapp found a correlation between use of more constructivist approaches and achievement gains in high-poverty schools. Weinberger & McCombs found that students who reported more learner-centered methods used in their classrooms performed at a higher level than other students. Still, much more research is needed to establish the conditions under which constructivist approaches are effective for enhancing student achievement.

Cooperative Learning and Instructional Methods

In *cooperative learning* instructional methods, students work together in small groups to help each other learn. Many quite different approaches to cooperative learning exist. Most involve students in four-member, mixed-ability groups, but some methods use dyads, and some use varying group sizes. Typically, students are assigned to cooperative groups and stay together as a group for many weeks or months. They are usually taught specific skills that will help them work well together, such as active listening, giving good explanations, avoiding putdowns, and including other people.

Cooperative learning activities can play many roles in lessons. After the formal lesson, students worked as discussion groups. Finally, students had an opportunity to work together to make sure that all group members had learned everything in the lesson in preparation for a quiz, working in a group study format.

Cooperative Learning Methods

Many quite different cooperative learning methods have been developed and researched. The most extensively evaluated cooperative learning methods are described in the following sections.

Student Teams-achievement Divisions (STAD)

In Student Teams-achievement Divisions (STAD), students are assigned to four-member learning teams that are mixed in performance level, gender, and ethnicity. The teacher presents a lesson, and then students work within their teams to make sure that all team members have mastered the lesson. Finally, all students take individual quizzes on the material, at which time they may not help one another.

Students' quiz scores are compared to their own past averages, and points are awarded on the basis of the degree to which students meet or exceed their own earlier performance. These points are then summed to form team scores, and teams that meet certain criteria may earn certificates or other rewards. In a related method called Teams-Games-Tournaments (TGT), students play games with members of other teams to add points to their team scores.

STAD and TGT have been used in a wide variety of subjects, from mathematics to language arts to social studies, and have been used from second grade through college. The STAD method is most appropriate for teaching well-defined objectives with single right answers, such as mathematical computations and applications, language usage and mechanics, geography and map skills, and science facts and concepts. However, it can easily be adapted for use with less well-defined objectives by incorporating more open-ended assessments, such as essays or performances. STAD is described in more detail in the next Theory into Practice.

Student Teams-Achievement Divisions (STAD)

An effective cooperative learning method is called Student Teams-Achievement Divisions, or STAD. STAD consists of a regular cycle of teaching, cooperative study in mixed-ability teams, and quizzes, with recognition or other rewards provided to teams whose members excel.

STAD consists of a regular cycle of instructional activities, as follows:

- *Teach*: Present the lesson.
- *Team study*: Students work on worksheets in their teams to master the material.
- *Test:* Students take individual quizzes or other assessments (such as essays or performances).
- *Team recognition:* Team scores are computed on the basis of team members' scores, and certificates, a class newsletter, or a bulletin board recognizes high-scoring teams.

The following steps describe how to introduce students to STAD:

1. Assign students to teams of four or five-members each. Four are preferable; make five-member teams only if the class is not divisible by four. To assign the students, rank them from top to bottom on some measure of academic performance (e.g., past grades, test scores) and divide the ranked list into quarters, placing any extra students in the middle quarters. Then put one student from each quarter on each team, making sure that the teams are well balanced in gender and ethnicity. Extra (middle) students may become fifth members of teams.
2. Make a worksheet and a short quiz for the lesson you plan to teach. During team study (one or two class periods) the team members' tasks are to master the material you presented in your lesson and to help their teammates master the material. Students have worksheets or other study materials that they can use to practice the skill being taught and to assess themselves and their teammates.
3. When you introduce STAD to your class, read off team assignments.
   - Have teammates move their desks together or move to team tables, and allow students about 10 minutes to decide on a team name.
   - Hand out worksheets or other study materials (two of each per team). Suggest that students on each team work in pairs or threes. If they are working problems (as in math), each student in a pair or threesome should work the problem and then check with his or her partner(s). If anyone missed a question, that student's teammates have a responsibility to explain it. If students are working on short-answer questions, they might quiz each other, with partners taking turns holding the answer sheet or attempting to answer the questions.
   - Emphasize to students that they are not finished studying until they are sure that all their teammates will make 100 percent on the quiz.
   - Make sure that students understand that the worksheets are for studying—not for filling out and handing in. That is why it is important for students to have the answer sheets to check themselves and their teammates as they study.

- Have students explain answers to one another instead of just checking each other against the answer sheet.
- When students have questions, have them ask a teammate before asking you.
- While students are working in teams, circulate through the class, praising teams that are working well and sitting in with each team to hear how the members are doing.

4. Distribute the quiz or other assessment, and give students adequate time to complete it. Do not let students work together on the quiz; at this point they must show what they have learned as individuals. Have students move their desks apart if this is possible. Either allow students to exchange papers with members of other teams or collect the quizzes to score after class.
5. Figure individual and team scores. Team scores in STAD are based on team members' improvements over their own past records. As soon as possible after each quiz, you should compute individual team scores, and write a class newsletter (or prepare a class bulletin board) to announce the team scores. If at all possible, the announcement of team scores should be made in the first period after the quiz. This makes the connection between doing well and receiving recognition clear to students, increasing their motivation to do their best. Compute team scores by adding up the improvement points earned by the team members and dividing the sum by the number of team members who are present on the day of the quiz.
6. Recognize team accomplishments. As soon as you have calculated points for each student and figured team scores, you should provide some sort of recognition to any teams that averaged 20 improvement points or more. You might give certificates to team members or prepare a bulletin board display. It is important to help students value team success. Your own enthusiasm about team scores will help. If you give more than one quiz in a week, combine the quiz results into a single weekly score. After 5 or 6 weeks of STAD, reassign students to new teams. This allows students to work with other classmates and keeps the program fresh.

Cooperative Integrated Reading and Composition (CIRC)

Cooperative Integrated Reading And Composition (Circ) is a comprehensive program for teaching reading and writing in the upper elementary grades. Students work in four-member cooperative learning teams. They engage in a series of activities with one another, including reading to one another, making predictions about how narrative stories will come out, summarizing stories to one another, writing responses to stories, and practicing spelling, decoding, and vocabulary. They also work together to master main ideas and other comprehension skills. During language arts periods, students engage in writing drafts, revising and editing one another's work, and preparing for publication of team books. Three studies of the CIRC program have found positive effects on students' reading skills, including improved scores on standardized reading and language tests.

Jigsaw

In *Jigsaw*, students are assigned to six-member teams to work on academic material that has been broken down into sections. For example, a biography might be divided into early life, first accomplishments, major setbacks, later life, and impact on history. Each team member reads his or her section. Next, members of different teams who have studied the same sections meet in expert groups to discuss their sections. Then the students return to their teams and take turns teaching their teammates about their sections. Since the only way students can learn sections other than their own is to listen carefully to their teammates, they are motivated to support and show interest in one another's work. In a modification of this approach called Jigsaw II, students work in four- or five-member teams, as in STAD. However, each student receives a topic on which to become an expert. Students with the same topics meet in expert groups to discuss them, after which they return to their teams to teach what they have learned to their teammates. The students take individual quizzes, which result in team scores, as in STAD.

Learning Together

Learning Together, a model of cooperative learning developed by David Johnson and Roger Johnson, involves students working in four- or five-member heterogeneous groups on assignments. The groups hand in a single completed assignment and receive praise and rewards based on the group product. This method emphasizes team-building activities before students begin working together and regular discussions within groups about how well they are working together.

Group Investigation

Group Investigation is a general classroom organization plan in which students work in small groups using cooperative inquiry, group discussion, and cooperative planning and projects. In this method, students form their own two- to six-member groups. After choosing subtopics from a unit that the entire class is studying, the groups break their subtopics into individual tasks and carry out the activities that are necessary to prepare group reports. Each group then makes a presentation or display to communicate its findings to the entire class.

Cooperative Scripting

Many students find it helpful to get together with classmates to discuss material they have read or heard in class. A formalization of this age-old practice has been researched by Dansereau and his colleagues. In it, students work in pairs and take turns summarizing sections of the material for one another. While one student summarizes, the other listens and corrects any errors or omissions. Then the two students switch roles, continuing in this manner until they have covered all the material to be learned. A series of studies of this *cooperative scripting* method has consistently found that students who study this way learn and retain far more than students who summarize on their own or who simply read the material. It is interesting that while both participants in the cooperative pairs gain from the activity, the larger gains are seen in the sections that students teach to their partners rather than in those for which they serve as listeners. More recent studies of various forms of peer tutoring find similar results.

Research on Cooperative Learning

Cooperative learning methods fall into two broad categories. One category might be called group study methods, in which students primarily work together to help one another master a relatively well-defined body of information or skills—what Cohen calls "well-structured problems." The other category is often called project-based learning or active learning. Project-based learning methods involve students working in groups to create a report, experiment, mural, or other product. Project-based learning methods such as those described by Blumenfeld, Marx, Soloway, and Krajcik, Palincsar, Anderson, and David ; and Sharan and Sharan focus on ill-structured problems, which typically have less of a clear expected outcome or instructional objective. Methods of this kind are often referred to as collaborative learning methods.

Most research comparing cooperative learning to traditional teaching methods has evaluated group study methods such as STAD, Jigsaw II, CIRC, and Johnson's methods. More than 100 studies have compared achievement of students in such methods to that of students in traditional classrooms over periods of at least 4 weeks. The results have consistently favored cooperative learning as long as two essential conditions are met. First, some kind of recognition or small reward must be provided to groups that do well so that group members can see that it is in their interest to help their groupmates learn. Second, there must be individual accountability. That is, the success of the group must depend on the individual learning of all group members, not on a single group product. For example, groups might be evaluated on the basis of the average of their members' scores on individual quizzes or essays, or students might be individually responsible for a unique portion of a group task. Without this individual accountability there is a danger that one student might do the work of the others, or that some students might be shut out of group interaction because they are thought to have little to contribute.

Studies of cooperative learning methods that incorporate group goals and individual accountability show substantial positive effects on the achievement of students in grades 2 through 12 in all subjects and in all types of schools. Effects are similar for all grade levels and for all types of content, from basic skills to problem solving . Although cooperative learning methods are usually used for only a portion of a student's school day and school year, one study found that students in schools that used a variety of cooperative learning methods in almost all subjects for a 2-year period achieved significantly better than did students in traditionally organized schools.

These effects were particularly positive for the highest achievers (compared to equally high achievers in the control group) and for the special-education students. Other studies have found equal effects of cooperative learning for high, average, and low achievers and for boys and girls . There is some evidence that these methods are particularly effective for African American and Latino students. More informal cooperative learning methods, lacking group goals and individual accountability, have not generally had positive effects on student achievement.

In addition to group goals and individual accountability, a few classroom practices can contribute to the effectiveness of cooperative learning. For example, students in cooperative groups who are taught communication and helping skills or are taught metacognitive learning strategies learn more than do students in usual cooperative groups. For example, King taught students generic question forms to ask each other as they studied, such as "compare and contrast and," or "how does affect?" Students in classes that used these discourse patterns learned more than students using other forms of cooperative learning. A great deal of research has shown that students who give extensive explanations to others learn more in cooperative groups than do those who give or receive short answers or no answers.

There is less research on the effects of project-based forms of cooperative learning focused on ill-structured problems; but the studies that do exist show equally favorable results of cooperative methods designed for such problems. In particular, a study by Sharan and Shachar found substantial positive effects of the Group Investigation method on higher-order objectives in language and literature, and studies by Cohen have shown that the more consistently teachers implement her Complex Instruction program, the better children achieve.

In addition to boosting achievement, cooperative learning methods have had positive effects on such outcomes as improved intergroup relations, self-esteem, attitudes toward school, and acceptance of children with special educational needs. Studies find that cooperative learning is very widely used, but the forms of cooperative learning most often used are informal methods lacking group goals and individual accountability. If this method is to achieve its full potential, educators will need to focus on more research-based strategies.

Teaching of Problem-Solving and Thinking Skills

Students cannot be said to have learned anything useful unless they have the ability to use information and skills to solve problems. For example, a student might be quite good at adding, subtracting, and multiplying but have little idea of how to solve this problem: "Sylvia bought four hamburgers at $1.25 each, two orders of french fries at 65 cents, and three large sodas at 75 cents. How much change did she get from a 10-dollar bill?"

Sylvia's situation is not an unusual one in real life, and the computations involved are not difficult. However, many students (and even some otherwise competent adults) would have difficulty solving this problem. The difficulty of most applications problems in mathematics lies not in the computations but in knowing how to set the problem up so that it can be solved. *Problem solving* is a skill that can be taught and learned.

General Problem-solving Strategies

Students can be taught several wellresearched strategies to use in solving problems. Bransford and Stein developed and evaluated a five-step strategy called IDEAL:

I Identify problems and opportunities

D Define goals and represent the problem

E Explore possible strategies

A Anticipate outcomes and act

L Look back and learn

IDEAL and similar strategies begin with careful consideration of what problem needs to be solved, what resources and information are available, and how the problem can be represented (e.g., in a drawing, outline, or flowchart) and then broken into steps that lead to a solution. In solving Sylvia's problem, the goal is to find out how much change she will receive from a 10-dollar bill after buying food and drinks. We might then break the problem into substeps, each with its own subgoal:

1. Figure how much Sylvia spent on hamburgers.
2. Figure how much Sylvia spent on french fries.
3. Figure how much Sylvia spent on sodas.
4. Figure how much Sylvia spent in total.
5. Figure how much change Sylvia gets from $10.00.

Means–Ends Analysis

Deciding what the problem is and what needs to be done involves a *means–ends analysis*. Learning to solve problems requires a great deal of practice with different kinds of problems that demand thought. All too often, textbooks in mathematics and other subjects that include many problems fail to present problems that will make students think. For example, they might give students a set of word problems whose solutions require the multiplication of two numbers. Students soon learn that they can solve such problems by looking for any two numbers and multiplying them. In real life, however, problems do not line themselves up neatly in categories. We might hear, "Joe Smith got a 5 percent raise last week, which amounted to $1,200." If we want to figure out how much Joe was making before his raise, the hard part is not doing the calculation, but knowing what calculation is called for. In real life this problem would not be on a page titled "Dividing by Percents." The more different kinds of problems students learn to solve, and the more they have to think to solve the problems, the greater the chance that, when faced with real-life problems, students will be able to transfer their skills or knowledge to the new situation.

Extracting Relevant Information

Realistic problems are rarely neat and tidy. Imagine that Sylvia's problem was as follows:

> Sylvia walked into the fast-food restaurant at 6:18 with three friends. Between them, they bought four hamburgers at $1.25 each, two orders of french fries at 65 cents, and three large sodas at 75 cents. Onion rings were on sale for 55 cents. Sylvia's mother told her to be in by 9:00, but she was already 25 minutes late by the time she and her friends left the restaurant. Sylvia drove the 3 miles home at an average of 30 miles per hour. How long was Sylvia in the restaurant?

The first part of this task is to clear away all the extraneous information to get to the important facts. The means-ends analysis suggests that only time information is relevant, so all the money transactions and the speed of Sylvia's car can be ignored. Careful reading of the problem reveals that Sylvia left the restaurant at 9:25. This and her arrival time of 6:18 are all that matters for solving the problem. Once we know what is relevant and what is not, the solution is easy.

Representing The Problem

For many kinds of problems, graphic representation might be an effective means of finding a solution. Adams provides a story that illustrates this:

A Buddhist monk has to make a pilgrimage and stay overnight in a temple that is at the top of a high mountain. The road spirals around and around the mountain. The monk begins walking up the mountain at sunrise.

He walks all day long and finally reaches the top at about sunset. He stays all night in the temple and performs his devotions. At sunrise the next day the monk begins walking down the mountain. It takes him much less time than walking up, and he is at the bottom shortly after noon. The question is: Is there a point on the road when he was coming down that he passed at the same time of day when he was coming up the mountain?

This can seem to be a difficult problem because people begin to reason in a variety of ways as they think about the man going up and down. Adams points out one representation that makes the problem easy: Suppose there were two monks, one leaving the top at sunrise and one starting up at sunrise. Would they meet? Of course they would.

In addition to drawings, there are many other ways of representing problems. Students may be taught to make diagrams, flowcharts, outlines, and other means of summarizing and depicting the critical components of a problem.

Teaching Creative Problem Solving

Most of the problems students encounter in school might require careful reading and some thought, but little creativity. However, many of the problems we face in life are not so cut-and-dried. Life is full of situations that call for creative problem solving, as in figuring out how to change or end a relationship without hurt feelings or how to repair a machine with a bent paper clip.

The following sections describe a strategy for teaching creative problem solving.

Incubation

Creative problem solving is quite different from the analytical, step-by-step process that was used to solve Sylvia's problems. In creative problem solving, one important principle is to avoid rushing to a solution; instead, it is useful to pause and reflect on the problem and think through, or incubate, several alternative solutions before choosing a course of action. Consider the following simple problem:

Roger baked an apple pie in his oven in three quarters of an hour. How long would it take him to bake three apple pies?

Many students would rush to multiply 45 minutes by 3. However, if they took some time to reflect, most would realize that baking three pies in the same oven would actually take about the same amount of time as baking one pie! In teaching this process, teachers must avoid putting time pressures on students. Instead of speed, they should value ingenuity and careful thought.

Suspension of Judgment

In creative problem solving, students should be encouraged to suspend judgment, to consider all possibilities before trying out a solution. One specific method based on this principle is called *brainstorming*, in which two or more individuals suggest as many solutions to a problem as they can think of, no matter how seemingly ridiculous. Only after they have thought of as many ideas as possible is any idea evaluated as a possible solution. The point of brainstorming is to avoid focusing on one solution too early and perhaps ignoring better ways to proceed.

Appropriate Climates

Creative problem solving is enhanced by a relaxed, even playful environment. Perhaps even more important, students who are engaging in creative problem solving must feel that their ideas will be accepted. People who do well on tests of creative problem solving seem to be less afraid of making mistakes and appearing foolish than do those who do poorly. Successful problem solvers also seem to treat problem-solving situations more playfully. This implies that a relaxed, fun atmosphere is important in teaching problem solving. Students should certainly be encouraged to try different solutions and not be criticized for taking a wrong turn.

Analysis

One method of creative problem solving that is often suggested is to analyze and juxtapose major characteristics or specific elements of a problem. For example, careful analysis of the situation might help solve the following problem:

> A tennis tournament was set up with a series of rounds. The winner of each match advanced to the next round. If there were an odd number of players in a round, one player (chosen at random) would advance automatically to the next round. In a tournament with 147 players, how many matches would take place before a single winner would be declared?

We might solve this problem the hard way, making diagrams of the various matches. However, careful analysis of the situation would reveal that each match would produce exactly one loser. Therefore it would take 146 matches to produce 146 losers.

Engaging Problems

One key to teaching of problem solving is providing problems that intrigue and engage children. The same problem solving skills could be involved in a context that is either compelling or boring to students, and this matters in the outcomes. For example, Bottge found that low-achieving secondary students, many with serious learning disabilities, could learn complex problem solving skills relating to building a cage for a pet or setting up a car racing track. Since John Dewey proposed it a hundred years ago, the motivational value of connecting problem solving to real life or simulations of real life has been demonstrated many times.

Feedback

Provide practice with feedback. Perhaps the most effective way to teach problem solving is to provide students with a great deal of practice on a wide variety of problem types, giving feedback not only on the correctness of their solutions but also on the process by which they arrived at the solutions. The role of practice with feedback in solving complex problems cannot be overemphasized.

Teaching Thinking Skills

One of the oldest dreams in education is that there might be some way to make students smarter—not just more knowledgeable or skillful but actually better able to learn new information of all kinds. Perhaps someday someone will come up with a "smart pill" that will have this effect; but in the meantime, several groups of researchers have been developing and evaluating instructional programs that are designed to increase students' general thinking skills.

The most widely known and extensively researched of several thinking-skills programs that are currently in use was developed by an Israeli educator, Reuven Feuerstein. In this program, called *Instrumental Enrichment*, students work through a series of paper-and-pencil exercises that are intended to build such intellectual skills as categorization, comparison, orientation in space, and numerical progressions.

Less intensive interventions, particularly those involving fewer than 80 hours of instruction, have rarely been successful. In one study done in Israel and one in Venezuela, positive effects of Instrumental Enrichment on aptitude test scores were still found 2 years after the program ended. Many reviewers of the research on Instrumental Enrichment have suggested that this method is simply teaching students how to take IQ tests rather than teaching them anything of real value. Many of the exercises are, in fact, quite similar to items that are used in nonverbal IQ tests. A similar pattern of results has been found for many other thinking-skills programs. In fact, researchers have now begun to question whether there are broadly applicable thinking skills— the evidence points more toward the existence of teachable thinking skills in specific domains, such as math problem solving or reading comprehension. In fact, researchers have combined teaching of thinking skills with instruction in specific content areas, and results of these combined models are more encouraging . Another approach to the teaching of thinking skills is to incorporate them in daily lessons and classroom experiences— to create a "culture of thinking". As an example of integrating thinking skills into daily lessons, Tishman, Perkins, and Jay describe an impromptu discussion in a class that has been taught a generic strategy for problem solving.

Critical Thinking

One key objective of schooling is enhancing students' abilities to think critically, to make rational decisions about what to do or what to believe. Examples of critical thinking include identifying misleading advertisements, weighing competing evidence, and identifying assumptions or fallacies in arguments. As with any other objective, learning to think critically requires practice; students can be given many dilemmas, logical and illogical arguments, valid and misleading advertisements, and so on.

Effective teaching of critical thinking depends on setting a classroom tone that encourages the acceptance of divergent perspectives and free discussion. There should be an emphasis on giving reasons for opinions rather than only giving correct answers. Skills in critical thinking are best acquired in relation to topics with which students are familiar. For example, students will learn more from a unit evaluating Nazi propaganda if they know a great deal about the history of Nazi Germany and the culture of the 1930s and 1940s. Perhaps most important, the goal of teaching critical thinking is to create a critical spirit, which encourages students to question what they hear and to examine their own thinking for logical inconsistencies or fallacies.

Beyer identified 10 critical-thinking skills that students might use in judging the validity of claims or arguments, understanding advertisements, and so on:

1. Distinguishing between verifiable facts and value claims
2. Distinguishing relevant from irrelevant information, claims, or reasons
3. Determining the factual accuracy of a statement
4. Determining the credibility of a source
5. Identifying ambiguous claims or arguments
6. Identifying unstated assumptions
7. Detecting bias
8. Identifying logical fallacies
9. Recognizing logical inconsistencies in a line of reasoning
10. Determining the strength of an argument or claim.

Beyer notes that this is not a sequence of steps but rather a list of possible ways in which a student might approach information to evaluate whether or not it is true or sensible. The key task in teaching critical thinking to students is to help them learn not only how to use each of these strategies but also how to tell when each is appropriate.

References

Furth, H.G. & Wachs, H. (1975). *Thinking goes to school: Piaget's theory in practice.* Oxford: Oxford University Press.

Glover, J, & Ronning, R. (Ed.). (1987). *Historical foundations of educational psychology.* New York, NY: Plenum Press.

Gronlund, N.E. (2000). *How to write and use instructional objectives* (6th ed.). Columbus, OH, USA: Merrill.

Seifert, Kelvin & Sutton, Rosemary. (2009). *Educational Psychology: Second Edition.* Global Text Project, pp. 33-37.

Zimmerman, B.J. &Schunk, D.H. (eds.) (2003). *Educational psychology: A century of contributions.* Mahwah, NJ, US: Erlbaum.

6

Understanding Learners Needs

Although explicit knowledge of learning theory may not be necessary for every lesson you teach, theory will be valuable for decision making and for understanding why some techniques promote learning more than others. As you begin teaching, you will continually ask yourself whether you are lecturing too much, providing enough examples, using too many or too few cues, giving enough feedback, allowing sufficient time for discussion, or providing sufficient opportunities for practice. A knowledge of learning theory can help answer these questions.

Such knowledge also helps teachers explain why their classroom techniques promote learning. By providing a focus or point of observation, learning theories help teachers reflect on what they do and why they do it. Reflection is considered one of the principal ingredients of both student learning and teacher self-renewal .

Behavioral Science Approach to Learning

Although educational psychologists disagree about the effectiveness of instructional methods based on behavioral science, the behavioral science approach to classroom learning has considerable significance for teaching. Its major contributions to your teaching lie in what it says about the learning of basic academic skills.

First we will present a historical overview of the behavioral science approach to learning. From this overview, you will learn about the principles that underlie classical and operant conditioning. Then we will describe how these principles of learning can be applied to the classroom to help learners acquire important academic skills.

What should teachers know about learning in order to deliver effective instruction to their students? Behavioral scientists have clear recommendations on this matter. Before examining these ideas and their historical antecedents, let's look at how a behavioral scientist describes the ideal classroom. Here is Ogden Lindsley's vision of the twenty-first century:

> The only adult in the classroom seems to be loitering....She is moving about the classroom from student to student, answering a question with a whisper here, offering a quiet suggestion there, helping with a chart decision here, and giving a pat and a smile of appreciation there. Now and then, she calls for a class one-minute practice session.

The students are busy at their desks, in teams of two, timing each other's practice, jumping up to take a chart down from the wall, or to post new data. The students are noisy, shouting correct answers as fast as they can at 200 words per minute, several shouting at once at neighboring desks....It is not the orderly class that student teachers were taught to manage....

> The precision teacher performs like a coach, an advisor, and an on-line instructional designer. She arranges materials and methods for the students to teach themselves, including self-counting, timing, charting, and one-on-one direction and support.

According to behavioral scientists like Lindsley, who advocates an approach called *precision teaching,* this classroom contains most of the basic conditions required for learning. These conditions are:

- An environment scientifically designed to elicit correct and rapid performance.
- A focus on observable behavior or performance.
- Opportunities for feedback and reinforcement following performance.

These three essential elements make up the *ABC model of learning*, which is illustrated. The ABC model of learning refers to antecedents in the environment (A) that elicit desired behavior (B), which then becomes strengthened when followed by appropriate consequences (C). This simple model includes all the essential elements of the behavioral science approach. Think of it as an overview of the behavioral model of learning as a whole and keep its main components—antecedents, behaviors, and consequences—in mind as we examine the historical roots of behaviorism and its three major components.

Classical Conditioning

Have you ever had the experience of taking a shower when suddenly someone in the apartment above you, or in a nearby bathroom, flushes the toilet? The shower's relaxing warmth turns to scalding heat! You flinch, tense up, maybe even scream in pain. But soon the water returns to its former temperature, and you relax once again—but this time your ears are alert to the sound. When you hear the flush again, you anticipate the burning water and jump back even before the temperature changes. Your body reacts reflexively.

Your body has learned an important lesson—that there is a predictable relationship or association between two events, a sound and a change in water temperature. It has learned this association through a process called classical conditioning.

Pavlov's Experiment

Ivan Pavlov, a Russian physiologist, discovered the phenomenon of classical conditioning nearly a century ago. He did this by demonstrating that dogs could "learn" to salivate at the sound of a bell that was rung before they were fed, even before they could see or smell the food.

Before a dog undergoes the conditioning process, the bell is a *neutral stimulus* (NS). In other words, a bell does not automatically elicit a physiological response from a dog. Food, on the other hand, automatically causes a dog to salivate. The food, therefore, is an *unconditioned stimulus* (UCS), meaning "naturally conditioned" or "conditioned by nature." Salivation is an *unconditioned response* (UCR), a reaction that automatically follows an unconditioned stimulus.

During the conditioning process, the bell is rung, and food is placed in the dog's mouth just seconds later. The food causes the dog to salivate. If these events are repeated, eventually the dog will salivate at the sound of the bell alone, without tasting, seeing, or smelling the food. When this occurs, the bell is no longer a neutral stimulus. Instead, it becomes a *conditioned stimulus* (CS). When a response, such as salivation, occurs following a conditioned stimulus, it is called a *conditioned response* (CR). The bell, which prior to conditioning had no effect on salivation, has become a conditioned stimulus that elicits a physiological response. While nature created the connection between food (UCS) and salivation (UCR), conditioning created the connection between salivation (CR) and the sound of a bell (CS).

Many learning theorists use the classical conditioning paradigm to explain how we learn relationships between environmental stimuli and behavioral, cognitive, and emotional responses. For example, how do we account for the following phenomena?

- The smell of a certain perfume reminds you of a close friend or loved one.
- You recoil at the sight of a snake when you've never encountered one before except in pictures or stories.
- As a first-grader you became anxious at the sound of the school bell.
- Your professor utters the word "exam" and you get a funny feeling in your stomach.
- A familiar song on the radio creates mental images that change your mood.

What these events have in common is that a neutral stimulus (an odor, the sight of an animal, a sound, a spoken word, a song) has developed the power to evoke an emotional (affective), physiological (a muscle contraction), behavioral (running away), psychological (a shiver), or cognitive (an image) response. Thus, classical conditioning theorists propose that many of our behavioral, emotional, and cognitive responses to people, places, and things have been acquired through a process of classical conditioning.

For example, how might a learner develop a fear of math? Math, in and of itself, is a neutral stimulus. There is no natural connection between it and the emotional responses associated with fear (increased adrenalin flow, constriction of blood vessels, increased blood pressure, rapid breathing). However, there is a natural (unconditioned) association between being reprimanded (UCS) by a teacher or parent and the fear (UCR) that might immediately follow answering a question incorrectly or receiving a failing test grade. Such events, repeated over time, can condition a learner to respond with intense fear at the sight of a math test—or even the announcement that one is forthcoming.

Relevance for Teachers

As a teacher, you will want your learners to acquire positive attitudes toward you and your subject. Initially, you and your learning activities will be neutral stimuli, but over time you and how you teach can become conditioned stimuli that elicit emotions (or conditioned responses) of interest and joy, evoke approach behaviors such as studying and asking questions, and even arouse physiological responses of comfort and naturalness.

Learning theorists remind us that classical conditioning processes go on in classrooms all the time. Your role is to be aware of the classical conditioning paradigm and use it to build positive associations between your teaching activities and learning.

While the classical conditioning paradigm can explain how children learn certain emotional, behavioral, and cognitive responses to neutral stimuli, it is not as successful in explaining how children learn to be successful in Lindsley's ideal classroom: to read and solve problems, follow directions, and work productively with others. Let's look at a second learning paradigm, which can explain how learners develop these skills in their learners.

Operant Conditioning

B.F. Skinner, a Harvard psychologist, has been one of the most influential psychologists of the twentieth century. His theories and research have been applied to education, business, health care, mental health, prison reform, and military training. Skinner was thoroughly familiar with the writings of Pavlov and accepted the basic principles underlying classical conditioning. But he viewed these principles as applicable only to the learning of physiological and emotional responses—those responses (for example, salivation) that are elicited by some type of stimulus (food) and can be conditioned to another type of stimulus (bell). He called this class of behavior *respondent behavior* because it occurred in response to a stimulus.

Skinner was most interested in the learning principles governing a different class of behavior, which he called *operant behavior.* Operant behavior, in contrast to respondent behavior, is not a physiological or emotional response to something that happens in the person's environment.

Rather, operant behaviors are actions that a person uses to meet the demands of the environment.

For example, riding a bicycle, going to a movie theater, pushing a vacuum cleaner, turning on the stereo, visiting a friend's house, cooking a meal, painting a picture, tuning a car engine, and writing a poem are examples of operant behaviors. These behaviors are called "operant" because they are operations that the individual carries out to help him or her deal with the environment in some way. Rather than being reactions to stimuli in the environment, they are actions or operations that the person purposely performs on the environment.

Many if not most of the operant behaviors we perform are complex, the result of years of skill acquisition. Speaking, writing, reading, problem solving, running, sewing, and making friends are complex skills, the building blocks of which can be traced to simple behaviors that the person first performed as an infant or toddler. These simple behaviors—grasping at a mobile, looking at a face, uttering a sound, pulling oneself up, balancing on two feet—were gradually shaped into more complex skills as a result of the interaction between the person performing the behavior and the people reacting to it.

Skinner used the expression *operant conditioning* to describe the process whereby simple operant behaviors are gradually transformed or shaped into more complex ones. Let's examine this paradigm to see first how an animal can learn a skill such as pressing a lever to get food, and then how humans can learn to speak, write, and even problem solve.

How Operant Conditioning Works

Figure 1 shows a "Skinner box"—an experimental chamber used for operant conditioning. A hungry rat is placed in the box. Inside the box is a lever, which, if pressed, releases a food pellet into a tray. There are also a red light, a green light, and an electric grid on the floor.

Suppose that your goal is to teach the rat to press the lever. When placed in the box, the rat will move about randomly. It will stand up, sniff, turn left, turn right, bump into walls, and so forth. These are all operant behaviors.

Given sufficient time, the rat will press the lever by accident and release a food pellet into the tray. Most rats will quickly learn the association between lever-pressing and food release, and they will keep pressing the lever again and again. In other words, operant conditioning will take place. If the rat is removed from the box after 30 minutes of lever-pressing and is placed back in the box the next day, it will press the lever to get food in a shorter period than it took the first time.

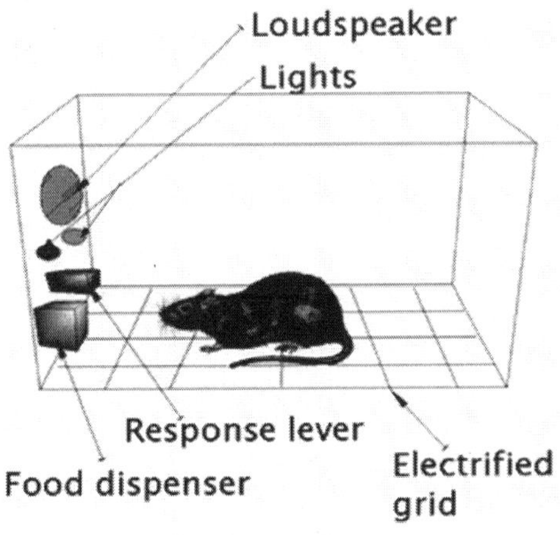

Figure 1. Skinner box

Reinforcement

Skinner emphasizes that what happens following a behavior determines whether it will be repeated and strengthened. He used the term *reinforcement* to refer to any event following a behavior that makes it more likely that the behavior will be repeated: the food the rat obtains reinforces the lever-pressing behavior. When the event following the behavior is desirable, so that the behavior is repeated in anticipation of a reward, *positive reinforcement* has occurred. Again, the food pellet is a positive reinforcer that makes the behavior more likely to recur.

Schedules of Reinforcement

Skinner discovered that to get the rat to repeatedly press the lever, reinforcement had to occur on a continuous schedule—after every occasion when the rat pressed the lever. He also showed that once reinforcement stopped, the rat would soon stop pressing the lever, a process called extinction. *Extinction* is the gradual disappearance of a learned behavior when it is no longer being reinforced. This naturally led to the question of how to reinforce behavior so as to increase or speed up the initial rate of learning and make it more resistant to extinction once reinforcement was discontinued.

Skinner studied how to increase the rate of response and make learned behavior more resistant to extinction by manipulating what he called schedules of reinforcement. A *schedule of reinforcement* is a rule for when reinforcers will be given after the desired behavior is performed. Reinforcers can be given every time a behavior occurs (a *continuous reinforcement schedule)*, or every now and then (an *intermittent reinforcement schedule*).

If reinforcers are given intermittently, you may choose, for example, to reinforce every other response or every third response (thus creating a *ratio schedule*), or you may decide to give the reinforcer after a set period of time, such as at the end of each 30-second or 60-second period during which the rat presses the lever *(an interval schedule*).

Ratio and interval schedules can be fixed or variable. A *fixed ratio schedule* is a rule that says, for example, "reinforce every fourth time the rat presses the lever." A *variable ratio schedule,* on the other hand, directs the experimenter to reinforce a certain proportion of responses in such a way that, on average, one out of every four responses is reinforced. Interval schedules can also be fixed (for example, every minute) or variable (so that, on average, the rat is reinforced every 60 seconds).

Skinner discovered that each schedule of reinforcement had a predictable effect on rate of learning and resistance to extinction.

Punishment

What would happen to the rate of lever-pressing if, after the rat pressed the lever, a mild electric shock was delivered by means of the electric grid at the bottom of the box? Skinner found that the rat would quickly stop pressing the lever. The speed with which it learned to stop pressing would depend on both the immediacy of the shock and its intensity. Skinner defined *punishment* as any action, following a response, that makes that response less likely to occur again. The key part of this definition is that punishment makes a response *less* likely to recur.

Negative Reinforcement

Punishment, which we described above, is distinguished from *negative reinforcement*, which is a way of making a response *more* likely to recur by removing an aversive (unpleasant) stimulus. For example, suppose you wanted to teach the rat to jump over a fence that divided the box in half. One means of accomplishing this would be to send an electric current through the floor on the side of the box where the rat was standing. The rat would become agitated and would eventually jump the barrier and land in the unwired portion of the box. The next time the rat was placed in the wired section and the shock was delivered, it would jump much sooner than the first time. Eventually, the rat would jump the barrier even before the shock was administered.

The rat learned to jump by means of negative reinforcement. The rat escaped or avoided a shock by performing a new behavior. In general, we tend to repeat behaviors that help us avoid, postpone, delay, or alter situations we find aversive or unpleasant. For example, when you postpone or cancel assignments or tests because students complain about them, you are negatively reinforcing their complaining behavior. If a student doesn't want you to call on her, and finds that she can get you to call on someone else by looking away, then you are negatively reinforcing her behavior.

Stimulus Control

Let's say that you want the rat to press the lever for food only when the green light comes on. In other words, you want the green light, but not the red one, to elicit or control lever-pressing behavior. This could be accomplished by reinforcing the rat with food pellets when the green light was on, but not the red one. Eventually, the rat would learn to press the lever for a reward only in the presence of a green light. This is an example of *stimulus control*—the rat's lever-pressing response has been brought under the control of the conditioned stimulus (the green light). Skinner called this type of training *discrimination training.* By reinforcing the rat only in the presence of a particular stimulus, the rat learns to discriminate the occasions when it will be rewarded from those when it will not.

In the classroom, this would be analogous to expecting learners to raise their hands to ask questions only when you have finished an explanation, which you signal by pausing and looking around the room. You then could bring hand raising under stimulus control by calling only on those who raise their hands and ignoring students who speak out without permission. Students quickly learn that when they raise their hands following your signal, they are more likely to be called on.

Relevance of Operant Conditioning for Teachers

Skinner points out that most of the behaviors that we want learners to acquire in school can be classified as operants. Complying with rules, following important routines such as lining up or changing learning groups, completing homework, writing legibly, speaking in complete sentences, dissecting a frog, reciting a poem, performing a cartwheel, getting along with others, and working independently are behaviors that teachers can gradually strengthen, shape, and refine. In addition, through discrimination training, you bring these behaviors under stimulus control—you let learners know when and under what circumstances it is appropriate to perform them.

Using the Behavioral Science Approach

In the introduction to this unit we asked the question, "What does a classroom teacher need to know about learning?" According to the behavioral science approach, the teacher must be able to:

1. Focus instruction on observable learner performance.
2. Assure that learners can perform the skills that are prerequisites to that performance.
3. Elicit a rapidly paced, correct performance.
4. Use appropriate consequences following performance.

Focus on Learner Performance

Behavioral scientists have traditionally defined learning as a stable change in behavior brought about by the environment. Cognitive theorists have expanded this traditional definition of learning to include such topics as cognitive changes in memory capacity, thinking, and mental processing. Behavioral scientists are opposed to this definition. Their opposition stems less from a denial that changes in cognitive (mental) activity occur than from a concern about the difficulty of measuring them.

Behaviorists believe that in order to establish a true science of instruction we must be able to explain how what teachers do affects what learners do—not what or how they think. Cognitive activity is something we cannot measure directly.

We can only infer it from observing performance—and inferences about cognitive activity can be wrong. Behaviorists believe that a focus on observable performance avoids incorrect inferences about learning and allows us to build a science of instruction on a firm foundation.

Distinctions between learning and performance and between cognitive and observable changes are important for teaching. By their strong advocacy of observable outcomes and performance objectives, behavioral scientists challenge teachers not to take learning for granted. This means that you should plan lessons with a clear vision of the important outcomes you want learners to achieve, and end your instruction with an assessment of those outcomes. Both of these recommendations are consistent with the behavioral science approach to learning. This premise of behavioral science—that the only valid measure of learning is observable performance—has been criticized by some educators and psychologists, who believe that this emphasis encourages teachers to write only those objectives that are easy to measure and thus to ignore educational outcomes involving complex intellectual skills.

Behavioral scientists, on the other hand, believe that a concern for performance will have the opposite effect—that it will persuade teachers to give more serious thought to what they want their learners to accomplish. This, in turn, will help teachers devise authentic ways to assess learning in terms of performance and thinking skills, not just the acquisition of facts.

Ensure the Learning of Prerequisite Skills

You may be wondering how someone's intelligence, abilities, aptitudes, or learning style enters into a behavioral scientist's theory of learning. After all, if someone lacks an aptitude for math or writing, or possesses little musical or painting ability, doesn't that affect his or her learning?

What characteristics of learners should classroom teachers be concerned about when planning their lessons? Behavioral scientists have a straightforward and (given their concern for observable performance) predictable answer to these questions: Other than a learner's physical capabilities to perform the learning task, the only characteristic that is relevant to a student's learning a skill is whether the learner possesses the prerequisites for it. In other words, if you expect your students to learn how to write a paragraph, you must first ask yourself whether they can write a complete sentence, a topic sentence, and transitions between sentences. At an even more basic level, can they spell words and form letters correctly? If some of your learners cannot learn to write a paragraph skillfully and effortlessly, behavioral scientists would attribute this to a lack of prerequisite skills (or poorly designed instruction)—not to a lack of ability, aptitude, or intelligence.

Behavioral scientists believe that the source of almost all learning failures can be identified if teachers analyze both the *internal conditions* (prerequisite skills) and the *external conditions* (instructional events) of learning. For example, if one of your learners can't seem to master long division, is it because he hasn't learned how to subtract? If he is having difficulty learning subtraction skills, has he learned how to regroup? If he hasn't learned to regroup, can he identify which of two numbers is larger? At no point would the behavioral scientist conclude that the learner lacks ability or intelligence. If the teacher analyzes and probes deeply enough, eventually she can identify the source of the problem and teach or reteach the skills necessary for learning to continue.

The idea of breaking complex behaviors into smaller component behaviors originated with Skinner. As we saw earlier, Skinner's experiments on shaping the behavior of rats demonstrated the usefulness of this method. Gagné, however, more so than any other behavioral scientist, demonstrated the importance to classroom learning of such an analysis.

Task Analysis

The process of analyzing the internal conditions necessary for learning is called *task analysis*. The outcome of a task analysis is an arrangement of prerequisite skills into a *learning hierarchy.* You begin a task analysis by identifying what task you want your learners to perform at the end of a lesson or unit of instruction. Then ask, "In order to perform this task, what prerequisite skills must my learners already have mastered?" The answer should be the most complex, highest-level prerequisite skills.

If you have trouble conducting a task analysis using the logical questioning process described above, do the task yourself and write down what you did, or observe someone doing the task and write down what you saw. Some curriculum guides are sufficiently detailed as to provide a task analysis for you.

Sequencing

Constructing a learning hierarchy is dependent on identifying the prerequisite skills in the correct sequence: you can't teach subtraction with regrouping before you teach place value. Behavioral scientists consider the sequence in which skills are taught to be especially important. They place a premium on correct responses, rapid responding, and efficiency. Therefore, incorrectly sequenced instruction results in errors, frustration, and inefficiency.

Englemann cautions that the sequence of skills presented in the published curriculum you use may create problems for your learners. Thus, it will be worth your while to examine this sequence and adjust it when necessary.

Also, solving complex problems in math, writing compositions, and interpreting difficult reading passages are all tasks that require learners to perform prerequisite skills automatically and effortlessly. Imagine the difficulty your learners would have writing an essay if they could not form letters, spell, punctuate, and construct grammatical sentences. Learners who cannot perform prerequisite skills effortlessly and with minimal errors find it difficult to transfer new learning to unfamiliar problem contexts. One of the key ingredients for transfer of new learning is the mastery of prerequisite skills.

Elicit Rapidly Paced, Correct Performance

As we saw in our study of operant conditioning, Skinner was able to elicit rapid correct performance by the skilled use of reinforcement and stimulus control. As you will recall, the basic elements of operant conditioning are:

(a) a response or behavior that you want to teach or shape,

(b) an effective reinforcer, and

(c) the delivery of that reinforcer immediately after performance of the desired response.

The challenge—both to psychologists in the lab and to teachers in the classroom—is to elicit a correct response. Let's analyze this challenge and explore further the topic of rapidly paced, correct performance.

The skilled teacher gets learners to respond correctly by bringing correct responses under stimulus control. Exactly how is this done? How does a teacher deliver instruction in a manner that minimizes the likelihood that learners will make mistakes? Four important factors are involved.

1. Assure the learning of prerequisite skills.
2. Present instructional material effectively.
3. Use prompts.
4. Use reinforcement.

We have already discussed the first of these factors. In this section, we explain the remaining three.

Effective Presentation

Behavioral scientists point out three areas for you to consider as you decide how to present instructional material: specific directions, opportunities for learner responses, and the pacing of response opportunities.

Specific Directions

Let's say that you want to teach some sight words to your learners. You want them to look at a word and pronounce it correctly. Here are two examples of possible directions:

- *Example 1.* This is the word "rabbit." Say "rabbit" and point to the word.
- *Example 2*: This is the word "rabbit." A rabbit is a small, furry animal with big ears. It likes to eat carrots. Point to the word "rabbit" and say it.

Example 1 is a better set of directions if your objective is to bring the response "saying and pointing to the word 'rabbit'" under the stimulus control of the word "rabbit." Example 2 contains information that may distract the learner from making the correct response.

Whether you are teaching word recognition to first-graders, subtraction to second-graders, paragraph construction to sixth-graders, or problem solving in physics to eleventh-graders, instructional directions should be specific to the behavior you want your learners to acquire. So think carefully about what you want learners to do and how you will direct them to do it. Discard information and explanations that are extraneous and serve only to distract the learner.

Opportunities For Learner Response

Behavioral scientists have conducted extensive research on the idea of opportunity to respond. They make a useful distinction between active and passive responding. *Active responding* requires the learner to do something: write sentences, calculate answers, focus a microscope, balance a scale, weigh rocks, and record observations. *Passive responding*, on the other hand, includes such activities as listening to lectures, paying attention to peers while they are reading, watching television, and waiting for teacher assistance.

Greenwood, Delguardi, and Hall report that nearly half of a learner's day is involved in passive responding. This is unfortunate, because their research also demonstrates a strong relationship between learner achievement and active responding. Behavioral scientists, therefore, urge you to plan your lessons so that learners spend at least 75 percent of their time engaged in active responding.

Research on opportunity to respond has also found that correct responses are more likely to come under stimulus control when you design your practice material (worksheets, seatwork drills, homework assignments, and so forth) to elicit correct responses 70 to 90 percent of the time. Many teachers purposely design materials for learner practice to be challenging—in other words, they design it so there is a strong likelihood that the learners will make mistakes. Behavioral scientists have demonstrated that learners acquire basic facts and skills faster when their opportunities for practice result in success most of the time.

Although you might predict that more errors would result from fast-paced lessons, research indicates just the opposite for the acquisition of facts and action sequences. In a series of studies on the pace of reading instruction, Carnine found that rapid presentations by teachers produced greater achievement, fewer errors, and more sustained attention by learners during letter and word identification tasks than did slower presentations.

In summary, the behavioral science approach to learning suggests that you deliver instruction in the following ways:

- Give directions that focus only on the response you want learners to make.
- Allow learners to engage in active responding during the majority of class time.
- Design instructional material for both initial learning and practice so that learners can produce correct answers 70 to 90 percent of the time.

Use of Prompts

During instruction teachers often provide prompts—hints and other types of supplementary instructional stimuli to help learners make the correct responses. Because, as we have seen, the behavioral science approach is concerned with minimizing mistakes, it places a high value on the use of prompts that increase the likelihood that learners will respond correctly.

Behavioral scientists identify three categories of prompts used by teachers to shape the correct performance of their learners: verbal prompts, gestural prompts, and physical prompts. We will discuss the use of all three kinds in the following sections.

Verbal Prompts

Verbal prompts can be cues, reminders, or instructions to learners that help them perform correctly the skill you are teaching. For example, saying "Leave a space between words" to a first-grader as he is writing reminds him what you previously said about neat handwriting. Or saying "First adjust the object lens" to a learner as she is looking at a microscope slide prompts her as she is learning how to use a microscope. Verbal prompts help guide the learner to correct performance and prevent mistakes and frustration.

Gestural Prompts

Gestural prompts model or demonstrate for learners a particular skill you want them to perform. For example, if you were to point to the fine adjustment knob on the microscope and make a turning gesture with your hand, you would be prompting the student to perform this step of the process. Gestural prompts are particularly helpful when you anticipate that the learner may make a mistake. Teachers use gestural prompts routinely to remind learners how to fold a piece of paper, to grasp a pair of scissors, to raise a hand before asking a question, or to hold a pen properly when writing.

Physical Prompts

Some learners lack the fine muscle control needed to follow a demonstration and imitate the action that is being modeled. For example, the teacher might verbally describe how to form the letter "A" and demonstrate this for the learner, and the learner may still be unable to write "A" correctly. In such a case, the teacher might use her hand to guide the learner's hand as he writes. This is called a physical prompt. With a physical prompt you use hand-over-hand assistance to guide the learner to the correct performance. Teachers routinely use physical prompts to assist learners with handwriting, cutting out shapes, tying shoelaces, correctly holding a dissecting tool, or performing a complex dance routine.

Least-to-most Prompting

Behavioral scientists generally recommend that you use the least intrusive prompt first when guiding a learner's performance. This is referred to as *least-to-most prompting.* Verbal prompts are considered the least intrusive, while physical prompts are considered the most intrusive. Thus it would be more appropriate to first say to a learner “Don’t forget the fine adjustment!” when guiding her in the use of a microscope than to take her hand and physically assist her. The reasoning behind using a least-to-most order of prompts to assist learners is that verbal prompts are easier to remove or fade than are physical prompts. Learners who are dependent on physical prompts to perform correctly will find it more difficult to demonstrate a skill independently of the teacher.

At this point, let’s summarize what we’ve learned about stimulus control and its relationship to correct responses. So far, we have learned that behavioral scientists view the eliciting of a correct response as one of the four basic elements of learning. Correct responses followed by reinforcement results in more permanent learning then correct responses intermixed with incorrect responses. Mistakes slow down the learning process and often lead to frustration and attempts by learners to avoid, or passively respond to, a learning activity.

Establishing stimulus control over learner performance is the key to errorless learning. In order to elicit rapidly paced, correct performance, you must pay particular attention to four important factors when planning your lessons:

1. Make sure your learners have mastered prerequisite skills.
2. Present your lessons in a way that will give learners frequent opportunities to make correct responses.
3. Use prompts to ensure correct responding.
4. Reinforce correct responses immediately.

Let’s turn now to the fourth basic element of the behavioral science approach, which tells us how to deliver consequences to learners following their performance.

Use Appropriate Consequences Following Performance

Picture the following situation: You have just begun a unit on converting fractions to decimals with your fifth-graders. After demonstrating how to perform this skill, you pass out a worksheet with 20 problems. You give your learners 10 minutes to complete the task. As the students work, you move from desk to desk checking on their answers. You notice several students getting answers wrong. What should you do? Here are some alternatives.

1. Circle the incorrect answers, show them what they did wrong, and encourage them to do better.
2. Circle just the correct answers, point out what they did right, and encourage them to do better.
3. Circle the correct answers, and praise the students for their good work.
4. Circle the incorrect answers, admonish the students, and have them do the problems again.
5. 1 and 4.
6. 2 and 3.
7. All of the above.

Educational psychologists using the behavioral science approach have researched the issue of how best to respond to the correct and incorrect responses of learners. They have arranged the possible consequences into three general categories:

(1) informational feedback,

(2) positive consequences, and

(3) negative consequences.

Let's examine each and see what behavioral scientists have learned about their effectiveness in promoting learning.

Informational Feedback

Correct Responses. If a learner correctly recalls the major historical events leading up to the Civil War, legibly forms a lowercase cursive letter, or accurately solves an algebra equation with two unknowns showing her work, you should do two things immediately: (1) tell the learner the answer is correct, and (2) briefly describe what she did to obtain the correct answer. For example:

> "That's right. You listed the five major events."
>
> "Those letters are slanted correctly and you wrote them on the line."
>
> "The answer is right and you showed all the required steps."

Behavioral scientists remind us that better learning results when you tell learners not only what they got right, but also *why* they got it right.

Incorrect Answers. Learners give incorrect answers for several different reasons: carelessness, lack of knowledge, or lack of understanding. In the first case, some teachers scold or use some form of verbal punishment. Behavioral scientists and many educators strongly advise against these consequences for careless performance. Instead, they recommend that you use the following types of feedback whenever students give incorrect answers, regardless of the reason:

1. If the problem involves only knowledge of factual information, simply give the correct response.
2. If the problem involves more complex intellectual skills, point out the rules, procedures, or steps to follow.
3. Ask the learner to correct the answer.
4. Ask the learner to practice some extra problems.

Here is an example of each:

> "The correct spelling is *t-h-e-i-r*."
>
> "End every sentence with a period, question mark, or exclamation point."
>
> "First draw the base. Then, draw the altitude. Now, retrace your steps."
>
> "Ask yourself: 'Who are the more talked-about people in this story?' Then answer the next set of questions."

Note that these examples do not include preaching, scolding, or focusing extensively on the student's error—even if the learner was being careless. Such responses often create feelings of anxiety and distaste for schoolwork, which encourage disengagement from the learning activity. Learning will occur more quickly if you simply tell your students what to do, have them try again, and provide practice with additional problems when an incorrect response is given.

Cautions for Correcting Mistakes

Research on feedback and error correction has shown that the recommendations given above improve learning for most students. However, there are two groups of learners for whom these procedures may not be beneficial: (1) those who make a lot of mistakes and (2) those who are excessively dependent on adult guidance.

When given material that is too difficult, low-achieving learners make many errors. Such learners experience low rates of positive consequences and high rates of negative ones. Consequently, they are likely to ignore corrective feedback and simply stop working. Research on low achievers affirms that when error rates are high, little is learned from informational feedback. This finding underscores the importance of designing your instruction to produce as few errors as possible in all learners.

The second case, learners who depend greatly on adult guidance, may involve attention-seeking behavior. In other words, some learners may persist in making mistakes because of the attention they receive after doing so. Hasazi and Hasazi and Stromer speculated that when a teacher's response focuses on the mistake itself rather than on the correct answer (for example, circling reversals of letters when the learner writes *b* for *d,* or circling digits when the learner writes *32* for *23*), it may inadvertently reinforce incorrect responses.

These researchers carried out experiments in which teachers circled only correct responses and drew no attention to those that were incorrect. They found dramatic improvements in the learners' ability to write digits and letters correctly after teachers made this change alone. This surprising finding reminds us that focusing on mistakes may actually reinforce the wrong response. This may be especially true in classrooms where teachers pay more attention to children who are misbehaving (talking out of turn, not following instructions) than to those who routinely follow class rules.

Positive Consequences

Following Performance. Behavioral scientists have conclusively demonstrated the crucial role played by positive consequences in promoting and strengthening learning in animals. They have shown that positive consequences play an equally critical part in the classroom learning of children. Thus, for the classroom teacher today, the important question is not whether to use positive consequences in the classroom, but what type of consequence to use and how.

Behavioral scientists make a distinction between positive consequences and positive reinforcers. They may or may not serve as positive reinforcers.

Something can be called a *positive reinforcer* only when it can be conclusively shown that it increases the frequency of a target behavior. When you praise a learner's correct punctuation with the intention of increasing the likelihood that she will continue her progress, you are using a positive consequence. In order to classify this consequence as a positive reinforcer, you must show that the learner continues to make progress and that your praise was the causal factor. Some teachers develop elaborate systems of positive rewards, hoping that they will energize their learners to achieve increasingly higher levels of both social and academic skills. However, the teachers believe they are using positive reinforcers when they are simply using positive consequences.

We will now extend our discussion of positive consequences following learning to address two additional issues:

(1) how to use positive consequences to promote and maintain learning and

(2) how to establish natural reinforcers (i.e., intrinsic motivators) for learners who require extrinsic ones.

The Expert Practice of Positive Reinforcement

Recall from our discussion of operant conditioning that positive reinforcement is the process of strengthening behavior by the presentation of a desired stimulus or reward. While this definition appears simple, reinforcement is nevertheless easily misunderstood and misused. Before we expand on the use of positive reinforcement in the classroom, let's see some examples of what it is *not.* These will help you grasp the complexity of positive reinforcement.

- Mr. Russo has snack time at 10:15 and 10:30 for his first-grade class. He gives his learners juice, cookies, fruit bits, and other types of reinforcers.
- Mr. Baker, the principal, decided to start a positive reinforcement program. At the end of the week, each teacher would nominate his or her "best student" to receive the "Principal's Pride Award" at a ceremony each Monday morning. Parents would be invited to attend.
- Mrs. Knipper allows students who finish assignments early to use the computer in the back of the room.
- Mr. French has a popcorn party every Friday if the class has not broken more than five major rules the entire week.
- Mrs. Reimer has a basketful of inexpensive trinkets and school supplies. She lets learners who have been particularly helpful on a given day select a prize from the basket.

Learners who read more than five books a year are treated to a special roller skating party at the end of the school year, hosted by the principal.

There is nothing wrong or inappropriate about these activities. Learners, their teachers, and parents generally like and support them. They even may have some beneficial outcomes on learning, but they are not necessarily examples of positive reinforcement. Positive reinforcement is a complex process that demands a substantial commitment of the teacher's time and effort, as we will now see. The Process of Positive Reinforcement

When behavioral scientists speak of positive reinforcement they refer to a sequence of actions by a teacher, trainer, or behavioral specialist that has a beginning, middle, and end. When you decide to use positive reinforcement you commit yourself to this specific sequence of steps, which we describe in the accompanying box, *Administering Positive Reinforcement.* Note that very few of these steps were followed in the examples given earlier. Reread the examples now, and ask yourself how many included: baseline measurement of specific behaviors; assessment of reinforcer preferences; immediate, continuous reinforcement for the performance of specific behaviors; and a gradual fading of the use of extrinsic reinforcers to natural reinforcers.

Box 1. Administering Positive Reinforcement

Step 1: Determine a specific, observable behavior to strengthen and decide at what level of strength or correctness you want the behavior to occur. Behavioral scientists emphasize that we reinforce observable behaviors, not people.

Step 2: Measure the frequency or duration of this behavior before beginning to reinforce it. Without a baseline measure of the behavior, it cannot be determined whether the behavior has changed.

Step 3: Determine what reinforcers for the given behavior are likely to be the most effective.

Step 4: Give the reinforcer to the learner immediately after he or she performs the desired behavior.

Step 5: Give the reinforcer to the learner every time he or she performs the desired behavior until it reaches the desired level of strength or correctness.

Step 6: Change reinforcers or alter the teaching if the behavior does not show progress.

Step 7: Change from a continuous schedule of delivery of reinforcers to an intermittent one. This will maintain the behavior at the desired level and prevent it from weakening as the behavior is reinforced less and less.

Step 8: Gradually transfer the control of the behavior from extrinsic reinforcers to natural reinforcers.

The point is that the expert practice of positive reinforcement is a demanding intellectual and physical challenge. When you decide to use it, you are committing yourself to a process that involves measurement, consistent delivery of reinforcers, and the responsibility to fade them. Because of this commitment, there may be few examples in regular school classrooms today where the science of reinforcement, as developed by behavioral scientists, is consistently and appropriately applied.

Therefore, it is important to recognize that most reward, recognition, and incentive systems used in today's schools do not constitute positive reinforcement as behavioral scientists use the term. In either case, users of positive reinforcement should be aware of the ethical issues involved in the use of extrinsic rewards, such as paying students for reading books or for staying off drugs.

Natural Reinforcers: Alternatives to Extrinsic Reinforcers

Behavioral scientists have often been criticized for creating a generation of learners who are hooked on artificial or extrinsic consequences in order to learn and behave in the classroom. However, an analysis of the writings of early behaviorists like B. F. Skinner, or other behavioral scientists like Ogden Lindsley and Baer, Wolf, and Risley, challenges this criticism. Such behavioral scientists have advocated the use of natural reinforcers, those that are naturally present in the setting where the behavior occurs. Thus, there are natural reinforcers for classrooms (grades), ballfields (the applause of fans), the workplace (money), and the home (story hour, parent attention). Examples of unnatural reinforcers are paying children or giving them treats for achievement in schools, or buying toys for children who behave well at home.

Skinner makes a further distinction in his definition of a natural reinforcer: he sees it as a change in stimulation resulting from the behavior itself. In other words, natural reinforcers occur when the behavior itself produces an environmental change that gives the person pleasure. For example, the natural reinforcer for hitting the correct keys on a piano is the pleasurable sound that the behavior brings. Similarly, the natural reinforcer for writing correct letters is the satisfaction the first-grader experiences when she sees the letters forming on the page. Thus to Skinner a natural reinforcer is a consequence that results from the very performance of the behavior we want the child to learn; that consequence in turn motivates the child to want to perform these behaviors again.

Children who enjoy solving puzzles are receiving natural reinforcement for doing so. Likewise, learners who write poetry, play the guitar, study history, read novels, or compete in gymnastics are receiving natural reinforcement. What these examples have in common is that children are engaging in the behaviors again and again without the need for external praise or other reinforcers delivered by another person.

Some learners are naturally reinforced by learning to write, read, color, answer questions, play sports, solve equations, answer textbook questions, and write essays, but others are not. Many learners require external reinforcers to engage in certain classroom activities that they do not find naturally reinforcing. For such children, external reinforcers have an important role to play. They can accomplish two things. They enable you to (1) shape and improve the behaviors you desire through the use of positive reinforcement and (2) transfer their control over the learner's behavior to natural reinforcers. Behavioral scientists refer to this process as *conditioning*

Conditioning a Natural Reinforcer. Over the past decade, the Communidad Los Horcones has developed a strategy for transferring the control of extrinsic reinforcers to that of natural, or intrinsic reinforcers. This process as a whole is referred to as *intrinsic reinforcement***.** The group's recommendations are listed in the Box 2, *Conditioning a Natural Reinforcer.* Note how the use of natural reinforcers relies on the learner's intrinsic motivation and thus allows you to transfer control of the behavior to the learner herself.

Positive Consequences

Behavioral scientists emphasize that there is nothing wrong with extrinsic reinforcers, particularly when they are used as a means to get learning started and to condition natural reinforcers. But there are drawbacks to their use. Some learners stop studying when they are removed. They are not always available for all learners at the same time nor available for individual learners when they are needed. This is not the case with natural reinforcers.

Moreover, extrinsic reinforcers can be effective only when they are consistently delivered by another person. It is impractical to expect teachers to reinforce the most important behaviors of all learners at the right moment. Natural reinforcers allow for this possibility.

Box 2. Conditioning a Natural Reinforcer

Step 1: Select the target behavior. Examples are forming letters correctly, solving multiplication problems, drawing geometric figures, bisecting angles, and writing compositions.

Step 2: Identify the natural consequences of the selected behavior. For example, writing on a piece of paper produces many natural consequences: a scratching sound, the formation of letters, the filling up of a page, the gradual wearing away of a pencil point. Writing an essay has similar natural consequences, but in addition produces sentences that express thoughts, ideas, and images.

Step 3: Choose intrinsic consequences. From the list of natural consequences just given, select those that are likely to be reinforcing to the person and relevant to the purpose of the activity. For example, the formation of the letters is a more appropriate consequence to focus on than the scratching sound on the paper or the filling up of the page.

Step 4: Identify those consequences that can be more easily noticed by the learner. The more conspicuous the consequence to the learner, the easier it is to condition this as a natural reinforcer. For example, the shape of a printed word is a conspicuous consequence of correct handwriting that may serve as a natural reinforcer. Likewise, writing a complete thought, coming up with an answer that matches the one in the back of the textbook, or the satisfied feeling after finishing a task can all serve as natural reinforcers.

Step 5: Design your lessons in such a way that you make conspicuous the occurrence of natural consequences. Rather than focusing only on the right answer to a problem, point out and describe for the learner the sequence that was followed. In general, focus on how something was done, not just on the end result. Some learners may not notice or direct their attention to the natural consequences of their work. By setting up instructional conditions to do this, you allow for natural reinforcers to acquire power over behavior.

Step 6: Select appropriate backup reinforcers. In order to transfer the power of an extrinsic reinforcer over behavior to a natural consequence, you must select extrinsic or backup reinforcers. These reinforcers should have educational value, be typically available in your classroom, and, ideally, involve you in the reinforcing activity.

Step 7: Condition the natural reinforcer. Have your learners engage in the behavior. As soon as possible, give informational feedback that points out the natural consequences you hope will become natural reinforcers. Immediately give the backup reinforcers. Gradually remove these reinforcers from the learning setting, but continue to point out and illustrate the natural consequences of what the learner did. Gradually point out the natural consequences less and less. Deliver and intermittently pair the backup reinforcers with the natural reinforcers.

Let's turn now to a discussion of the third type of consequence that teachers can use following learner performance: negative consequences.

The Use of Negative Consequences

We will end our discussion of the use of the behavioral science approach with the final type of consequence teachers can use: negative consequences. Here are some examples of negative consequences:

- Mr. Holt's fourth-period math class was just before lunch. His students often failed to complete their seatwork during this period. He decided to delay the lunch period for any learners who did not finish their work.
- Ms. Tolbert wanted to help her learners spell more accurately. She made them write each misspelled word 25 times in their notebooks.
- Mr. Blandon was a stickler for correct punctuation. Any student who failed to capitalize a sentence or place a period at the end received a firm lecture on carelessness.
- Mr. Thomas decided to do something about students who weren't doing homework—students who didn't turn in homework assignments were required to do them after school.
- Mr. Altman sent "sad-grams" home to the parents of students who were doing poorly in his math class.

These are all examples of negative consequences, things that teachers (or other adults) do to learners after inappropriate behaviors in the hope that such behaviors will not occur again. Types of negative consequences typically used in schools are these:

- *Verbal reprimands:* Speaking harshly to the student: "That work is sloppy and careless, and you should be ashamed of yourself for doing it."
- *Overcorrection:* The learner not only corrects what he did wrong but engages in repetitive, boring practice on the same skill: "After you correct all the spelling mistakes, write each misspelled word correctly 50 times."
- *Response cost:* The teacher takes away some right or privilege: "Whoever fails to complete the assignment loses the first 15 minutes of recess."
- *Exclusion*: The learner is removed from one setting and placed in another, often called "time out": "If you don't cooperate in your groups, you will be removed and put in the back of the room for the rest of the period."

Negative Consequences Versus Punishers

Negative consequences may or may not be punishers. As we have seen, to a behavioral scientist, a *punisher* is something you do following a behavior to reduce the frequency of that behavior for as long as the punisher is used. In other words, your overcorrection of spelling mistakes is a punisher only if you keep good records that show that spelling mistakes have been substantially reduced. If not, then overcorrection is not a punisher—it is simply a negative consequence, which has no real effect on mistakes and may or may not cause the learner discomfort.

Behavioral scientists are very particular about what they call a punisher (just as they are very particular about what they call a reinforcer). Something is a punisher only if you have demonstrated that it reduces the behavior you targeted. Scolding, overcorrection, sending someone to the principal's office (exclusion), taking away recess (response cost), and even corporal punishment are all negative consequences, but they may not be punishers.

The distinction between a negative consequence and a punisher is significant for two reasons. First, some teachers persist in the use of negative consequences in the belief that they are helping their learners in some way. However, after a scolding, a learner may appear chastened and remorseful. He may even stop the inappropriate behavior for the next hour or day. But the same behavior soon reappears; the teacher, in frustration, scolds or reprimands again; and the cycle repeats itself.

Scolding in this case does not reduce the target behavior. It is not a punisher. It is simply a negative consequence, which the teacher uses to relieve frustration with the learner and which gives the illusion of effectiveness. By distinguishing between negative consequences and punishers, behavioral scientists remind us of the importance of gathering evidence that a behavior is changing before we persist in the use of any technique. They highlight an important ethical question: What is the justification for the continued use of negative consequences in the absence of proof of their effectiveness?

Second, the distinction between negative consequences and punishers is also significant because it raises the question of what is required to turn a negative consequence into an effective punisher.

The Use of Punishment

As often as you hear the lament "I tried positive reinforcement and it didn't work," you will hear the assertion "Punishment isn't effective." And just as we can attribute the failure of positive reinforcement to ineffective practice, so we can attribute the failure of punishment to ineffective application.

Many myths have arisen over the past two decades concerning the use of punishment in schools. These myths pertain to both the effectiveness and the ineffectiveness of punishment in reducing undesirable behavior. In the former case, we often hear statements like these: Punishment stops unwanted behavior.

When all else fails, use punishment! Children must experience negative consequences for misbehavior! Spare the rod and spoil the child! In the latter case, punishment is frequently criticized because it makes children hate school or teachers, creates emotional problems, only temporarily suppresses behavior, or deals only with the symptom of the problem and not the cause.

In response to these beliefs, behavioral scientists cite hundreds of studies, carried out with both animal and human subjects over the past half century, that have led to a set of tested conclusions about punishment and its use. Here is what these studies tell us about the use of punishment:

- Punishment can result in long-term elimination of undesirable behavior, but so can techniques that involve the exclusive use of positive reinforcement to strengthen appropriate behavior.
- Some individuals engage in severe, chronic, life-threatening behaviors that cannot be eliminated by positive reinforcement alone.
- When punishment to eliminate inappropriate behaviors is used in conjunction with positive reinforcement to teach alternative behaviors, emotional side effects such as fear and dislike of teachers, attempts to escape or avoid school or schoolwork, or anxiety are less likely to occur.
- The failure of some nonaversive and positive reinforcement techniques to suppress undesirable behavior does not automatically justify the use of punishment. Usually this failure is due to the ineffective use of positive reinforcement.
- The failure of less intense punishment to suppress behavior does not necessarily justify the use of more intense punishment. In fact, increasing the ratio of positive reinforcement to create a contrast with punishment usually precludes the need for increased punishment.

From their studies on the effective use of punishment, behavioral scientists have identified several conditions as essential for the suppression and eventual elimination of undesirable behavior. They include the following:

1. Precise identification and baseline measurement of the target behavior.
2. Precise identification of an alternative, positive behavior.
3. An assessment of the most effective potential punisher for the target behavior prior to its use.
4. Consistent, immediate reinforcement and punishment on a continuous schedule until changes in both the target behavior and the alternative behavior are evident.
5. Fading of both reinforcers and punishers.

References

Alberto, P. & Troutman, A. (2003) *Applied behavior analysis for teachers* (6th ed.). Columbus, OH, USA: Prentice-Hall-Merrill.

Phillips, D. C., & Soltis, J. E. (1991). *Perspectives on learning* (2nd ed.). New York: Teachers College Press.

Sulzer-Azaroff, B., et al. (1988). *Behavioral analysis in education,* reprint series, vol. III. Lawrence, KS: Society for the Experimental Analysis of Behavior, Inc.

Whaley, D. L., & Malott, R. W. (1971). *Elementary principles of behavior.* Englewood Cliffs, NJ: Prentice-Hall.

7

Understanding Effective Thinking

Cognitive psychologists are concerned with studying good thinking—both the content of good thinking and its processes. We called this "gaining freedom from stimulus control" and described cognitive development as the learner's gradual accumulation of cognitive skills and abilities that allow her to think about both the real and the imaginary.

We cannot see good thinking. Nor can we see its content or its processes. As a result, cognitive psychologists use metaphors to describe what they cannot see or touch. Their metaphors are ways of talking about things too abstract to describe literally or precisely. When Forrest Gump says "Life is like a box of chocolates," he is using a metaphor to describe the intangible.

Cognitive scientists use a variety of metaphors to describe the content and processes of good thinking. They use these expressions not with the intent of stipulating what thinking actually is like, but with the goal of offering us a suggestion. They are saying, "Since you can't see or touch good thinking, why not think of it as a computer, or a filing system, or as an information management system." If thinking with the use of a metaphor is helpful to you, then the metaphor has value.

Almost all cognitive approaches to learning are concerned with how everyday experiences are transformed or processed into mental images or sounds and stored for later use. In other words, they are concerned with how information is processed. It is logical, therefore, that cognitive psychologists have chosen the information processing model or computer as their metaphor of choice.

The cognitive approach to learning has a unique set of beliefs and assumptions about each of these elements. Moreover, their research examines how characteristics of learners (such as memory capacity or cognitive development) and instructional manipulations (such as certain teaching practices) influence good thinking.

Cognitive vs. Behavioral Approaches

Cognitive approaches to learning differ from behavioral approaches in three respects:

(1) types of learning examined;

(2) research methodology; and

(3) extent of human learning examined.

It makes no assumptions about what or how learners are thinking while they are learning.

Cognitive approaches to learning examine human learning exclusively. They have no interest in animal learning, which is of prime concern to behavioral scientists. Consequently, cognitive psychologists use methods that allow them to infer what people are thinking. They give people complex learning tasks and measure variables like eye movements, eye fixations, time taken to react to a stimulus, self-reports of what the learner is thinking while engaged in the act of learning, or lists of pictures or words that the learner committed to memory and recalled. From these sources of data, cognitive psychologists make inferences about the content and processes of human thought.

Finally, cognitive psychologists limit their interest in learning to complex human thinking, such as concept and strategy learning, decision making, problem solving, and how learners construct knowledge. Unlike behavioral scientists, they do not study simple motor responses, right or wrong answers, or simple observable behaviors. Moreover, behavioral scientists have attempted to erect a system that can account for all human learning—behavioral, emotional, and social. Cognitive psychologists, in contrast, have limited their theorizing to those aspects of human functioning related to complex thought processes.

Content of Good Thinking

Good thinking involves three elements: strategies, metacognition, and knowledge. Expert thinkers in any field of study possess these three characteristics. As a teacher who is interested in teaching learners to be good thinkers, you will want to focus your lessons on these three areas. Let's examine what each contains.

Cognitive Strategies

In the exercise below, fill in the blanks with terms that you have learned so far, such as *information processing, good thinking, cognitive strategies, metacognition,* and *knowledge base.* Place your selections in the blanks in ways that make sense, but without trying to find the "best" or most correct answer.

- How are .... and .... alike?
- What is the main idea of .... ?
- What are the strengths and weaknesses of .... ?
- In what way is related to .... ?
- How does affect .... ?
- What do you think causes .... ?
- What would happen if a learner were to use .... ?
- What do I still not understand about .... ?

King gave these generic questions to students in her undergraduate psychology class. She taught them how to use these questions in three different ways:

(1) during class to learn more from her lectures,

(2) after class to learn more from studying, and

(3) as a basis for group discussion. She found that the use of these questions significantly improved what her students learned from her lessons.

If you use these questions on your own to learn what we are presenting in this text, you will have learned what cognitive psychologists call a cognitive learning strategy. *Cognitive strategies* are general methods of thinking that improve learning across a variety of subject areas. Cognitive strategies go beyond the processes that are naturally required for carrying out a task. For example, as you read this paragraph you are engaged in decoding processes (moving eyes from left to right, instantly sounding out each word, and so on). Therefore, decoding is not a cognitive strategy, because it is naturally required, or obligatory, for reading. However, if before you began to read and scanned the headings and asked yourself questions about the subject matter, and if, as you were reading, you regularly paused and asked yourself if you understood what you were reading, then you would be using cognitive strategies.

Similarly, a student is not using a cognitive strategy when he regroups and borrows to solve a subtraction problem—he is doing what is naturally required to perform the task. However, if before solving the problem and during the act of problem solving, the learner prompted himself with statements such as "What am I supposed to do? What information am I given? First, I'll draw a picture of what the problem is asking," he would be using a cognitive strategy.

There are cognitive learning strategies to improve memory, reading comprehension, math problem solving, and problem solving in general. In the following sections, we will describe a number of strategies and demonstrate how you can use them in your classroom.

Strategies to Improve Memory

As we will see in our discussion of human memory processes, learners have only a limited capacity for recalling information. Permanent recall depends on how well the learner takes in new information and stores it. Cognitive psychologists have discovered a number of strategies for improving memory that you can teach to your students. These strategies typically involve rehearsal, elaboration, and organization.

Rehearsal involves repeating to yourself what you are reading or hearing. This could involve repeating the lines in a poem, letters that spell a word, or a list of steps to be followed.

School-age learners are expected to learn the names of letters, associate sounds with particular letters and letter combinations, and memorize addition, subtraction, and multiplication steps, facts, dates, scientific terminology, and word definitions. Learners who experience difficulty memorizing such information are often helped by learning a memory strategy called *elaboration.* Learners use elaboration when they associate a particular image with something they are learning (for example, a learner recalls an image of an apple to learn the sound of the letter "a"). They might also relate something they have already learned to new material. Van Houten taught letter sounds and multiplication facts to learning disabled students using an elaboration technique that he calls *color mediation.* A child who has learned to label several colors correctly is taught to apply color labels to letters or number facts printed in a particular color. The number or letter in question is printed in the color associated with its verbal label. The child learns to label the letter or recall the number fact by matching it with its color.

The *keyword method* is an elaboration strategy in which the learner transforms one or two related pieces of information into a "keyword" already familiar to her. For example, students in high school are often required to learn foreign language words and definitions. The students have two pieces of information to associate—one of which is an unfamiliar term (the foreign word).

The foreign word can be transformed into something familiar, thus making its definition easier to remember. For example, to learn that *pollo* means "chicken" in Spanish, a learner would identify a word that looks or sounds like *pollo.* Either "pole" or "polo" could serve as a keyword for *pollo.* Thus the learner might imagine a chicken scratching the ground at the North Pole or a team of chickens playing polo. The potency of this memory strategy has been demonstrated in scores of studies used with learners from elementary school through college.

Organization is a term applied to memory strategies in which the learner groups or arranges the information being studied according to some system. *Chunking* is an organization strategy in which the learner places information in related groups. Another organization strategy is to arrange information into some type of outline form with headings and subheadings. Teaching students to employ such mental organizers gives them creative alternatives by which to manipulate ideas and information, retain mental strategies for learning, and thus internally reinforce their own learning.

Strategies to Improve Reading Comprehension

The goal of reading instruction is to train learners not how to say words but how to get meaning out of them. *Comprehension monitoring* is a term applied to a host of strategies learners can use to derive meaning from what they read. These comprehension strategies have in common the following skills:

1. *Setting goals for reading:* Learners learn to ask themselves "What do I have to do?" and "Why am I reading this story?"
2. *Focusing attention:* Learners learn to prompt themselves with questions such as "What am I supposed to do as I read?"
3. *Self-reinforcement:* Learners learn to say to themselves "Great, I understand this. Keep up the good work," or "This strategy really works."
4. *Coping with problems:* When they encounter difficulties, learners learn to say to themselves "I don't understand this. I should go back and read it again," or "That's a simple mistake. I can correct that."

Strategies for General Problem Solving

Many systems for problem solving can be taught to learners . There are problem-solving strategies to improve general problem solving, scientific thinking, mathematical problem solving, and writing during the elementary years and during adolescence.

A problem-solving system that can be used in a variety of curriculum areas and with a variety of problems is called IDEAL. IDEAL involves five stages of problem solving:

1. *Identify the problem.* Learners must know what the problem is before they can solve it. During this stage of problem solving, learners ask themselves whether they understand what the problem is and whether they have stated it clearly.
2. *Define terms.* During this stage, learners check whether they understand what each word in the problem statement means.
3. *Explore strategies.* At this stage, learners compile relevant information and try out strategies to solve the problem. This can involve drawing diagrams, working backward to solve a mathematical or reading comprehension problem, or breaking complex problems into manageable units.
4. *Act on the strategy.* Once learners have explored a variety of strategies, they select one and now use it.
5. *Look at the effects.* During the final stage of the IDEAL method, learners ask themselves whether they have come up with an acceptable solution.

There is abundant evidence that learners as young as 2 years use problem-solving strategies. Good learners at all grade levels know and use strategies to accomplish school tasks in reading, math, science, and social studies. They know how to use memory strategies to improve recall, comprehension strategies to learn more from reading, and general problem-solving strategies to improve math and science understanding.

METACOGNITION

Pressley, Borkowski, and O'Sullivan reviewed a series of experiments that demonstrate that knowing how to use a cognitive strategy is no guarantee that learners will use it when they need to. In these experiments, one group of learners was taught a strategy for a particular task. A second group was taught the same strategy for the same task but was also told that using the strategy would increase learning. As predicted, learners who were informed about the usefulness of the strategy were more likely to use and remember it than those who were not informed.

O'Sullivan and Pressley found that groups of children who were given information on when and where to use a strategy for which they were trained used that strategy on a greater variety of tasks than those not given such information. From this research and that of others, we know that the long-term use of strategies by your learners depends on how well you supplement the teaching of strategies with instruction on when and where to use them. Students who are aware of when to use strategies are said to possess *metacognition*—or knowledge about their cognition.

Development of Metacognition

While children as young as 2 years use cognitive strategies, they are not aware that they are using them and thus do not do so intentionally. The capacity to think metacognitively appears to develop as children enter the concrete operational stage of development. Nevertheless, learners who use strategies typically fail to notice that the strategy is helping them, and often fail to use it when the opportunity arises.

Ghatala, Ghatala, Levin, Pressley, and Goodwin, and Pressley and Ghatala conducted a series of studies on metacognition with school-age learners. They taught fifth- and sixth-grade learners two strategies for learning vocabulary words, one of which was clearly more effective than the others. To their surprise, the learners did not notice that one was more effective. Only when this was pointed out did the learners choose the more effective strategy for subsequent vocabulary-learning tasks.

The surprising conclusion from this research is that learners in second through sixth grades do not automatically acquire metacognitive knowledge. In other words, while engaged in using strategies, they don't automatically realize that one strategy may be better than another, spontaneously compare the effectiveness of the strategies, or use information about the effective use of the strategy to make future decisions.

Learners at this age can learn to make these decisions, but they need explicit instruction.

Teaching Metacognition

The work of Ghatala and Pressley on the development of metacognition in young children makes two main points:

(1) learners as young as second grade can learn to regulate their use of cognitive strategies, but

(2) they require systematic instruction to do so.

Thus, if you want your learners to use cognitive strategies to improve their learning of vocabulary, spelling, number facts, reading comprehension, or problem solving, you must not only teach these strategies systematically, but also teach learners to regulate their use. Metacognitive instruction involves teaching your learners to:

(1) attend to the effectiveness of strategies,

(2) attribute differences to the relative effectiveness of a particular strategy, and

(3) use the more effective strategy in future decision making.

Otherwise, learners may not use a given strategy, not notice whether it is effective, or fail to use it when they should.

Knowledge

If you plan to teach history, social studies, science, literature, or the cultural arts to children in elementary, junior, or senior high school, you have probably asked yourself the following questions: Is it really important that my learners have a lot of factual information about the subject I'm teaching? What difference does a knowledge of important facts, concepts, and principles in my field make in my learners' ability to think? What can a learner with a large amount of knowledge do that a learner with limited knowledge can't? As you will see from the next section, the answer is: A lot.

Effect of Knowledge on Learning

Suppose you gave the same memory task to two groups of learners—fourth graders and twelfth graders. If the memory task involved recalling specific information from the sports page of a daily newspaper, which group would remember more? Make your choice before reading on.

Now suppose we were to tell you that the fourth graders were all sports buffs and that the twelfth graders didn't know the sports page from the society column. Now who would you predict would remember the most from the memory task? If you predicted the fourth graders, you are most likely correct.

Let's change the task. Suppose the memory task involved recalling the names of pictures of 20 common objects including a bike, a car, a ring, and a hairbrush that the learners saw for 60 seconds. Who would recall more? Here the older learners would do better. Why? The answer has to do with the role of knowledge. In the first example, the fourth graders have specific knowledge about sports. Therefore, when they read the sports page they understand and recall much more than the twelfth graders, who are unfamiliar with such terms as zone defense, nickle defense, the blue line, sacrifice, infield fly rule, and point guard.

The fourth graders possess what cognitive psychologists call *domain-specific knowledge,* or knowledge of facts, concepts, and principles pertaining to a specific area or topic. Domain-specific knowledge is different from *general knowledge,* which is knowledge useful for learning across a variety of school tasks.

Examples of general knowledge are how to write or spell, how to use a dictionary or encyclopedia, and how to use a computer. Domain-specific knowledge allows the fourth-graders to think about and process information about their domain of expertise better than learners who are unfamiliar with the domain . General knowledge, however, allows the twelfth-graders to do a better job of recognizing familiar objects.

Here's another demonstration of the importance of a knowledge base in learning. Schneider, Korkel, and Weinert (1989) and Schneider and Korkel asked 8-, 10-, and 12-year-old children to read passages about soccer, a sport popular in Germany, where they conducted their research. After reading the passages, the children were asked questions that assessed recall of specific information, the making of inferences, and detection of contradictions. Some of the children across all age levels knew a lot about soccer, some very little. In addition to measuring the soccer expertise of the children, the researchers also measured their general intelligence by means of an IQ test.

The researchers found that age had a lot to do with performance on the reading tests—12-year-olds made more correct inferences than 8-year-olds, as you would expect. But they also found that prior knowledge of soccer was associated with higher learning, regardless of age level. Knowledgeable 8-year-olds did better on the tests than did novice 12-year-olds. Even more striking was the fact that general intelligence was not a strong determinant of performance. Learners with a lot of soccer expertise and average general intelligence outperformed novice learners with high general intelligence.

These results have been confirmed in this country with both children and adult learners. Walker found that baseball experts with low general intelligence learn more from a baseball passage than do baseball novices with high general intelligence. Ceci and Liker went to a racetrack and located both experts and novices at race handicapping who were comparable in years of education, years going to the track, and job prestige. The range of IQ in both groups was from 80 to 130. The task given to the subjects was to handicap 50 two-horse races. They were given a variety of statistics and asked to compute the odds for each of 50 races that pitted an unnamed horse against a horse that was the same in each race. The researchers found that the complexity of the reasoning of the low-IQ experts was far greater than that of the high-IQ novices.

Thus, domain-specific knowledge appears to be much more important in determining good thinking and performance on a given task than general intelligence. The message for teachers who want to teach their learners to be good thinkers is clear: Teaching cognitive strategies and metacognitive knowledge is necessary for good thinking, but it is not sufficient. You must also ensure that your learners have mastered the critical information in the area in which you want them to think well.

Types of Expert Knowledge

What types of knowledge do experts have that allow them to think so productively? Cognitive psychologists have classified knowledge in a variety of ways. We have already discussed one such type: domain-specific versus general knowledge. Another way of categorizing knowledge is declarative knowledge versus procedural knowledge.

Declarative knowledge is another name for verbal information: the facts, concepts, principles, and theories that we learn from lectures, studying textbooks, or watching television.

Procedural knowledge is know-how: knowledge of the action sequences involved in booting a floppy disk, writing an outline, tying your shoes, focusing a microscope, or playing a trombone.

To give you a better feel for the distinction between declarative and procedural knowledge let's examine what researchers have found about the knowledge bases of expert teachers.

Researchers in teaching expertise typically ask experienced and beginning teachers to view videotapes of real-life classroom episodes and to then make judgments about what is happening in the classroom. The teachers record their judgments on tape or write them down. Researchers then analyze these tapes for what they reveal about the knowledge bases of expert and novice teachers. What they find is that expert teachers are able to classify the types of instruction and activities they view (discovery learning, lecture, discussion, and so forth), relate the activities of the lesson to the behavior of the learners, categorize the behavior of the learners (attention-seeking, power struggle, and so on), and suggest alternative courses of action.

Novice teachers, on the other hand, have little understanding of what is going on in the classroom, see few connections between teacher behavior and learner behavior, and have few suggestions. In short, expert teachers possess a great deal of declarative knowledge about specific subject area teaching practices, curriculum materials, the characteristics and cultural backgrounds of learners, theories of instruction, and theories of learner behavior that allows them to make sense out of what they see in classrooms.

Other researchers who have studied the procedural knowledge of expert teachers have shown that expert teachers draw up extensive lesson plans, know how to prevent behavior problems from escalating, monitor students as they are learning, develop efficient techniques for grading papers and giving students immediate feedback on learning, and know how to ask questions that elicit reflective comments by students.

Characteristics of an Expert's Knowledge Base

So far we have learned that experts in any area have a large base of knowledge that includes both declarative and procedural knowledge. This knowledge base allows experts not only to think well, but also to think quickly. Experts are fast: they solve problems faster than novices and with fewer mistakes.

One reason they solve problems faster is because their procedural knowledge is automatic—a characteristic of the knowledge base often referred to as *automaticity*. Automaticity means that a procedure has been learned so thoroughly that it is carried out with little thinking and little effort. Good readers decode automatically—they don't have to think about sound/symbol associations. Good writers construct sentences automatically—they don't have to think about grammatical rules as they are writing. Expert problem solvers in math perform math operations automatically—they don't spend a lot of time thinking about how to regroup in subtraction, carry in addition, or find the least common denominator when working with fractions.

This organization of information is often *hierarchical:* for example, the mind organizes the information in a specific area, such as "earthquakes," from the most general principles to the most specific details. In other words, general principles of plate tectonics (geologic activity occurs where plates converge) subsume concepts (pressure, crust, tectonic plates), which, in turn, subsume specific facts (location of plates, mountain ranges, number of continents). According to these researchers, it isn't simple cognitive strategies that allow experts to reason and solve problems quickly. Rather, it is the organized nature of the information base that allows the learner to quickly access information and use it to expertly perform a task.

Educational Implications

As the saying goes, "Knowledge is power." A knowledgeable learner with an average IQ is a better thinker in a given area than is a learner with a high IQ who lacks domain-specific knowledge. Therefore, the message for teachers who want their learners to be good thinkers is clear: Teach important declarative and procedural knowledge. Make sure that you help your learners organize and categorize the verbal information so they can access it from memory quickly and efficiently. In addition, provide extensive practice with procedural knowledge so learners can perform operations like decoding text, writing sentences, or carrying out basic math procedures automatically and effortlessly.

Cognitive psychologists tell us that good thinkers or good information processors in any area of expertise have

(1) an extensive knowledge base, characterized by

(2) organization, and

(3) automaticity.

They use cognitive strategies when thinking and know when and where to use these strategies. The expert teaching of good thinking requires that teachers attend to all three components of good thinking.

But how do learners come to learn, retain, and use these processes? Cognitive psychologists can't see the processes of good thinking at work. So to help understand them, they use models. In the next section, we will examine the most popular of these models—the information processing model—and study some of its more recent variations.

The Information Processing Model

In the preceding section, we learned what makes good thinking. By now you are probably asking yourself "What is the best way to teach strategies, metacognition, and knowledge to my learners?" This is also a goal of cognitive psychologists—designing instruction to make learners better thinkers. However, cognitive psychologists realize that another question must be answered before we can answer the question of how good thinking can be taught. This question is: "What does good thinking look like?"

Cognitive psychologists have some ideas about what makes up good thinking. But how do knowledge, cognitive strategies, and knowledge about the use of cognitive strategies get into our heads in the first place? And once this content gets there, what happens to it? How does it get organized and sorted? Where exactly is the information stored? How is it retrieved?

All these questions have to do with how the mind works—the processes involved in good thinking. Accurate answers to these questions would greatly help us in our efforts to teach learners to think better. For example, knowing how the mind takes in new information would allow you to make better decisions about how to present new information. Knowing how the mind categorizes or organizes this information would allow you to present new information in the most efficient way.

The information processing model seeks to describe what happens to information the first time it is presented to a learner. For example, the first time a ninth-grade biology student hears about the structure of the circulatory system, what happens to all the related facts, concepts, and principles? How is the biology information processed? They do not correspond to physical locations in the brain; they represent only functions. Arrows in the model represent the sequence in which these functions occur, while ovals stand for control processes or executive routines that govern or regulate information flow. Control processes include goal setting, strategy selection, expectations, monitoring progress, and metacognition (when we consciously regulate control processes).

Reception of Information

Information processing begins when the learner starts reading an assigned history, watching a science demonstration, or listening to the explanation of the legislative process in a political science class. *Receptors* (such as rods and cones in the eyes, bones in the middle ears) take in light and sound energy, transform these different energy forms into electrical impulses, and send the impulses to the brain. These impulses are registered in *immediate memory* (IM). IM holds this wealth of sensory information for the briefest period of time—Sperling estimates a visual stimulus decays in about a fourth of a second. Nevertheless, these impulses linger just long enough for the control processes involved in selective perception to impose some organization or meaning on them. Thus, not all information coming into IM is lost.

Selective perception occurs when the learner attends to what is most important in the information coming in through the receptors and attaches some meaning to it. When the stimulus itself provides the meaning, *bottom-up processing* is said to occur . In other words, when the light patterns from a motorcycle are received on the rods and cones, your mind analyzes the patterns and instantly recognizes it as a motorcycle—something that has meaning to you. But we also selectively perceive through *top-down processing.* For example, when a learner is reading a history assignment dealing with the Protestant Reformation, she will more quickly recognize the word "schism" because she already possesses *prior information* about schisms and has certain *expectations* for what the homework is about. Thus, selective perception, whether top-down or bottom-up, is influenced by visual, auditory, or tactile stimulus patterns, prior knowledge, and expectations.

Attention also has a great deal to do with selective perception. It is particularly important during the early stage of processing unfamiliar information. Attention maintains the learner's vigilance, which keeps the selective perception process going and enhances sensory acuity, which in turn makes one aware of new stimulus cues. Thus, gaining and holding a learner's attention, particularly at the beginning stages of a lesson, is a pivotal challenge to teachers.

Working Memory

Working Memory is often referred to as *short-term memory,* although there are some subtle differences between the two concepts. Pressley refers to both working memory and short-term memory as "attentional capacity." If the learner attends to and selectively perceives the data that enter immediate memory (IM), these data next enter working memory (WM). Try to picture the function of WM in terms of awareness. What you are aware you are thinking about at any given moment is said to be in your WM. WM is of limited duration—current research suggests that it retains new information for about 10 to 20 seconds. After that, the information is either lost or transformed.

For example, we've all had the experience of getting a number from the telephone operator but having no pencil to write it down. The number gets into WM, but it is quickly lost unless you either write it down or repeat it a few times (a process called *rehearsal*). This is an example of the limited capacity of WM. Estimates are that its capacity is limited to five to nine isolated bits of information—in this example, numbers.

WM is where conscious thinking occurs—consider it a kind of mental workplace. When you try to solve a math problem in your head (for example, "If pencils cost 69 cents a dozen, how much will nine pencils cost?") you are using your WM. Because of its limited capacity and duration, WM is not a good place to perform several different mental operations at the same time. Try comprehending the main point of a sentence you are reading in a foreign language when at the same time you have to sound out and then think about the meaning of half the words. Reading comprehension occurs in working memory, which is why learners who are slow in word decoding are also weak in comprehension.

Why We Forget

Several theories try to explain why WM is of such limited duration and capacity. *Decay theory* holds that information simply leeches out of WM or dissolves. The energy impulses dissipate with the passage of time unless we rehearse the new information. While decay theory presents some vivid metaphors, it is not as convincing as displacement theory. *Displacement theory* suggests that there are only so many "slots" in WM that can be filled. Once new information comes into WM, the existing information is pushed out and replaced by the incoming data. Displacement theory is closely related to *interference theory*, which posits that subsequent learning competes with prior learning and somehow interferes with what's contained in WM.

Information in WM is like information in the working memory of your computer. If you want to save it, you must transfer it to a long-term storage device. WM helps process information into a form that is acceptable for more permanent storage in long-term memory—like saving a document on the hard drive in your computer.

Implications for Teaching. The function of WM has important implications for your teaching. Two of these implications are as follows:

1. Unrelated facts are quickly forgotten unless the learner organizes them in some way or unless you help the learner to do so (remember that different learners have different storage capacities in WM).
2. The more you allow learners to think about information in WM, the more likely they are to put that information into more permanent storage. Active processing or thinking about new information, such as taking notes, discussion, and practice, are essential learning strategies for accomplishing this.

Long-Term Memory

Information from WM may be stored in *long-term memory* (LTM). Storage is a term or metaphor that describes a series of processes whereby new information is integrated with information that is already known or residing in LTM. The principal storage processes, as you have already learned, involve rehearsal, elaboration, and organization.

Form of Knowledge in LTM

There is considerable discussion among cognitive psychologists about what exactly is stored in long-term memory. At one level, we know that declarative and procedural knowledge are stored there. But what form does this information take in long-term memory? This is an important question, because if we know in what form information is stored in LTM, we could present information to learners in that form to facilitate remembering. For example, if information is stored in long-term memory in the form of visual images, then teachers could help their learners to encode information visually. Cognitive psychologists propose a number of theories about how knowledge is represented in LTM: dual-coding theory, propositional networks, and schemas.

"Don't think about pink elephants." As soon as you hear this, what do you do? If you're like most people, you think about pink elephants. In thinking about *how* we think, we all depend on images to help us. We also depend on words, particularly when we can't construct an image (for example, try to imagine a heffalump). Paivio has developed a *dual-coding theory* of long-term storage. He believes that information in LTM is composed of complex networks of verbal representations and images. A good example of the verbal imaging of information is when you think about the concept "dental cavity." Your experience probably includes images of drills, excruciating pain, needles, chairs, and New Age music.

In addition to verbal images, however, you also think in terms of connected ideas (for example, "If A is bigger than B, and B is bigger than C, then A is bigger than C"). Anderson proposes that much declarative knowledge is stored in LTM in the form of extensive networks of interconnected ideas called *propositional networks*. Cognitive psychologists propose that if we could see into a learner's brain and examine those neurons that contain information about Benjamin Franklin, it would look something like this web of ideas, concepts, and facts. If LTM actually stores information in the form of propositional networks, teaching learners how to outline and make connections during a lesson would greatly facilitate remembering.

A third hypothesis about the form of information in LTM is called *schema theory* . They are cognitive structures that organize large amounts of information about objects (the Taj Mahal), events (the first landing on the moon), or text readings (Willa Cather's *The Lost Lady*). Your learners have schemata for "a birthday party," "the first day of school," "the senior prom," and so forth, which organize a vast array of information about events, people, feelings, and their relationships. These schemata influence how learners perceive and make sense of what they hear and read.

Capacity of LTM

Most cognitive psychologists stipulate that information in LTM lasts a lifetime. Then, you may be asking yourselves, how come we forget so much? Cognitive psychologists believe that your experience of forgetting things you once "knew" is due more to your failure to find a good way to retrieve the information than to any permanent loss of data. A good example of the permanence of LTM comes from a study by Williams and Hollan . They asked people who had graduated from high school between 4 and 19 years earlier to recall as many names of individuals as possible from their high school classes. At first the subjects were slow to come up with names. But as they began to use clues, such as "the kids who lived on my block," "the kids I rode to school with," or "the kids in my physics class," recall dramatically improved. The subjects in the study recalled large percentages of their graduating classes despite the fact that these classes were quite large.

Retrieval Processes

As this example shows, when we actively search our memories for information to use in a thinking task (to get it into working memory) we are engaged in *retrieval processes.* Cognitive psychologists use the term *activation* to refer to cognitive processes involved in becoming aware of what we have learned and in establishing connections between this prior learning and the task in which we are currently involved. This connection-building is facilitated by the use of retrieval cues.

Retrieval cues are hints or things we say to ourselves to help us remember what we have already learned and stored in LTM. In the experiment about remembering one's high school classmates reported above, retrieval cues were the hints, such as "the kids who lived on my block." Retrieval cues are particularly effective when the cue you are using to recall information matches information that you stored at the time of original learning. For example, the cue "who are the kids in my physics class?" would be of no help if, at the time you were taking high school physics, you never noticed who was in your class.

Tulving believes that good recall of memorized information is largely cue-dependent. You forget the meaning of a word that you once knew, such as *homunculus,* because you don't have a cue that emphasizes remembering it. You forget how to spell a particular word because you fail to use a cue that emphasizes sound. Depending on the type of recall you want (meaning, spelling, date, name, address, phone number), there are cues to match it.

The information processing model of how the mind works is a metaphor. This model can help you think about what you can do during your lessons to help your learners better understand and retain what you are teaching.

Parallel Distributed Processing Model

Cognitive psychologists have only just begun to understand how the mind works. The information processing model has contributed greatly to the development of the cognitive science of learning. Nevertheless, alternative models of the architecture of the mind reflect both the latest advances in computer science and our understanding of cognitive processes.

McClelland and Rumelhart believe that the information processing model encourages a perspective on thinking that is inconsistent with our experience. According to the information processing model, the mind is a system that performs one action after another very rapidly (reception followed by flow into working memory followed by storage into long-term memory followed by retrieval and transfer to working memory, and so on).

Rumelhart's view, on the other hand, is that the mind does a lot of things not one at a time, but rather all at once, much like the various processing units of a powerful computer. Inside a computer are complex arrangements of memory chips, processors, disks, switches, and drives. These components don't perform complex operations in an orderly, sequential fashion. Rather, they do a lot of things simultaneously as they solve problems.

So, too, the brain is made up of complex collections or arrangements of neurons that form *neural networks.* The brain contains many neural networks that perform a variety of specialized functions involved in complex thinking. There are neural networks for decoding text, solving arithmetic word problems, playing chess, and so forth. These networks are made up of smaller units, called *nodes,* that contain particular types of information (words, letters, sounds, images, rules) important to completing the task of the network.

No central processor or organizer governs how these nodes work together. Instead, the nodes are simultaneously active—they activate one another; they build new connections among one another; and eventually they learn and solve the problem at hand.

As a specific example of a neural network model, Gagné, Yekovich, and Yekovich considered Marshall's work on how students distinguish among five types of arithmetic word problems. Marshall studied the five types of word problems exemplified. *Change* problems are characterized by a change in the state of one quantity. *Group* problems involve situations in which two or more groups can be logically combined into a larger group. *Compare* problems contrast the values associated with two objects. *Restate* problems require rephrasing a verbal description into a different set of quantitative terms. Finally, *vary* problems depict direct or indirect variation.

Marshall postulated that through practice and feedback in identifying these five kinds of problems, students begin to form "pattern-recognition" units that fit specific problem types. Certain features of the word problems are associated with certain types of problems. For example, phrases like "how much bigger" or "how much more" are almost always associated with "compare" problems. Thus, these phrases come to be part of the pattern-recognition unit for such problems. These units are said to exist in long-term memory.

After learning, when a student reads a new problem, he represents its features in working memory. These features then activate the same features coded in long-term memory, and the features coded in long-term memory start to activate the pattern-recognition unit to which they belong. The large circle represents working memory, and the elements within this circle represent features and pattern-recognition units stored in long-term memory. Notice that elements of three different problem types (change, compare, and restate) have been activated by their connections to the representation of the current problem.

How does the learner decide which of these problem types best fits the current problem? Usually, more features of one pattern-recognition unit are activated than of any other. The unit with the most activated features is selected as appropriate. This is a characteristic assumption of neural network models. As you can see, this model involves a great deal of metaphorical thinking, which can make the model difficult to understand and apply. However, your own experience of thinking and problem solving may help: when engaged in problem solving, you are aware of many things at once: ideas, images, facts, rules, principles, and sounds pop in and out of your consciousness, and eventually some closure comes about. This kind of experience suggests that the PDP model is a valid metaphor for human thought.

The neural network models of cognitive functioning suggest that the minds of your learners may not always work in orderly, sequential ways. They may construct their own meanings or make their own sense of things without considering all the facts, advantages and disadvantages, similarities and differences.

The PDP model reminds you that thinking is not simple and orderly, based on neatly stored knowledge. Rather, a lot of thinking goes on at the same time the learner is gathering new knowledge and pondering over ongoing situations. PDP theorists believe that learning depends largely on the interactions between what is in the learner's head and what is outside it.

Cognitive Approaches to Learning and Intelligence

One of the goals of understanding how the mind works is to develop instructional methods that teachers can use to help learners become better thinkers. This goal inevitably raises the question: "If we can teach learners to think better, can we teach them to be more intelligent?" In other words, when we use the expression "good thinking" or "good information processing," do we really mean "good intelligence"? What is the difference between intelligence and the cognitive processes of good thinking?

Views of Intelligence

There are two major views of intelligence. The *classical tradition* attempts to understand the content, or *structure,* of intelligence, while the *revisionist tradition* seeks to understand its *processes.*

Intelligence as Structure

For most of the twentieth century, psychologists studying human intelligence have created tests to help them understand the underlying abilities that make up intelligence. They asked questions such as "Is intelligence one *general* ability or many *specific* abilities ?" These psychologists agree on several points:

1. Tests that contain questions to which there are clearly right and wrong answers are the best way to learn about intelligence.
2. The ability that underlies intelligence (in other words, the structure of intelligence) exists within the person and is largely inherited.
3. Intelligence is largely neurophysiological, involving such factors as the speed of transmission of nerve impulses.
4. Intelligence cannot be significantly improved through instruction or training.

Intelligence as Process

Rather than seek to understand the content or elements of intelligence, other psychologists have sought to understand what people do when they are engaged in intelligent behavior. Largely influenced by cognitive psychology, these psychologists view intelligence from an information processing framework. For them, what is important is the way in which people combine knowledge, strategies, and metacognitive processes to solve problems important to them. These theorists also share a common set of beliefs.

1. Intelligence may have a structure (abilities, and so on), but what's more important in studying and describing it is an understanding of its underlying processes.
2. Intelligence can be significantly improved by education and training.
3. Standardized tests are not the best way to explore the nature of intelligence. Instead, the best way to measure intelligence is to have people solve problems that are culturally relevant and to then examine the processes they used to do so.
4. There is a genetic component to intelligence, but it does not account for the majority of intelligent behavior.
5. Intelligence is strongly influenced by one's cultural environment. The study of intelligence must take into consideration the different environments to which people must adapt.

Two of the most prominent theorists of intelligence who work within the information processing tradition are Gardner and Sternberg. In the next sections, we will describe their recent work and discuss its relevance to classroom teaching.

Gardner's Theory of Multiple Intelligences

For Gardner, intelligence involves the ability to solve problems or fashion products (compose music, write poems, choreograph a dance) that are of consequence in a particular culture or community. He rejects the notion that we can learn about intelligence by studying how people answer questions on tests. For Gardner, we can only learn about intelligence by studying the cognitive processes people use when they are solving important cultural problems or creating important cultural products.

Gardner has identified seven intelligences that are involved in solving problems and fashioning products, and he believes that all seven can be taught in school. He has also developed a curriculum to do so, called Project Spectrum .

For Gardner, problem solving is essential to intelligence. This is consistent with many traditional notions of intelligence. However, Gardner insists that problem solving can be studied only by observing people solving problems or creating products that are important to them, not by administering standardized tests.

Gardner believes that by observing people solving the naturalistic, culturally important problems his seven intelligences represent, we will eventually map out the cognitive processes involved in good thinking. But he also predicts that no single model of cognitive functioning will be found to underlie all human problem solving. Rather, cognitive processes vary depending on the task a learner is involved in.

Sternberg's Triarchic Theory of Intelligence

Sternberg agrees with Gardner that the best way to study intelligence is to examine how people solve the problems that are important to them in their environments; that is, to study the cognitive processes by which people shape themselves and their environments to meet their needs. But he disagrees with Gardner in this important respect: Sternberg believes that regardless of the type of problem people are confronted with, they use a common set of cognitive processes to solve them. According to Sternberg, this is true whether the problems involve mathematical, spatial, linguistic, or interpersonal issues.

Sternberg identifies three components involved in any type of problem solving, components that represent basic information processes that act on information we take in through the senses. He calls these *metacomponents, performance components,* and *knowledge-acquisition components.*

Metacomponents of Intelligence

When attempting to solve real-world problems, intelligent people must make decisions about which strategies to use to solve them; how much time to allocate to arrive at a solution; the resources necessary; the best way to monitor a solution; and how to set up a system for obtaining feedback, attending to the feedback, and making sense of it. Sternberg refers to these as *executive skills.* As you can see, they relate to the regulation and control of problem solving. Thus they are similar to the metacognitive skills we studied in the information processing model above. Conventional intelligence tests do not test these metacomponents. Nevertheless, Sternberg stipulates that these executive skills are essential features of intelligent behavior, and, more importantly, that they can be taught.

Performance Components

Metacomponents regulate planning, monitoring, and decision making. Performance components actually carry out the processes involved in problem solving. They involve the use of cognitive strategies and include such matters as attending to stimuli, storing them in long-term memory, analyzing the features of problems, and retrieving information from working memory. These performance components work best to solve problems when they have become automated—when they are performed effortlessly and rapidly without conscious thought. Again, conventional intelligence tests do not assess these components very well. But as we have seen in our discussion of cognitive strategies, they can be taught.

Knowledge-Acquisition Components

To solve real-world problems, learners must perform cognitive strategies with automaticity and regulate their use, and they must also acquire knowledge about the problem itself. Some of the skills involved in acquiring knowledge include distinguishing relevant from irrelevant information while reading, forming internal connections with incoming information so that concepts and principles can be formed, and building external connections with prior learning (what we have called *activation*). Sternberg believes that conventional intelligence tests can serve as good measures of the knowledge-acquisition components of intelligence. But he also believes that the skills involved in knowledge acquisition are learned and can be taught.

For Sternberg, intelligence and good information processing are one and the same. His message to teachers is clear—you can make your learners more intelligent in the following ways.

1. Give them real-world problems that are important in their culture and environment to solve.
2. Teach them general cognitive strategies that they can use to solve any problem.
3. Teach them metacognitive skills to help them regulate their use of cognitive strategies.
4. Show them how to acquire knowledge and provide practice opportunities, so that these skills become automatic.

Making Learners Active Thinkers

Current cognitive models of learning and thinking (such as the information processing and PDP models) stipulate that the mind learns not by passively recording or absorbing information, but by actively trying to make sense of it. These models tell us that in the process of making sense of information, active learners build internal connections or relationships among the ideas and facts they are learning. In addition, they build external connections between the new information and what they already know. This approach to learning emphasizes the active role of the learner, in contrast to the behavioral science approach, which emphasizes the active role of the teacher. *Constructivism* is a term used by cognitive psychologists to represent this approach to learning.

Over the past decade, the term "constructivism" has come to mean more than a theory about learning. It has become associated with a theory of knowledge that says that the world is inherently complex, that there is no objective reality, and that much of what we know is constructed from our beliefs and the social milieu in which we live. Here is how a leading constructivist, Ernst von Glasersfeld, describes this philosophy of knowing:

From the beginning, in the 5th century B.C., the skeptics have shown that it is logically impossible to establish the "truth" of any particular piece of knowledge. The necessary comparison of the piece of knowledge with the reality it is supposed to represent cannot be made because the only rational access to that reality is through yet another act of knowing.

The skeptics have forever reiterated this argument to the embarrassment of all the philosophers who tried to get around the difficulty. Nevertheless, the skeptics did not question the traditional concept of knowing.

This is where constructivism, following the lead of the American pragmatists and a number of European thinkers at the turn of this century, breaks away from the tradition. It holds that there is something wrong with the old concept of knowledge, and it proposes to change it rather than continue the same hopeless struggle to find a solution to the perennial paradox. The change consists of this: Give up the requirement that knowledge represents an independent world, and admit instead that knowledge represents something that is far more important to us, namely *what we can do in our experiential world, the successful ways of dealing with the objects we call physical and the successful ways of thinking with abstract concepts.*

In addition to being associated with a philosophical theory on the existence of knowledge, the term "constructivism" has also become associated with an educational movement that restores learners to the forefront of the instructional process. The goal of this movement is to redesign educational practice so that lessons are planned and sequenced to encourage learners to use their experiences to actively construct understanding in a way that makes sense to them. The constructivist movement in education has resulted in numerous curriculum reforms in the teaching of reading, writing, mathematics, social studies, and science.

Thus, for our purposes, constructivism is the application to classrooms of learning principles derived from cognitive models that provide learners the opportunity to construct their own ways of knowing.

Constructivist instructional practices, whether in the areas of science, social studies, mathematics, reading, or writing, have the following characteristics in common:

1. They organize learning and instruction around important ideas.
2. They acknowledge the importance of prior learning.
3. They challenge the adequacy of the learner's prior knowledge.
4. They provide for ambiguity and uncertainty.

5. They teach learners how to learn.
6. They view learning as a joint cognitive venture.
7. They assess a learner's knowledge acquisition during the lesson.

Let's examine each of these elements in more detail.

Organize Learning Around Important Ideas

Rene Jordash was unhappy with the way her world history text discussed World War I. In particular, she felt that its discussion of the causes of the war led her tenth-grade students to think that it all started because someone got shot in his carriage. She wanted her students to understand that the causes of major wars have their roots in religious, ethnic, economic, and other conflicts, which fester over long periods of time. So, to help her learners appreciate the complexity of causes underlying conflicts such as

World War I, she started her third-period class with the question: "What would have happened if the Archduke Ferdinand of Austria hadn't been shot?"

Extensive interviews with learners of various ages reveal that, in comparison to adults, school-age learners typically do not see learning as a goal of instruction. In other words, they do not attend to a lesson with the explicit intention of learning, but rather with the idea of completing assignments and activities, passing tests, and doing homework.

Cognitive psychologists believe that learners' view of learning as an activity rather than a goal leads them to be passive during classroom instruction. In other words, they sit in classrooms waiting for the spelling worksheet or biology lab sheet to be passed out, homework to be assigned, and test dates to be given. So how does a teacher help learners view learning as a goal rather than an activity? To do this, most cognitive approaches to instruction advocate that teachers focus their lessons on and make explicit to learners the primary concepts, generalizations, and underlying themes of the content they are teaching rather than focus on isolated facts or bits of information. Let's look at some ways teachers can do this.

Curriculum guides and textbooks don't always identify these larger ideas, generalizations, or principles for you. Often they may, instead, be compilations of facts or activities. For example, a U.S. history text typically devoted to different wars: the French and Indian War, the American Revolution, wars with Mexico, the Civil War. Students typically learn facts about these wars—names, dates, places—and fill out maps and take tests to assess that learning. A constructivist approach to teaching about important wars might instead involve students' learning about the theme of human conflict: its underlying causes and its outcomes. Wars would be presented as a *group* of events to help learners construct a larger understanding of American history.

In advocating that teachers organize instruction around primary concepts, generalizations, and underlying themes, cognitive psychologists are not denying the importance of factual knowledge; prior knowledge is considered a requirement of good thinking. Rather, they are saying that factual knowledge can be acquired in a variety of ways (for example, from reading, lectures, peers), and that the best way for learners to retain and apply this knowledge is to put it in a larger, more lifelike context that stimulates learners to reflect, organize, analyze, and problem solve.

The importance of focusing lessons around important ideas as opposed to facts has resulted in numerous curriculum reforms during the past decade. Science curricula are being developed that organize information around "conceptual themes" like cause and effect, change and conservation, diversity and variation, and energy and matter, rather than around topics such as the digestive system, the planets, nutrition, or electricity. Language arts curricula present readings in the context of themes such as fantasy/realism, reflection/impulsivity, reactive/proactive, and freedom/responsibility, rather than in genre-specific units, like poetry, prose, mythology, and nonfiction.

The rationale behind these curricular changes is that learners acquire meaning and understanding by organizing information for themselves, connecting it to other information, and storing it as networks or schemata, rather than by being told isolated bits of information. The more that lessons can be focused on larger units of knowledge—concepts, generalizations, and underlying themes—the more likely learners are to connect the new subject matter with what they already know.

Acknowledge the Importance of Prior Knowledge

Cognitive psychologists believe that learners, even at the earliest grade levels, have some information about nearly every topic they study. This information may be in the form of ideas, however vague; unconnected facts; implicit rules; or images. Frequently, this information consists of mistaken beliefs, such as "the world is flat," "the sun moves around the earth," "the cause of the Civil War was the firing on Fort Sumter," or "all microorganisms are bad." This prior knowledge affects learners' attempts to construct meaning out of what they are hearing, seeing, or reading. Unlike the behaviorists, who view the learner as passively absorbing and storing new information, cognitive psychologists assert that learners are continually engaged in trying to make sense out of what they learn.

At this point you might ask yourself, "Isn't the emphasis placed on *prior knowledge* by cognitive psychologists similar to what the behaviorists mean by *prerequisite skills?*" The answer is that although prior knowledge and prerequisite skills have some similarities, the former term, as cognitive psychologists use it, connotes far more than the latter.

Behaviorists view prior knowledge in terms of readiness for instruction. When prior knowledge is lacking, they see the teacher's role simply as one of giving it to the learners so that they can acquire new knowledge. Cognitive psychologists, on the other hand, view prior knowledge as a cognitive structure—or *schema*—which suggests deeper understandings, interconnectedness with other data, and connections to incoming knowledge. The teacher's concern with prior knowledge is not simply to fill up an empty vessel, as the behaviorists contend, but rather to help learners gain entry to that knowledge, understand its conceptions and misconceptions, and swap inappropriate cognitive structures for better ones.

Organizing Prior Knowledge

David Ausubel was one of the first American educational psychologists to advocate the importance of prior knowledge as a cognitive structure or schema for achieving meaningful learning. Ausubel held that people learn when they (1) assimilate new material into existing schemata and (2) reconstruct or accommodate new material to existing schemata by transforming it in idiosyncratic ways. He championed the concept of an "advance organizer" to provide learners with instructional supports to facilitate meaningful learning.

An *advance organizer* is a summary of the concepts, generalizations, and themes to be learned, presented at a general and inclusive level. When presented to learners at the beginning of a lesson, it can help learners both recall familiar material (material the learners had prior knowledge of) and learn unfamiliar material. Ausubel believed that advance organizers help learners construct new knowledge. They do this both by providing a cue for recalling existing schemata and by providing a conceptual peg on which to hang new information.

Recognizing Learner Opinions, Beliefs, and Ideas

Learners who have little prior knowledge in a given area may have difficulty learning anything new. For example, suppose you were teaching a unit on World War I and you began by focusing on specific facts and details about which your learners had little prior knowledge. As a consequence, the learners would be unable to build bridges to what they already know, they would not make an effort to construct their own understanding of what is being taught, and, at best, they would passively attend to your lesson. On the other hand, if you recognize that your learners already have opinions, beliefs, or general notions about what your next lesson will cover, and if you try to organize this lesson around larger ideas that your learners can build on, they are more likely to engage in active thinking that results in meaningful learning and retention.

Anticipating Misconceptions

Cognitive psychologists caution that prior knowledge, in the form of misconceptions, may hamper the acquisition of new knowledge when these misconceptions are not anticipated by the teacher. For example, learners sometimes come to science classes with prior knowledge that is inconsistent with the content they are being asked to learn. Sometimes erroneous prior knowledge is so entrenched in the learners' minds that they continue to use mistaken ways of thinking even when alternative methods have been taught. And sometimes prior beliefs are so strong that learners ignore statements that they disagree with or they choose not to believe what they see.

To show the power of prior knowledge, Gunstone and White constructed a demonstration involving a weight and a bucket of sand, which were hanging in balance on opposite sides of a pulley and extending downward an equal distance from the wheel of the pulley. A small amount of sand was added to the bucket—so small that its addition caused no movement. Yet students who believed that the bucket would sink reported that they observed movement!

Next, the experimenters pulled the bucket down (which raised the weight) and asked students to predict what would happen if they let go of the bucket. Students predicted that the bucket would return to its original position, which it did not. Some students reacted to what they saw not by learning a new rule or generalization, but by trying to explain it away, arguing that something was wrong with the pulley.

The best way to ensure that your learners' prior knowledge works to enhance meaningful and conceptually accurate learning is to ask these questions as you prepare a unit:

1. What important ideas, principles, generalizations, or beliefs do I want my learners to construct at the end of this unit?
2. How might this topic already look to my learners? How might they already perceive it or think about it?
3. What is the best way to represent or introduce these new ideas to my learners so that they connect them with what they already know and thus challenge the adequacy of their existing knowledge?

Challenge the Adequacy of Prior Knowledge

What is the best way to get your learners to compare what they know with what you are teaching? Constructivist educators propose that teachers deliberately plan their lessons to create "conceptual conflict". For example, imagine introducing a biology unit on the body's defense mechanisms with the following assertion: "Germs are not trying to hurt us when they settle in our bodies. They just want to live quietly, eat, and prosper."

Undoubtedly, many learners view germs as targeting the body and intentionally harming it rather than as just wanting to find a way to reside peaceably in the new environment.

Conceptual conflict comes about when our existing beliefs or ways of explaining things don't produce the outcomes we predict. Conceptual conflict is a useful teaching tool in many different subject areas. Social studies teachers create conceptual conflict when they challenge long-established beliefs about the significance of certain events. Reading teachers create conceptual conflict when they ask learners to make predictions about what may happen next in a story. Science teachers create conceptual conflict when they ask learners to guess what will happen when a certain chemical is added.

Some cognitive psychologists and constructivist educators suggest that the most effective way to get learners to challenge the adequacy of prior knowledge is to design lessons that deliberately create the opportunity for conceptual conflict. They believe that learners will attempt to resolve the conflict by constructing new meanings for themselves and that they will thereby retain what they have learned and apply it in new contexts.

Posner, Strike, Hewson, and Gertzog developed an instructional framework teachers can use to promote conceptual conflict and resolution in science instruction that is applicable to any academic discipline.

Provide for Ambiguity and Uncertainty

Constructivist educators point out that problem solving in the real world rarely results in quick, simple, and correct solutions. Rather, real-world problems are complex, messy, and unstructured, and they often have multiple solutions. Consequently, such educators argue that the problem-solving situations in which we place learners should be "authentic." *Authentic problems* are those that people encounter in the real world. They involve hands-on exercises or problems whose solutions are uncertain. Ideally, the tasks should yield multiple solutions, each with its own advantages and disadvantages. This creates the initial uncertainty and ambiguity necessary for meaningful learning to occur.

Many new approaches to instruction underscore the importance of ambiguity, complexity, uncertainty, and multiple solutions. Cognitive psychologists who study the development of writing skills, for example, urge that writing be viewed as problem solving . They suggest that the task of writing involves problem exploration, planning, brainstorming, organizing ideas, testing for connections and coherence, editing, and revising. But writing typically has not been viewed as problem solving. Rather, Applebee reports that writing assignments, even in high school, tend to be limited in scope and confined to a narrow topic. The typical assignment is a first-and-final draft, one page or shorter in length, to be completed in class, and the topic is usually chosen by the teacher to test previous learning or skills. Hence the students' task is to get the answer "right," rather than to convince, inform, or entertain a prospective audience.

Since Applebee's study, cognitive psychologists and constructivist educators have introduced numerous innovations into the teaching of writing . At the heart of these innovations is the notion that good writing instruction teaches learners to approach writing as a problem-solving activity. Learners are encouraged to pursue their own topics for writing rather than writing on a teacher-prescribed topic. They also learn the importance of planning: establishing goals for writing, outlining, and identifying the important information they need to gather. Finally, they learn to revise their writing in light of their goals, a process that leads writers to change their goals and be flexible in light of inconsistent or contradictory information.

Writing from a constructivist point of view is much more than learners trying to convince their teachers that they learned what they were taught. Rather, it is a process of solving an unstructured problem through planning, writing, and revising. The goal of instruction is for learners to appreciate the complexity of the writing task and to view it as a way of communicating ideas that are important to *them.*

Teach Learners How to Learn

We reviewed strategies to help learners remember, comprehend, write, and problem solve in a variety of academic areas.

A constructivist approach to classroom instruction includes cognitive strategies that teach students learning-to-learn skills and how to regulate those skills. Carl Bereiter, a prominent cognitive psychologist, refers to this goal of teaching as helping students become “intentional learners”. Students become *intentional learners* when they learn or find their own approaches or systems for achieving educational goals. Becoming an intentional learner requires the ability to find and allocate resources for learning, overcome obstacles to learning, and know how to sustain effort.

Intentional learners see themselves as being in charge of their learning—that is, they see themselves, not the teacher, as responsible for directing their learning efforts. In fact, cognitive psychologists have evidence that suggests that learners’ use of cognitive strategies depends on their willingness to accept responsibility for their own learning. In other words, they know how to monitor their understanding as they work. According to cognitive psychologists, better learners attend more closely to and assess more correctly the state of their understanding than do poorer learners. The importance of learners’ knowing cognitive strategies and how to regulate their use is summarized by Bereiter and Scardamalia as follows:

By several different routes we arrive at the same conclusion: In order to learn what is ostensibly being taught in schools, students need to direct mental effort to goals over and above those implicit in the school activities. Without such intentional learning, education degenerates into the doing of schoolwork and other activities.

View Learning as a Joint Cognitive Venture

Instruction that is focused on knowledge construction is a joint cognitive effort rather than a solitary search for knowledge or an exclusively teacher-controlled activity. A *joint cognitive venture* is focused on a clear cognitive goal, and different components of the venture are carried out by different classroom participants: learner, peers, and teachers. According to cognitive instructional theory, genuine knowledge construction is not a solitary enterprise involving a learner working in isolation from peers and adults.

Research continues to document the superiority of collaborative cognitive ventures over individualistic ones . One benefit of collaborative learning is that less-informed learners acquire knowledge and learning strategies by observing and imitating more knowledgeable ones. A number of factors contribute to the importance of learning in a social context. Let's look at some of them.

Conceptual Growth

Social or group learning is a principal force for promoting conceptual growth. Group instruction forces learners to accommodate their thinking to that of others. Conceptual growth is more likely to occur when learners have to think about the alternative viewpoints of group members, elaborate and defend their own ideas in the presence of others, and debate the merits of other viewpoints.

Social Support

Groups provide social support to their members in the form of encouragement and praise. Group instruction and group problem solving allow learners to assume different responsibilities. Group members encourage one another to fulfill the responsibilities of these roles so that the group can accomplish its task.

Cognitive Modeling

When students are given the opportunity to learn in a social setting, they observe the thinking processes of group members as they carry out their roles. As group members argue and discuss with one another, thinking strategies often become explicit. Research into social learning demonstrates that children can learn good thinking from one another. Thus students can learn how to define problems, brainstorm solutions, identify standards, collect data, and evaluate solutions by observing what different group members do.

Shared Expertise

Group learning assignments often involve different members learning different aspects of a large body of material. For example, a group project about the life of a famous scientist might require group members to acquire knowledge about different aspects of her life: education, culture, accomplishments, important historical events during her lifetime. Each member of the group becomes a subject specialist and communicates his or her knowledge to other group members. Thus, group learning becomes an efficient vehicle for acquiring new information.

Assess a Learner's Knowledge Acquisition During Lessons

Most educators agree that testing is an important feature of successful instruction. But testing traditionally takes place after a lesson or unit of study is completed, or at the end of a semester or marking period. Cognitive psychologists, however, believe that separating tests from lessons this way can have unfortunate results. First, learners do not receive feedback on the adequacy of their answers until sometimes long after their actual performance. In addition, learners may miss the connection between what happens in class and what happens on test day, reducing the motivation both to learn in class and to study for tests.

Classroom Instruction that Promotes Good Thinking

As we have seen, cognitive learning theory emphasizes three related aspects of learning:

(1) learning is a process of knowledge construction, not a matter of simply taking in what is heard or read;

(2) because learners construct new knowledge based on what they already know, learning depends on prior knowledge; and

(3) learning is an inherently social activity.

As you read about each one, ask yourself these questions:

1. Does this method allow learners to learn for themselves, or is knowledge already digested for them?
2. Does this method acknowledge that learners have preexisting ideas, information, and beliefs, or does it assume that their minds are blank slates?

3. Does this method allow learners to acquire and construct new knowledge through extended interactions with peers and adults, or is the learner viewed as a solitary investigator?

Discovery Learning

Bruner states that the mind organizes knowledge in a hierarchical fashion, with the more general, all-encompassing ideas at the top of the hierarchy, and the more concrete, factual ideas toward the bottom. Much of Bruner's cognitive theory is built around the idea of categorization or organization. He reasons that so much information comes in through the senses that the mind must find ways to simplify and make sense of it. *Categorization* is how the mind simplifies information that enters short-term memory. *Organization* involves arranging information in coding systems.

Bruner theorizes that the mind spontaneously organizes information in a hierarchical manner with the organization of knowledge in long-term memory. He believes that all subject matter has a similar structure: facts are supported by concepts, which, in turn, are supported by generalizations.

These generalizations, concepts, and facts tell us how instruction should be organized. Bruner stipulates that good teaching involves helping learners *discover for themselves* the generalizations under which lie related concepts and facts, rather than simply *telling them* to the learner. This *discovery learning* is facilitated when teachers organize the knowledge they present around fundamental themes and principles rather than discrete facts. This type of organization is similar to the way in which knowledge is organized in long-term memory.

Mrs. Greer has identified the important facts, concepts, and generalizations of her unit on fractions. But rather than teach children directly the rules and techniques for mathematically manipulating fractions in order to compare them (as did Mr. Robbins), she tries to help her learners *construct* the rules and generalizations for themselves. By doing so, Mrs. Greer (and Bruner) believe that students will have greater retention, understanding, and ability to use knowledge about (in this instance) fractions to solve future problems.

The essence of discovery learning is that the important facts, concepts, and generalizations of a subject area are not presented to learners in a final, organized form. Rather, they are taught in such a way that learners discover the relationships among facts, concepts, and generalizations and organize them in long-term memory on their own. According to Bruner, teaching by the discovery method makes it more likely that learners will remember new knowledge and be able to apply it to solve real-world problems.

Basic Features

Classroom instruction that is built around discovery learning has five important features: instructional set, motivational set, knowledge base, multiple examples, and hierarchically organized curriculum. Let's see what each contains.

Instructional set is the purpose or goal the teacher gives the learners at the start of the lesson. As we stated above, students can view learning as activities to be completed, or they can view it as an end in itself. In discovery learning, the teacher explains the purpose of the lesson in a way that is appropriate for the developmental level of the student. For example, you might tell kindergartners, "Today we are going to look for patterns using these blocks and buttons"; you would tell fourth-graders, "Work with these tiles to see how many different number patterns you can show. Then we'll write our results in numbers and letters"; to high school students, the message would be, "We are going to derive the equations for the graphs you drew yesterday." In this way learners approach the task with the goal of acquiring understanding rather than memorizing facts, filling out a worksheet, or taking a test.

Motivational set involves what the teacher does to stimulate, excite, or arouse learners to accomplish the goal of the lesson.

Knowledge base refers to the extent of a learner's declarative and procedural knowledge relevant to the content of the lesson. Thus, learners are more likely to see important relationships and discover important principles and generalizations if they have acquired the specific information necessary to do so.

Multiple examples means giving learners as many different instances or circumstances as possible in which the knowledge they are about to learn is included. For example, if the purpose of the lesson is to help learners discover how supply and demand affect price, you would provide a number of different examples: low interest rates cause people to refinance their mortgages, drought causes higher food prices, handmade sweaters are more expensive than mass-produced ones. Furthermore, discovery will be facilitated if you present the material through a variety of sensory modalities (audio, visual, tactile, and so forth).

A hierarchically organized curriculum stresses that the curriculum itself must be organized along the lines of a hierarchy of generalizations, concepts, and facts. Bruner feels that teachers must plan their lessons with an understanding of the hierarchical structure of the information they wish to convey. In that way, learners are exposed to specific facts from which they discover new concepts, from which they in turn derive generalizations.

As you read the following example of discovery learning, try to identify how it incorporates the five elements—instructional set, motivational set, knowledge base, multiple examples, and hierarchically organized curriculum.

An Example. Here is a principle of force and motion that Mr. Lyon will be teaching his junior high school science students:

The turning effect of a force depends, in part, on how far the force acts from the center of turning (which is called the axle or pivot).

Rather than simply explaining this principle to his learners and giving them examples, Mr. Lyon devised a lesson to help them discover it on their own.

Since he would be using terms and expressions like *force, turning effect,* and *center of turning,* Mr. Lyon first ensured that his learners were familiar with the required terms. Then he brought to the classroom devices that make use of the principles of force and motion and arranged them on a table. These included nuts and bolts of various sizes, a variety of manual can openers and cans, socket wrenches of various lengths and sizes, hand-operated drills of various lengths, and paper clips.

At the start of the class he divided his students into pairs and gave each pair one paper clip. He instructed each pair to straighten the paper clip, and then have one partner hold one end and make it turn in the other partner's fingers without bending it. He asked them to note if it turned easily when the partner really squeezed the wire.

Next, he told them to make a right-angle bend in the wire about two centimeters from either end. He instructed one partner to turn the bent part as a crank, while the other squeezed the wire to keep it from turning. He asked them to note who was more successful. If both tried to turn the wire in opposite directions, who succeeded?

Finally, before allowing the pairs to experiment with the various tools and devices arranged on the table, Mr. Lyon told them that he wanted the groups to explain to him at the end of the lesson what causes a force to have a greater turning effect.

Goals for Discovery Learning Lessons

Here are some important generalizations that could serve as goals for discovery learning lessons. Think about the knowledge required of learners to discover the generalization and try to plan a lesson to help them do so:

— Measurements are really comparisons with other known or accepted dimensions.

— The number of swings a pendulum makes in a given period of time depends mostly on its length.

— Major civilizations usually developed at the confluence of rivers and near natural harbors.

— Assuming no change in the quantity demanded by consumers, if producers increase the supply of a given good or service to the marketplace, then the price of that good or service can be expected to fall.

Cognitive Apprenticeship

Classrooms traditionally have been successful places for conveying large bodies of information. They have not been as successful in teaching learners how experts gather or use that information.

Cognitive apprenticeship is a model of teaching and learning that views the classroom learner as a novice who will be apprenticed to an expert. In a cognitive apprenticeship, the novice learns the cognitive strategies and metacognitive skills necessary to handle complex learning tasks. The teacher's role is not to fill the learner's mind with information, facts, and procedures, but rather to teach the "apprentices" how to explore, organize, question, and learn independently.

Cognitive apprenticeships are focused on teaching strategies and metacognition and are organized around specific learning areas such as reading, math, or writing. Thus, a novice learner learns strategies of expert thinking in a specific field: how a journalist writes, how a historian studies the past, how a mathematician solves problems. The facts and concepts that the student learns during a cognitive apprenticeship are those that are important in the expert's chosen field.

Basic Features

Cognitive apprenticeships can be organized in any field of study: science, social studies, literature, art. The most common models are in the areas of math, reading, and writing. All have common features: (1) they teach cognitive and metacognitive strategies, and (2) the skills learned are specific to an academic discipline (math, reading, writing, and so on). Collins, Brown, and Newman call these conditions *situated learning.* Other common elements of cognitive apprenticeships are the use of modeling, coaching, scaffolding, articulation, and reflection.

We have already discussed *modeling* in connection with the important work of cognitive social learning theorists. For novice learners in reading, math, or writing, modeling means they *see and hear* their teachers explain how they go about doing things. They hear their teacher thinking through a math problem. They hear and see their teacher as he reads a piece of writing and figures out how to revise it. They listen to their teacher as she explains how she determined the main ideas of a story. The challenge to the teacher is to make explicit these thinking skills, which are usually carried out automatically and covertly.

Consider how you would model for your learners the thinking strategies used to solve the following problem: "The price of bananas is four for 51 cents. What is the cost of one dozen bananas?" An expert math problem solver might think aloud to her learners like this: "Well, how do you solve a problem like this? What does the problem tell me? I know four bananas cost 51 cents. One way in which to find out how much a dozen cost is to find out the price of one banana. How can I find out how much one banana costs?"

The teacher then writes on the board while speaking to the class: "Let's see, 51 cents divided by 4 equals 12.75 cents for one banana. Now, if I multiply 12.75 cents by 12 bananas, I'll get the cost of all the bananas. So, the cost of a dozen bananas is $1.53. By finding out how much one banana costs, I can find out how much any number of bananas cost."

Coaching occurs during apprenticeships when a teacher observes his learners' attempts to imitate expert problem solving, writing, or reading while he offers feedback, hints, and guidance. As the teacher watches the learners, he may offer additional modeling, explanation, or suggestions.

Scaffolding is a technique for providing guidance to learners as they practice. The key to good scaffolding is to achieve the right balance between too much support and too little. Offering too much help to learners as they attempt to master a strategy can diminish their motivation to complete the task on their own, while providing too little assistance can quickly lead to frustration .

Scaffolding occurs when a teacher recognizes that a learner is in need of assistance and offers prompts, suggestions, and hints to help the learner solve the problem. As soon as the teacher sees that the "scaffold" is working, she gradually begins to remove the prompts and cues used to construct it. Expert scaffolding requires that the teacher be familiar with the demands of the task, and that she anticipate the difficulties the learners are likely to encounter.

Good scaffolded instruction involves getting learners to explain the reasoning they used or the steps they went through to solve a particular problem. This is your way of determining if the learner understands the process that you have modeled. This stage of cognitive apprenticeship is called *articulation.* It involves learners' explaining to the class what they are doing. For example, you might ask a learner to think out loud as he is solving a math problem. Or in reading, you might ask a learner to articulate why one sentence is a better topic sentence than another.

In the final stage of a cognitive apprenticeship, the teacher asks learners to compare their methods of solving a problem or their use of a particular strategy with that of an expert. This is called *reflection.* In the example of map instruction, the teacher could have given the learners a copy of the route she planned and asked them to compare it to the one they had chosen. The teacher would then ask each learner to describe the steps he or she used to plan the route, to compare them with the teacher's route.

Cognitive apprenticeship can be applied in your classroom with a strategy called *reciprocal teaching*. Reciprocal teaching provides alternative representations or elaborations of the content to be learned through the vehicle of group discussion. At the center of reciprocal teaching are group discussions in which students and teacher take turns leading discussions about the text. Gall observed that most discussion that takes place in classrooms amounts to little more than recitation of facts by students with the aid of question-and-answer sequences in which all or most of the answers are known. This leaves little opportunity for students to construct their own meaning and interpretation of content in order to reach higher levels of understanding. Most classroom discussions are further driven by content in the text, representing rapid-fire questions and answers that stay close to the facts as they are organized and presented in the textbook.

Reciprocal teaching attempts to make class discussion into a more productive and self-directed learning experience. It accomplishes this through four activities—*predicting, questioning, summarizing,* and *clarifying*—which unfold in the following sequence, as described by Palincsar and Brown (1989). In the *predicting* stage, the discussion begins by generating predictions about the content to be learned from the text based on (a) its title or subheading in the text, (b) the group's prior knowledge about the topic, and (c) the group's experience with similar kinds of information.

After the group members predict what they expect to learn from the text, the group reads and listens to a portion of it. Next comes the *questioning* stage, in which one learner leads a discussion of each portion of the text that was read. The discussion leader asks questions about the information in the text, and students respond and raise additional questions.

In the *summarizing* stage, the discussion leader summarizes the text, and other students are invited to comment or elaborate on the summary. In the final, *clarifying* stage, points are discussed until clarity is achieved. In this case, more predictions may be made and portions of the text may be reread for greater clarity.

The teacher's aim is to engage as many students as possible in the learning process. This is accomplished by elaborating on student responses and allowing ample opportunity for students to participate in the dialogue from their own perspectives. As the discussion continues, more responsibility for reading and developing the dialogue is gradually given over to the students until, over time, the teacher becomes more of an advisor—or coach—whose role is to refine, not provide, the appropriate responses. By the end of the discussion, the students' responses represent their own internalizations of the text.

The goal of reciprocal teaching is to sufficiently engage students in the learning process, by whatever means, so that they become conscious of their reasoning process and refine it through their own, other students', and the teacher's modeling of that process in the context of classroom dialogues. To attain this goal, teacher and learners together must continually monitor both the meanings students are deriving from the text and the ongoing dialogue. The teacher must also continually adjust the instructional content to meet the students' current levels of understanding. As students gradually accept the shift in responsibility from teacher to student, the teacher reduces the amount of explaining, explicitness of cues, and prompting that marked the earlier part of the lesson.

Cooperative Learning Activity

Cooperative Learning is a teaching activity that involves a heterogeneous group of students who are responsible for one another's learning of a common goal. In most classrooms, learning is not cooperative but, rather, individualistic or competitive. *Individualistic learning* occurs when the student works independently to achieve some learning goal. The success or failure of this effort depends on the learner's efforts and is unaffected by the achievement or lack of achievement of other class members. In *competitive learning* classrooms, student performance is judged against the typical or average performance of all class members. Grades are assigned as a reference to the performance of the class as a whole.

In cooperative learning, students are organized into small groups, each with an objective to accomplish. The lessons are structured so that the group objective can only be achieved if all group members perform their assigned tasks. A learner's final grade is a combination of the group score and an individual score.

Cooperative learning, like other constructivist approaches, is suitable when the teacher's goals involve the learning of problem-solving skills, cognitive strategies, meta-cognitive knowledge, or social interaction skills. It is not an efficient method for learning factual knowledge or simple procedural routines, such as subtraction or multiplication skills.

During cooperative learning, students are arranged into *heterogeneous groups* of four to five learners. Group members should be diverse in terms of gender, ethnicity, scholastic achievement, and interpersonal skills. The teacher thereby ensures that each group contains a range of achievement levels in the subject area, gender and ethnic proportions that reflect the composition of the class as a whole, and a mixture of socially assertive and nonassertive learners. Slavin and others have found that such arrangements not only promote high levels of scholastic achievement; they also have positive effects on intergroup relations and self-esteem .

Cooperative learning lessons should foster *positive interdependence.* In other words, activities are planned so that group members depend on one another for the accomplishment of the group's goal. If, for example, the objective of the lesson is to conduct a critical review of *Lord of the Flies,* then each group member is assigned a different responsibility. For example, one member may examine characters; another, plot. One member may be responsible for synthesizing the ideas discussed, while another writes them down. Each member must complete his or her task, or the group will not achieve its goal.

Positive interdependence can also be achieved when each learner receives a group participation grade in addition to an individual grade. For example, individuals can rate each other on a five-point scale that measures active group involvement. The average of all scores assigned by the team members would be each learner's score for individual effort. Another method is for you to rate the group's end product on a five-point scale. Scores from these scales can be recorded either independently of one another (e.g., individual effort=4, group product=5) or as a ratio (e.g., 4/5=.80). If the ratio method is chosen, each individual in the group is given the same group score, determined either by you or by averaging all group members' evaluations of each other. Ratios smaller than 1.0 indicate that the group product exceeded this individual's contribution. Ratios greater than 1.0 indicate that the individual's contribution exceeded the group product.

One reservation expressed about cooperative learning concerns whether individual learners will feel responsible for their own learning or, instead, let others do all the work. However, cooperative learning builds *individual accountability* through peer pressure and individual assessments. For the group to succeed, every member has to fulfill his or her assigned responsibilities. If one student slacks off, every group member's grade or evaluation suffers. In addition, teachers give learners individual tests or assignments to assess learning and rate the performance of each member in terms of how it contributes to overall group success. Thus, each student's final grade includes a group grade, an individual test grade, and a rating of how well he performed certain interpersonal skills important for positive group functioning.

The final feature of a cooperative learning lesson is the teaching and evaluating of *interpersonal skills.* Effective group functioning requires that learners be prepared to elicit and listen to one another's opinions, reflect on what has been said, give reasons for their statements, and allow everyone to contribute. Thus a central feature of cooperative learning is preparing learners to cooperate.

Direct Explanation Teaching

Direct Explanation Teaching is a label for a variety of teaching methods that make explicit to learners at the outset of a lesson the academic competencies, strategies, generalizations, or procedures to be taught . It encompasses such teaching models as *expository learning* and *reception learning*, and includes some elements of the *direct teaching model* .

Many have questioned whether direct explanation is "constructive enough" to be identified as a constructivist instructional practice. Pressley explains its constructivist roots this way:

Direct explanation is a decidedly constructivist approach: Students do not passively learn from explanations but rather actively learn from them. They do not completely understand what the teacher is saying or doing, but the teacher's explanation and modeling are a starting point for the student. As the student struggles with the process the teacher modeled, he or she adapts it to the particular tasks at hand and modifies it in ways that are sensible to him or her. If a classroom of children hears and watches a demonstration and then practices what was taught in the lesson, there will be much struggling, adaptation, and reflection on the part of the students, with the result that at the end of the instructional day, all will have somewhat different understandings of multiplication of fractions.

Basic Features

The most critical feature of direct explanation is the teacher's description, modeling, or demonstration of cognitive strategies. The teacher models the use of cognitive strategies in an authentic context and in an authentic manner. The students hear and see the teacher struggle with the task and arrive at new strategies to accomplish it. Students thus deepen their understanding and appreciation for the significance of the "cognitive struggle" in learning when they observe teachers coping with difficult tasks. The key ingredients of direct explanation teaching are up-front demonstration and explanation of the lesson goal, mental modeling of authentic problem solving, guided practice, and provision of metacognitive information. Let's learn more about each of these.

— *Up-front Demonstration and Explanation.* Up-front demonstration and explanation of the lesson goal requires that the teacher begin the class by telling learners what they should expect to get out of the lesson. Many models of good teaching emphasize the importance of capturing learners' attention at the start of a lesson and letting them know what they are going to accomplish. Hunter refers to this as *anticipatory set.* During this phase of direct explanation teaching, the teacher presents a task to learners that requires the use of a problem-solving strategy. The teacher informs the students that they will need the strategy to complete the assignment and then explains the strategy to them.

— *Mental Modeling of Authentic Problem Solving.* During mental modeling of authentic problem solving, the teacher thinks aloud to the learners and shows them how to apply a particular cognitive strategy. However, mental modeling involves more than just thinking aloud. It also involves saying things that indicate to learners that you are struggling or puzzling over the task. Statements like, "I'm stuck at this point.

— *Guided Practice.* During guided practice, the teacher uses prompts, questions, and hints to get learners to use the strategy that was modeled. Feedback, praise, and encouragement from the teacher accompany the learner's efforts. The level of assistance is determined using scaffolding techniques. As learners become more successful using the strategy, the teacher gradually fades the "scaffold" by providing fewer hints, questions, and prompts until the learner can use the strategy independently.

We also pointed out that learners do not always use strategies, despite their proven effectiveness. Therefore, during direct explanation instruction, teachers provide learners with metacognitive information about the strategy they are using. For example, one would model when and where to use them and how to notice or monitor whether they are helping. This involves (1) showing learners how to assess or monitor the effectiveness of a strategy, (2) prompting them to attribute their own improvement in performance to the strategy, and (3) prompting them to make a commitment to use the strategy in the future.

References

Brooks, J. G., & Brooks, M. G. (1993). *The case for constructivist classrooms.* Alexandria, VA: Association for Supervision and Curriculum Development.

Demetriou, A. & Valanides, N. (1998). A three level of theory of the developing mind: Basic principles and implications for instruction and assessment. In R.J. Sternberg & W.M. Williams (Eds.), *Intelligence, instruction, and assessment* (pp. 149–99). Hillsdale, NJ: Lawrence Erlbaum.

Kalyuga, S.; Chandler, P.; Tuovinen, J. & Sweller, J. (2001). When problem solving is superior to studying worked examples. *Journal of Educational Psychology*, 93, 579–88.

Resnick, L.B. (Ed.). (1989). *Knowing, learning, and instruction: Essays in Honor of Robert Glaser.* Hillsdale, NJ: Lawrence Erlbaum

Steffe, L. P., & Gale, J. (Eds.). (1995). *Constructivism in education.* Hillsdale, NJ: Lawrence Erlbaum.

8

Motivating Learners in the Classroom

Motivation as an internal drive that directs behavior towards some end. It is cause for an organism's behavior or the reason that an organism carries out some activity. Human behavior is complex and people are naturally curious. Therefore, instructional designers should meet the challenges of designing instruction assisted by motivation; because it is of paramount importance to student success. Students work longer, harder and with more vigor and intensity when they are motivated than they are not. In other words, motivation helps individuals overcome inertia.

This happens so because in the teaching-learning process, as in other various activities, there should be something that propels their mind or dangles in front to make them more active and vibrant, in classroom teaching, the major task is to nurture student curiosity as a motivation for learning. This is important because curiosity is motivation that is intrinsic to learning. The source of motivation is complex. It can be categorized into external and internal. The latter sustains behavior. Intrinsic and extrinsic motivations are two types of motivation that affect achievement of students. However, the value of external motivation, for instance, reinforcement, is questioned from those who suggest that once it is withdrawn the behavior stops. Critics go on to say that students must have intrinsic motivation to accomplish the required activities. In intrinsic motivation the "doing" is the main reason for finishing an activity whereas in extrinsic motivation the "value" is placed at the end of an action. Infants and young Children appear to be propelled by curiosity, driven by an intense need to explore, interact with, and make sense of their environment.

Learning often becomes associated with drudgery instead of delight. A large number of students-more than one in four-leave schools before graduating. Many more are physically present in the classroom but largely mentally absent; they fail to invest themselves fully in the experience of learning. Awareness of how students' attitudes and beliefs about learning develop and what facilitates learning for its own sake can assist educators in reducing student apathy towards learning. Therefore, the role and importance of motivation is worth looking at in this regard.

STUDENT MOTIVATION

Student motivation has to do with students' desire participate in the learning process. But it also concerns the reasons or goals that underlie their involvement in academic activities. Although students may be equally motivated to perform a task, the source of their motivation may differ. A student who is intrinsically motivated undertakes an activity "for its own sake, for the enjoyment it provides, the learning it permits, or the feelings of accomplishment it evokes". An extrinsically motivated student performs "in order to obtain some reward or avoid some punishment external to the activity itself" such as grades, stickers, or teacher approval. As stated above, the term motivation to learn has a slightly different meaning. It is defined by some author as "the meaningfulness, value, and benefits of academic tasks to the learner-regardless of whether or not they are intrinsically interesting".

Motivation to learn is characterized by long-term, quality involvement in learning and commitment to the process of learning. Factors that influence the development of students' motivation: According to educators, motivation to learn is a competence acquired "through general experience but stimulated most directly through modeling, communication of expectations, and direct instruction or socialization by parents and teachers. Children's home environment shapes the initial constellation of attitudes they develop toward learning. When parents nurture their children's natural curiosity about the world by welcoming their questions, encouraging exploration, and familiarizing them with resources that can enlarge their world, they are giving their children the message that learning is worthwhile and frequently fun and satisfying. When children are raised at home that nurtures a sense of self-worth, competence, autonomy, and self-efficiency, they will be more apt to accept the risks inherent in learning. Conversely, when children do not view themselves as basically competent and able, their freedom to enlarge in academically challenging pursuits and capacity to tolerate and cope with failure are greatly diminished.

Once children start school, they begin forming beliefs about their school-related successes and failures. The source to which children attribute their successes and failures have important implications on how they can approach and cope with learning situations. The beliefs teachers themselves have about teaching and learning and the nature of the expectations they hold for students also exert a powerful influence. As one notable educator remarked, "To a very large degree, students expect to learn if their teachers expect them to learn". School-wide goals, policies, and procedures also interact with classroom climate and practices affirm or alter students' increasingly complex learning-related attitudes and beliefs. Developmental changes comprise one more strand of the motivational web as well. For example, although young children tend to maintain high expectations for success even in the face of repeated failure, older students do not. Although younger children tend to see effort as uniformly positive, older children view it as a "double-edged sword". To them, failure following high effort appears to carry more negative implication-especially for their self-concept of ability-than failure that results from minimal or no effort.

Intrinsic Motivation

When intrinsically motivated, students tend to employ strategies that demand more effort and that enable them to process information more deeply. Students with an intrinsic orientation also tend to prefer tasks that are moderately challenging whereas extrinsically oriented students gravitate toward tasks that are low in degree of difficulty. Extrinsically oriented students are inclined to put forth the minimal amount of effort necessary to get the maximal reward. Although every educational activity cannot, and perhaps should not, be intrinsically motivating, findings suggest that when teachers can capitalize on existing intrinsic motivation, there are several potential benefits. How can motivation to learn be fostered in the school setting? Although students' motivational histories accompany them into each new classroom setting, it is essential for teachers to view themselves as "active socializing agents capable of stimulating student motivation to learn".

Classroom climate is important. If students experience the classroom as a caring, supportive place where there is a sense of belonging and everyone is valued and respected they will tend to appreciate more fully in the process of learning. Various task dimensions can also foster motivation to learn. Ideally, tasks should be challenging but achievable. Relevance also promotes motivation, as does "contextualizing" learning, i.e., helping students to see how skills can be applied in the real world. Tasks that involve "moderate amount of discrepancy or incongruity are beneficial because they stimulate students' curiosity", and this is an intrinsic motivator. Extrinsic rewards, on the other hand, should be used with caution, for they have the potential for decreasing existing intrinsic motivation. What takes place in the classroom is critical; but "the classroom is not an island".

Depending on their degree of congruence with classroom goals and practices, school wide goals either dilute or enhance classroom efforts. To support motivation to learn, school-level policies and practices should stress "learning, task mastery and effort" rather than relative performance and competition. What can be done to help unmotivated students? A first step is for educators to recognize that even when students use strategies that are ultimately self-defeating; their goal is actually to protect their sense of self-worth. A process called attribution retraining, which involves modeling, socialization, and practice exercise, is sometimes used with discouraged students.

The goals of attribution retraining are to help students to: Concentrate on the tasks rather than becoming distracted by fear of failure; respond to frustration by retracting their steps to find mistake or figuring out alternative ways of approaching a problem instead of giving up; and attribute their failures to insufficient effort, lack of information or reliance on effective strategies rather than to lack of ability. Other potentiality useful strategies include: portray effort as investment rather than risk; portray skill development as incremental and domain specific and focus on mastery. Because the potential payoff-having students who value learning for its own sake-is priceless, it is crucial for parents, teachers, and school leaders to devote rekindling students' motivation to learn.

Intrinsic motivation influences learners to choose a task, get energized about it, and persist until they accomplish it successfully, regardless of whether it brings an immediate reward. Intrinsic motivation is present when learners actively seek out and participate in activities without having to be rewarded by materials or activities outside the learning task. The first-grader who practices handwriting because she likes to see neat, legible letters like those displayed on the letter chart is intrinsically motivated. The fourth-grader who puts together puzzles of states and countries because she likes to see the finished product and wants to learn the names of the capital cities is intrinsically motivated. The ninth-grader who repeats typing drills because he likes the feel of his fingers hopping across the keys, and connects that sense with the sight of correctly spelled words on the page, has intrinsic motivation.

Motivated learners have more than just a vision of a goal they want to achieve. They have a passion or interest for achieving that goal. Motivated learners initiate actions, expend effort, and persist in that effort. As you become acquainted with the various theories, think about how they apply to your learners and keep this question in mind: How can this theory account for the energy and direction of a motivated learner?

Person-as-Machine Metaphor

How to win the hearts and minds of learners has been a concern of educational psychologists since the foundation of their science. In any given classroom, some learners will participate enthusiastically while others will not, but the explanation for this disparity is not always apparent. Over the years educational psychologists have used the term "motivation" to account for variations in the energy and direction of learners' behavior. But as we will see, motivation means very different things to different psychologists.

Since no one has ever seen, touched, or weighed motivation, educational psychologists typically use metaphors to help them describe this phenomenon. Likewise, various other metaphors have been the principal source of motivation theory and research.

The earliest theories of motivation assumed that the forces that give energy and direction to human behavior were beyond human control. These theories propose that either internal or external forces beyond our control cause people to display motivated or unmotivated behavior. Weiner proposes "person-as-machine" as a metaphor for describing these theories.

According to Weiner, the person-as-machine metaphor has the following attributes:

- Machines have parts (a structure).
- There is a desired end or function.
- The whole functions as a unit of mutually interacting parts to reach this end.

- The behaviors are involuntary, or without volition. Hence, the actions are like reflexes.
- The behaviors are performed without conscious awareness.
- The reactions are necessary or predetermined by a set of circumstances or activating stimuli.
- The actions are fixed and routine.
- Forces and energy are transmitted. The forces may be in balance or equilibrium (no tendency to change), or out of balance, promoting a tendency toward change.

By categorizing certain theories of motivation under the person-as-machine metaphor, Weiner alerts us to various distinctive characteristics pertaining to human motivation.

Instinct Theory

Instinct Theory was the earliest theory of motivation. Instincts are inherited, unlearned forces that help all species survive. Animals like salmon, bears, and turtles are preprogrammed at birth to engage in specific instinctive reproductive and feeding patterns. For example, salmon instinctively return to the same stream in which they were spawned to lay their eggs.

Humans are also born with instincts. The extent to which these instincts are under conscious control has been a subject of vigorous debate. Psychologists like William McDougall saw instincts as volitional and purposive:

> The human mind has certain innate or inherited tendencies which are the essential springs or motive powers of all thought and action, whether individual or collective, and are the bases from which the character and will of individuals and of nations are gradually developed....

McDougall states that instincts are inherited tendencies whose characteristics are energy, direction, and action.

According to Freud, instincts are neither conscious nor predetermined. They exist to satisfy biological needs and create a certain psychic energy or tension within the individual. This energy is bottled up, under pressure, like steam in a steam engine. It seeks release by driving us to pursue satisfactory (usually sexual) objects. Freud saw life as a struggle between the primal instincts of life (Eros) and death (Thanatos). Followers of Freud, as well as other psychologists, identified thousands of specific instincts by the 1920s.

Instinct theory came under heavy attack in the 1920s and 1930s, especially from cultural anthropologists. These scientists pointed out that what were assumed to be human instincts were really cultural—or learned—patterns of behavior. Instinct theory was soon replaced by drive theory as the principal explanation for the energy and direction of human action.

Drive Theory

Clark Hull is the psychologist principally identified with *drive theory*. *Drives,* according to Hull, are of two types: primary and acquired. *Primary drives* are forces within the individual that are triggered by biological needs such as hunger and thirst. Whatever behavior satisfies the need eventually becomes learned as a habit through the processes of drive reduction and reinforcement.

Acquired drives include desires for money, for love, to play sports, to write, or to create music. They do not spring from a biological need. Rather, they are acquired through a process of association with a primary drive. Drive theory assumes that almost all psychological motives are acquired drives.

Hull believed that all activity is directed toward reducing the tension triggered by needs and drives. Drive reduction, therefore, is the psychological mechanism underlying both activity and learning. Whatever behavior results in lessening the tension (and consequently the drive) will be repeated until it becomes habitual.

The drive theory of motivation provides the foundation for behavioral learning theory and, unlike instinct theory, still has its proponents. Extrinsic reinforcers (for example, money or good grades) are viewed as incentives that activate acquired drives. The behavior that is instrumental in getting each incentive is learned through a combination of both drive reduction and reinforcement processes.

Deficiency/Growth Needs Theory

Abraham Maslow's perspective on motivation, *deficiency/growth needs theory,* has both similarities to, and differences from, instinct and drive theory. Like the originators of those theories, Maslow proposes that people are born with innate needs that they strive to satisfy. However, in contrast to Freud and Hull, Maslow believes that the ultimate direction of this energy is not simply satisfaction of biological needs or tension reduction but a striving for self-actualization. Consequently, his theory accentuates the positive, intellectual, uplifting (not simply hedonistic) side of human beings. For Maslow, innate forces and an innate hierarchy of needs give human behavior its distinctive energy and direction.

Instinct, drive, and deficiency/growth motivation theories use the machine metaphor to describe motivated behavior. These theories agree that humans, for the most part, give energy and direction to their own behaviors without thinking about it. Instinctual, inherited needs present at birth give behavior its direction. The drive to satisfy these needs explains how behavior becomes energized. Individuals are largely unaware of these two aspects of behavior.

Person-as-Rational-Thinker

Early motivation theories, such as those just described, use biological and mechanical concepts including drives, energy, tension, and forces to explain the energy and direction of behavior. They present a picture of humans as passive and reactive, at the mercy of internal forces (needs and drives) or external forces (reinforcement and punishment) that they cannot control.

These mechanistic theories have been replaced in the last few decades by theories that use the person-as-rational-thinker metaphor. The two principal examples of these theories are *attribution theory*, developed by Heider, and Weiner, and *self-efficacy theory,* whose major proponents are Bandura and Schunk. Both of these theories posit that motivated behavior can be best explained by reference to conscious cognitive processes involving the ability to anticipate goals and rewards and to the use of judgment, evaluation, and decision making rather than unconscious biological or mechanical processes.

Attribution Theory

At this point in your life—if you're like everyone else—you've succeeded at some things and failed at others. Think about one of your more recent successes or triumphs. Were you successful because you really made an effort, had the ability, were lucky, or exercised some combination of the above? Another way to ask this question is this: Do you attribute your success to internal forces (effort, ability) or external forces (luck)?

Now think of one of your failures. Did you fail because you didn't work as hard as you should have, lacked the ability, simply ran into bad luck or difficulties you had no control over, or some combination of these? In other words, do you take personal responsibility for your failure or blame it on someone or something else?

Proponents of attribution theory, like Bernard Weiner, begin their analysis of motivation with the assumption that people inevitably seek to understand why they succeed or fail. In doing so they attribute their accomplishments or losses to a host of antecedents: good or bad luck, difficult or easy tasks, supportive or unfriendly people, their own hard work or lack thereof, or the degree to which they possess certain abilities.

Locus of Causality refers to the origin of the cause or causes to which people attribute success or failure. The origin can be either within or outside the person. Effort and ability are internal causes—they originate from within the person. The amount of energy a person expends to accomplish a goal is under that person's control. Innate ability also comes from within and is relatively immune to outside influence. People who attribute their success or failure to either of these two causes are said to be *internally oriented.*

Luck or degree of task difficulty are the typical external causes to which we attribute success or failure. If you believe you passed your last exam because it was easy (degree of difficulty) or because the professor just happened to choose questions you had studied (luck), you are using external causes to account for your success. Similarly, if a girl attributes her failure to make the baseball team to bad weather (luck) or the weight of the baseball bat (degree of difficulty), she is using external causes for her failure. Should this be a persistent feature of her thinking, we would label her locus of causality *externally oriented.*

Stability is another dimension of causal attributes. Some causal attributes can be changed, while others cannot. You can change the amount of effort you put into a task; you can get more help; you can study a different way. These are changeable attributes. However, if you attribute failure to your lack of innate ability you implicate a cause that is relatively unchangeable and stable.

The final dimension is *controllability.* Sometimes we attribute success or failure to antecedents that are out of our control. IQ is an example of an uncontrollable cause. So is luck. Effort, on the other hand, is something we have control over.

As you can see, attributes can be classified along all three dimensions. Luck, therefore, is an uncontrollable, unstable, external cause of success or failure, while effort is a controllable, stable, internal cause of success or failure.

Attributions and Motivated Behavior

You are probably asking yourself what these causes of success or failure have to do with motivation. Weiner believes that your causal attributions affect your future efforts to succeed at any given task. According to Weiner, your attributions produce both emotional reactions regarding your future performance and expectations for success or failure. These emotional reactions and expectations explain both the energy and direction that characterize your motivated behavior.

Attribution theory implies that the energy that drives motivated behavior comes from two sources: (1) an inherited, biologically based drive to achieve success and avoid failure; and (2) an emotional reaction to your cognitive appraisal of past achievements and defeats. These emotional reactions affect subsequent behavior. They either energize or restart efforts to achieve.

The direction of motivated behavior—the goals or accomplishments you pursue—derives from the following factors:

- past experiences with tasks
- the causal attribution of success or failure that you made during these tasks
- your expectations about what is likely to happen the next time you face a similar situation

For example, consider Evelyn, an eleventh-grader who is being encouraged by her teacher to take a course in calculus. Evelyn likes to try new things. She likes challenges. Her parents describe her as always having had a strong need to please and to achieve. She consistently earns high grades on both classroom and standardized math tests. Evelyn, however, is reluctant to take the course, and this puzzles both her parents and her teacher.

As it turns out, she took an advanced level algebra class in tenth grade and earned a C. She found the work difficult, and it required skills she had not learned in ninth-grade algebra. Furthermore, the teacher graded on a curve, and there were many eleventh- and twelfth-grade learners in the class.

The tests were multiple choice, and Evelyn dislikes multiple-choice tests, believing they give an advantage to the good guesser over the good thinker.

Evelyn attributed her low grades to two causes: task difficulty and luck. The work was hard and so were the tests. In addition, she was unfortunately matched against older and better-prepared learners. Moreover, Evelyn felt that the tests rewarded good guessing (luck), and she considered herself a poor guesser. She felt discouraged, frustrated, and angry.

In deciding whether to take calculus, Evelyn didn't see how things would be much different. She felt unprepared for such a tough course. Some of her friends from last year had failed it. She believed the grading system and tests would be the same this year.

Weiner believes that Evelyn's feelings of anger and discouragement and her low expectations for success are the direct result of her causal attributions, not of the situation itself. Evelyn attributed her C grade to causes that were uncontrollable, unstable, and external (luck, task difficulty). Given these attributions for failure, it is no wonder that she was reluctant and unmotivated to try calculus.

Two issues arise from Evelyn's predicament. First, what leads learners like Evelyn to decide whether effort or ability, luck or task difficulty, and circumstances outside or within their control are the causes of success or failure? What are they looking at, perceiving, or sensing that influences their choice of attributions? Second, since causal inferences affect learner motivation, what can you do to influence them? As we will see, answering the first question provides clues to the second.

Antecedents of Causal Attributions

People are naturally curious about *antecedents* behind their success or failure. School learners are especially interested in this question and typically assign blame or credit to task difficulty ("That teacher is easy" or "He never passes anyone"), effort ("I was too tired to study"), luck ("I guess I studied the right things"), or mood ("I had a fight with my girlfriend and couldn't concentrate").

How do learners decide what causes them to pass or fail tests, get A's, C's, or F's on assignments, or receive good or poor course grades? On what basis do they assign success or failure to internal or external causes, stable or unstable characteristics, and controllable or uncontrollable factors? Weiner maintains that learners' attributions spring from three general sources of information: (1) *situational cues,* (2) prior beliefs, or *causal schemata,* and (3) *self-perceptions.*

Situational Cues

In any learning task, a variety of environmental factors, or *situational cues*, help learners decide why they did well or poorly. One such cue is past experience with that task. If a learner has consistently done well on spelling assignments or word problems in math, she is more likely to attribute her success to ability (which is internal, stable, and uncontrollable) than to luck. A prior record of consistent failure will produce the same attribution. By the same token, a learner with a history of getting A's, C's, and F's on compositions will probably decide that luck or effort, more than ability or task difficulty, is behind his accomplishments.

Learners also note their own performance success and that of their peers when deciding why they succeeded or failed. A sixth-grader who usually gets good grades on geography tests will say that strong ability is behind her high grade on the last quiz. Conversely, if this same learner got a low grade on that quiz, as did most of her peers, she would likely attribute this to the difficulty of the test (external, stable, uncontrollable).

A third cue that learners use to explain their accomplishments is time-on-task. A ninth-grader who spent the weekend preparing for an English test and worked diligently throughout the exam period will probably conclude that his A was due to effort . If this same learner got an A without studying, he might say that the test was easy.

Finally, learners note how much help they received during the task when assigning attributions for the achievement. A learner who cheated on a test and received an A would not credit ability as the causal factor, nor would the learner who received a blue ribbon for a science project that was largely the work of an older brother.

Causal Schemata

We often hear the following expressions and may in fact believe them:

— Success is 10 percent inspiration and 90 percent perspiration.

— Nothing comes easy.

— A fool blames failure on others, a wise man on himself.

We all have certain *causal schemata,* or enduring beliefs about success and failure. We acquire them in a variety of ways—through experience, reading, listening to parents and teachers, or absorbing the wise sayings of renowned thinkers. Some learners believe that effort, not ability, is the key to success; others believe just the opposite.

Weiner asserts that attributions for success and failure depend not only on situational factors but also on the enduring beliefs learners have about what underlies achievement. Consider the student who never studies (or who we believe never studies) and gets A's on all his tests. We inevitably attribute this to natural ability, native intelligence, or IQ. It couldn't have been due to effort, we assume, because the person doesn't appear to have exerted any. By the same token, we perceive that the learner whose exceptional efforts consistently produce unexceptional results lacks ability. The learner herself may believe this.

Self-perceptions

In addition to situational factors and cognitive beliefs, learners also incorporate *self-perceptions* into their decisions about causal attributions. Learners high in self-esteem typically say that effort or ability, rather than luck or task difficulty, is the root of their success. Students high in achievement motivation usually identify effort as the key to success, while those low in this quality blame failure on luck or task difficulty.

We have identified three antecedents of the causal attributions of your learners: situation, causal schemata, and self-perception factors. Since Weiner's research demonstrates that causal attributions affect achievement behavior, and because these attributions stem from the three antecedents just given, the issue of what you can do to influence your learners' causal attributions naturally arises. Let's turn, therefore, to what attribution theory has to say about your role in motivating learners.

Teacher Influence on Attributions

Attribution theory and research tell us that the causal attributions your learners make about their accomplishments have important consequences.

- They affect future learners' expectations for accomplishing learning goals.
- They engender emotional reactions such as anger (when failure is attributed to luck), guilt or shame (when failure is attributed to effort), or discouragement (when failure is attributed to lack of ability).

- They contribute to self-esteem. Learners feel good when hard work produces success or when they believe they have a natural ability for some task.
- They affect the classroom behavior of learners.

  Consequently, you will want to do everything in your power to ensure that learners attribute their classroom accomplishments and setbacks in ways that elicit effort rather than discouragement. You can accomplish this in five ways.
- Recognize that your behavior conveys attributional information to your learners and carefully monitor the attributional messages you send.
- Focus on learning strategies.
- Refrain from grouping that promotes ability as the only source of success.
- Set up instructional arrangements that promote cooperation.
- Teach realistic goal setting.

Let's examine each of these responsibilities.

Monitor Your Attributional Messages

Although ability is an internal attribute of success, it is also an uncontrollable and stable one. Immediate effort, on the other hand, is not only internal but also unstable and controllable. In other words, effort is a cause of success that a learner can do something about. Clearly, then, it is in both the teacher's and the learner's best interests to stress the role of effort over ability in achievement. Nevertheless, many teachers inadvertently communicate the opposite, particularly to low achievers. Here are some examples:

Mr. Barker teaches seventh-grade reading. He wants his low achievers to experience success. However, their reading level is several years below that required by their reading text. He has brought fourth- and fifth-grade materials into class and given them to his slower learners. He then lavishly praises these students for correctly reading the words and answering the easy comprehension questions that follow.

Mrs. Johnson likes to challenge her learners by throwing out thought-provoking questions as she lectures and explains. She is hesitant to ask such questions of her low achievers out of concern over embarrassing them in front of the group. As a result, she has inadvertently fallen into the noticeable (to all her learners) habit of asking only yes/no questions to this group or giving them the answers when they hesitate, rather than probing, and rephrasing questions, as she does for the higher achievers.

Mr. Nkruma doesn't want his learners to doubt their ability at math, particularly those who are struggling. He wants them to believe that if they only make an effort, they can succeed. But in his concern to protect his learners from the consequences of failure, he makes excuses for them when they do poorly on tests or answer questions incorrectly in class. For example, he'll say things like "I'm sorry that you didn't do as well as you hoped," "I guess you studied the wrong material," "This was an unusually hard test," or "I probably didn't allow enough time for this test" to his learners when going over their work.

According to Good and Brophy, teachers who, however well intentioned, express sympathy at their learners' failure, show surprise at their success, give excessive unsolicited help, or lavishly praise success on easy tasks are telling students that they lack ability. As McQueen points out in her discussions with low achievers, these students are painfully aware what the teacher's behavior is suggesting.

Ginott advocates that teachers practice *congruent communication* when giving feedback to learners about their achievements. An important aspect of this type of communication is the use of encouragement instead of praise. According to Ginott, encouragement has the following attributes:

- Encouraging statements are directed at a student's actions—not at his or her character or person: "Your answers show thought," not "You are a good thinker."
- Encouraging statements reflect an accurate or honest evaluation of learner performance: "Your answers to these questions are too brief and need to show more thought. The other answers are thorough, thoughtful, and show understanding of the material," not "Some of your answers are fantastic. All of them show real effort," or "I feel bad that you got such a low grade."
- Encouraging statements help learners believe in themselves and their own ability: "Your handwriting is much improved. I appreciate the effort you're putting into it," not "Here's a happy face for that neat work."

- Encouraging statements attribute learner achievement to internal rather than external factors: "You have good ideas; you should want people to understand them. That's why it's important to write clearly," not "Write grammatically correct sentences or else I'll take off a point for each mistake."

Although as a general rule you should behave as if you value effort more than ability, Spaulding advocates that teachers exercise some caution. Her reasoning is that learners who believe that their success depends almost entirely on effort may begin to doubt their ability. For example, a student may believe that learners who are competent or who have ability don't have to try very hard to succeed. But since she has to spend several hours every night practicing French in order to get good grades, she concludes that she has little ability. This reasoning may influence her to drop the study of a foreign language from her plans even though she has a genuine interest in this area.

Hermine Marshall believes that teachers who believe that lack of success should be attributed to lack of effort may cause learners to feel frustrated and hopeless. She raises the issue of what to say to the child who is trying as hard as he can but not succeeding. Do you continue to imply that he's not working hard enough?

Spaulding recommends that teachers help learners understand the connection between effort and ability rather than lead them to believe that learning depends almost exclusively on either one. According to Spaulding, learners must realize that abilities are fluid. While abilities may give certain learners initial advantages, effort helps them develop. Marshall urges teachers to focus learners on the cognitive processes or strategies they use to accomplish a task, rather than putting undue emphasis on effort.

Similarly, when giving feedback to learners who are performing poorly, ask your learners how they came up with their answers. Marshall believes that focusing on strategies is an "attitude that teachers need to develop." She states that doing so accomplishes two things: (1) it reveals the thought processes of learners; and (2) it conveys to them that the process, as well as the product, is important. This puts the focus on learning and not just on coming up with the correct answer.

Refrain From Grouping That Exclusively Promotes Ability

Learners are acutely aware of, and often puzzled by, both school-wide and classroom ability grouping arrangements. Such arrangements can suggest that teachers value ability exclusive of effort. This perception on the part of learners inevitably affects their expectations of themselves, which may lead them to see no value in hard work. Attribution theory highlights a disadvantage of some types of ability grouping that may influence learners to assign greater importance for learning to ability (something they have less control over) in relation to effort or the use of learning strategies.

For now, we wish to point out that in terms of causal attributions for success or failure, cooperative learning arrangements emphasize the importance of learning processes and effort at least as much as ability. In competitive learning arrangements, on the other hand, students work alone to achieve grades and rewards, and thus tend to emphasize ability over effort and learning processes. Research suggests that competitive arrangements diminish intrinsic motivation.

Teach Realistic Goal Setting

Attribution theory tells us that learners should believe that their efforts to learn and master new tasks will not be in vain. The likelihood of this depends to a large extent on whether their goals are realistic. Failure to meet goals that are unrealistic may cause learners to doubt their abilities and to approach the learning task with a lessened commitment to learning.

Teaching learners how to set realistic goals, therefore, is an important aspect of any instructional program that aims to build intrinsic motivation. Goal setting and the beliefs of learners in their ability to achieve goals are principal elements of the next motivation theory we will discuss, the self-efficacy theory.

Attribution theory holds that the key to understanding learners' motivations for achievement can be found by analyzing their assumptions about what causes their success or failure. Additionally, this theory tells us that the most direct way to enhance learners' intrinsic motivation is to teach in ways that convince learners that success is largely due to factors under their control.Teachers influence causal attributions that energize and give direction to learner behavior by:

- carefully monitoring their attributional messages
- focusing on learning strategies
- refraining from ability grouping

- promoting cooperation among learners
- helping learners set realistic goals.

Self-efficacy Theory

The best-laid plans never work out. At least mine didn't. Not that first semester anyway. Most of the kids in my seventh grade showed no interest in my lessons. Now I know why. They were too difficult, and the kids knew it. Everyone knew it but me. Now I plan my lessons with one thing in mind. When I tell the class what we will be doing, I want everyone to say "I'm good enough at this to do what the teacher wants."

Self-efficacy theory holds that intrinsic motivation for academic tasks depends on learners giving a resounding "Yes!" to the question "Am I good enough to do what the teacher wants?" Bandura, one of the principal founders of self-efficacy theory, defines *self-efficacy* as "people's judgments of their capabilities to organize and execute courses of actions required to attain designated types of performance" . Bandura believes that learners initiate, work hard during, and persist longer at tasks they judge they are good at. This judgment is what Bandura refers to when he uses the term *self-efficacy.*

Self-efficacy is not a personality trait or disposition. There is no such thing as a self-efficacious person. It is not a biological drive or a psychological need. Instead, it is an appraisal or evaluation that a person makes about his or her personal competence to succeed at a particular task. Self-efficacy, therefore, is situation-specific. A person may have high self-efficacy for writing poetry but low self-efficacy for writing short stories. Another individual may judge herself to be competent at soccer but not at swimming. Nevertheless, the judgment, once made, goes a long way toward explaining the level of persistence and effort expended on a learning task as well as the level of achievement obtained.

You may be wondering how self-efficacy differs from attributions. Both appear to involve the cognitive process of judgment, and both affect internal motivation. Attributions, as you will recall, are perceived causes of success or failure. They influence expectations of success and subsequent behavior. Attributions are one type of information (we will soon identify others) that learners use to make their judgments about self-efficacy. An individual who succeeds at a hard task only after exerting high effort will judge himself less capable at that task than at a task of equal difficulty at which he succeeds with relatively little effort.

Antecedents of Self-efficacy Judgments

In addition to attributions, what other sources of information do learners use when appraising their self-efficacy for a given achievement? Dale Schunk, a leading researcher on self-efficacy, identifies four such sources: past experience, encouragement, physiological cues, and modeling effects.

Past Experiences of Success or Failure

Suppose you are conducting a lesson on fractions. Those learners who have earned high grades on the three previous math tests will have higher self-efficacy than those who failed them. Similarly, learners who have consistently earned high marks on the last several writing assignments will have greater self-efficacy and consequently greater effort and persistence for the current writing project than will those who earned low grades.

Encouragement or Persuasion from the Teacher

Learners who believe that they are not capable of a task, such as debating, can often be persuaded that they are by a convincing and inspirational teacher. However, while persuasion can enhance self-efficacy, its effects will be fleeting if the learner's efforts produce failure.

Physiological Cues

Learners who recognize symptoms of anxiety during a spelling bee (such as rapid breathing, increased heart rate, and sweating) may interpret them as signs that they lack ability. This may lead them to lower their self-efficacy.

Modeling Effects

Learners who hear peers make positive self-efficacy statements during a learning task, and who observe successful performances, will increase their self-efficacy judgments accordingly. The opposite is also true. Observing failure by peers or hearing about how hard a task is causes learners to lower their estimates of self-efficacy.

Self-efficacy in the Classroom

Appraisals of self-efficacy are dynamic, ongoing, changeable judgments of competence, which learners base on a variety of personal and situational information. No one source of information determines self-efficacy. Nor are appraisals of self-efficacy, once made, necessarily firm. Rather, the learner continually weighs and combines information from a variety of sources and situations. This information includes task difficulty, number and patterns of prior successes and failures, amount of help given, current and past feelings of anxiety, credibility of the person making encouraging statements, and perceived similarity to peer models.

But a learner's favorable appraisal of ability to achieve during a lesson does not necessarily predict successful or even persistent performance. As Schunk cautions, high self-efficacy for dissecting a frog in the absence of skill, for example, will not earn a high grade in biology class. Similarly, learners who do not value the goal that a teacher identifies for a geography lesson are unlikely to participate in it with great effort and enthusiasm regardless of their self-efficacy for map-making. Nevertheless, given sufficient skill to perform an academic task, and given that learners value the goal of that task, their judgments of self-efficacy will be the principal determinants of the direction of their behavior and energy for it.

Now, let's apply these ideas about self-efficacy to analyzing the behavior of Evelyn, the reluctant math student. Evelyn, as we know, had a bad prior experience with an advanced math class. In addition, she attributes her failure to factors out of her control: luck and task difficulty. Consequently, her initial appraisal of self-efficacy for calculus is low. Still, she knows she has an aptitude for math based on her test scores. Moreover, she rises to challenges. In other words, she has the skill and a positive attitude. Consequently, if we could only change her self-efficacy, she might take calculus and do well.

A conversation with a counselor might help Evelyn reappraise her self-efficacy for calculus. The counselor might point out that Evelyn has good preparation and adequate skill to do well (persuasion). In addition, the counselor could encourage Evelyn to talk to her friends who took calculus last year and did well (modeling). Finally, the counselor could help Evelyn reexamine her goals for the course, which may be unclear or unrealistically high (outcome expectations).

Assuming that Evelyn takes her counselor's advice and enrolls in the course, her self-efficacy would now hinge on such factors as anxiety, continued encouragement from teachers and parents, and her actual performance, as well as the similarity she perceives between herself and her peers and her observations of their performance.

Enhancing Self-efficacy

School programs designed to influence learners' self-efficacy and change achievement-related behavior have focused primarily on three activities: goal setting, information processing, and modeling. Let's examine each and see what you can do to improve your learners' judgments of self-efficacy.

Goal Setting

Researchers of self-efficacy, such as Schunk, Bandura, and Elliot and Dweck, have found an important link between lesson goals and self-efficacy. They have discovered that when teachers give learners a goal or help them identify their own goals for an activity, there is an initial boost in self-efficacy for that activity.

This initial appraisal is soon followed by a commitment to attempt the task. As learners work toward a goal and receive feedback on their progress, their self-efficacy is validated and enhanced. As self-efficacy heightens, so do effort, persistence, and skill development.

Information Processing

"I'm just not good at word problems." "I have trouble figuring out main ideas." "Reading comprehension is my real weak point." "I just can't remember a lot of what I read." You have probably heard learners make these comments. You may have even said something similar yourself at some point. They all indicate low self-efficacy for higher-level cognitive tasks.

Schunk postulated that learners who believe that they will encounter difficulty in complex learning tasks have lower self-efficacy than learners who feel confident about handling the information processing demands of these tasks. He reasons that learners who begin reading comprehension or math problem-solving activities already doubting their ability to succeed will cease efforts to master these tasks when they encounter difficulties. If, however, they sense that they understand what they are reading or are successfully solving a problem, their self-efficacy will increase, as will their motivation to persist and learn the material.

One way to help learners improve their ability to process information during reading or math activities is to teach learning strategies. As you will recall, learning strategies are systematic plans that learners use to help with the information processing demands of complex learning tasks. Such strategies, when used consciously, allow learners to sense that they are learning. The perception that they are learning enhances their self-efficacy, motivation to learn, mastery of the learning task, and willingness to use the strategies again.

Some suggestions for enhancing students' use of learning strategies are given here:

- Teach learning strategies to enhance motivation for complex learning tasks.
- Have learners observe a peer using a learning strategy, and listen to that person comment on how it helps him or her.
- Videotape your learners using a cognitive strategy and show the tape to them. This approach has been shown to enhance self-efficacy and skill learning.
- Have learners verbalize the strategy out loud as they are using it. Then gradually fade this technique so that the learner's comments become less and less audible and eventually are uttered covertly. Learners who talk about strategies as they are using them increase their attention to tasks, perceptions of learning, and self-efficacy.

Modeling

Nothing succeeds like success! A corollary to this proverb might be: Nothing reinforces success like seeing someone else succeed! And this is the major point of self-efficacy research on the impact of peer models. Such research has clearly shown that when learners see someone else succeeding, they believe more in their own capabilities. In these studies the following peer modeling activities increased the self-efficacy of observers for learning tasks such as subtraction, division, word puzzles, and complex problem solving:

- hearing a peer express confidence at being able to solve a learning task
- observing a peer showing high persistence and high confidence
- hearing a peer explain how she solved a problem
- hearing a peer make helpful statements like "I need to pay more attention to what I am doing"
- seeing and hearing several peer models instead of just one

- having learners observe videotapes of themselves (called *self-modeling*) using strategies and making positive self-efficacy statements.

Teachers interested in enhancing the self-efficacy of learners should therefore make use of the abundant modeling opportunities in their classrooms.

Self-efficacy theory holds that the key to a learner's motivation for achievement lies with the learner's own beliefs in his ability to organize and execute the actions required for a successful performance. These beliefs derive from

- past experiences of success or failure
- encouragement or persuasion from others
- physiological cues, such as rapid breathing and increased heart rate, that tell the learner something about his or her capabilities to complete the task
- modeling by peers, which may make the task appear easy or difficult.

Teachers can influence the self-efficacy of learners through the teaching of realistic goal setting and learning strategies and by having peers model successful performances.

Self-determination Theory

The cognitive motivational theories of attribution and self-efficacy have been criticized for focusing more on the direction than on the energy dimension of motivated behavior. Let's explore this important distinction.

Pintrich believes that both attribution and self-efficacy theory make motivation appear too cognitive, too abstract, too devoid of energy and passion. Similarly, Deci and his colleagues argue that most current approaches to intrinsic motivation fail to deal with the question of why learners desire certain goals or outcomes.

For example, Deci believes that attribution and self-efficacy theory emphasize too strongly the role of beliefs when accounting for intrinsic motivation. He questions how these theories account for the needs of learners to feel competent and independent. He claims that such theories make the motivational process appear too rational, too cold, too isolated from the day-today emotions and feelings that characterize the classroom behavior of children.

Deci offers an alternative, *self-determination theory.* He contends that this theory reintroduces a component of motivation that has long been neglected by most modern cognitive motivational theories: human needs. Moreover, it does so while still assigning a critical role to the learners' thought processes. Let's examine the self-determination perspective and see how it can be applied.

Human Needs

In our presentation of attribution theory, we pointed out that a learner's intrinsic motivation for a particular task depended on her beliefs about what was responsible for past successes or failures. We outlined teaching practices that lead learners to believe that success results from factors under their control.

Self-efficacy theory tells us that learners' intrinsic motivation for a task rests with their beliefs about whether they are good at it and can achieve its goals. We learned about instructional practices that promote positive self-efficacy beliefs.

Self-determination theory is more complex. It tells us that underlying intrinsic motivation is an attitude of self-determination to accomplish a goal. This attitude is more than just a belief in one's self-efficacy, although that is a component of self-determination. Likewise, self-determination involves more than beliefs about the causes of success or failure. Rather, self-determination theory focuses on three innate human needs: competence, relationships, and autonomy.

Competence needs involve the learner's knowledge of how to achieve certain goals and the skill for doing so. Deci believes that learners have an innate psychological need to believe that they are competent. *Relationship needs* are innate requirements for secure and satisfying connections with peers, teachers, and parents. Finally, *autonomy needs* refer to the ability to initiate and regulate one's own actions.

Deci believes that classrooms promote intrinsic motivation by helping learners acquire an attitude of self-determination. In other words, they meet learners' needs for competence, relationships, and autonomy. Furthermore, self-determination theory underscores that all three needs must be satisfied if the learner is to develop an attitude of self-determination. Learners who believe in their own competence will not feel self-determined if the classroom does not allow them to accomplish tasks with some degree of independence. Thus, classrooms characterized by teacher-directed instructional techniques are less likely to satisfy learners' needs for autonomy than are classrooms that incorporate constructivist instructional approaches, including cooperative learning. Similarly, classrooms that rely heavily on extrinsic rewards and punishments to control behavior will not meet learners' autonomy needs.

Deci also contends that meeting a learner's needs for competence and autonomy while at the same time ignoring needs for relationships will fail to enhance self-determination and intrinsic motivation. How can this be? Doesn't a need for relationships imply a certain degree of dependence on the part of learners? And doesn't this detract from feelings and beliefs about autonomy?

Deci resolves this seeming contradiction between needs for autonomy and needs for relationships by explaining that autonomy means that learners initiate and regulate their own learning behaviors. Self-initiation and self-regulation can develop only in a classroom where such behavior is supported and encouraged by peers and adults. Thus, self-determination theory tells us that learners will develop intrinsic motivation and the self-determination underlying such motivation only in a social milieu that supports competence and autonomy.

Enhancing Self-determination

Self-determination theory is a new and ambitious attempt to reconcile the early need and drive theories of motivation with more modern cognitive motivational perspectives that focus on a learner's attribu-tions and beliefs. While research into the antecedents of self-determination has just begun, we can still provide some recommendations for promoting it.

Self-determination theory tells us that learners have innate needs to feel competent, relate to other people, and be autonomous. They come to school, in other words, with built-in energy and a desire to achieve, and they possess the basic ingredients for developing the internal motivation to do so. The questions teachers should ask themselves as they scan the eager faces of their learners on the first day of school are these: "What can I do to meet their needs for competence, relationships, and autonomy? What is the best way to focus and give direction to this energy?" Self-determination theory holds that the answer to these questions lies in designing a classroom that

- places a premium on skill development

- allows learners to feel that they control this development
- encourages relationships that support the development of competence and autonomy.

With these three principles as guides, let's explore an approach to teaching and learning called project-based learning.

Project-based Learning

Teachers who practice *project-based learning,* or build their instructional programs around projects, provide learners with an environment ideally suited to the nurturing of intrinsic motivation . Whether your perspective on motivation leans toward attribution theory, self-efficacy theory, self-determination theory, or all three, project-based learning offers some solutions to the age-old problem of how to give energy and direction to the classroom behavior of learners.

Before we describe project-based learning, let's briefly review attribution theory, self-efficacy theory, and self-determination theory.

- *Attribution theory* emphasizes teaching methods that assure learners that their success depends on factors they control. Teachers do this by (1) stressing the importance of the learning process, not just the product; (2) helping learners set goals; and (3) using instructional groupings to promote cooperation.
- *Self-efficacy theory* emphasizes instructional programs that help learners set their own goals, acquire learning strategies, and observe successful peer models to enhance self-efficacy beliefs and intrinsic motivation.
- *Self-determination theory* emphasizes the important role of teachers in fostering intrinsic motivation by arranging their classrooms, designing lessons, and speaking to learners in ways that meet their needs for competence, relationships, and autonomy. The specific recommendations for doing this are nearly identical to recommendations for promoting effort-enhancing attributions and positive self-efficacy.

Project-based learning (PBL) makes extensive use of the ideas and research of Weiner's attribution theory, Bandura's and Schunk's self-efficacy theory, and Deci's self-determination theory in designing its comprehensive approach to classroom teaching and learning. It uses these motivational approaches to help delineate the roles of its three principal components: *tasks, learners,* and *teachers.*

In PBL, intrinsic motivation is not viewed as a feature of learning tasks, a disposition of learners, or the sole responsibility of teachers. Rather, intrinsic motivation is marshaled, generated, and sustained in a learning environment where it is recognized that each of these elements has a necessary role to play, though each alone is not sufficient. When each of these components carries out its assigned role, intrinsic motivation results. Let's examine these components of PBL and see how each incorporates elements of the cognitive motivational theories we have studied.

Role of Tasks

PBL assigns a critical role in the development of intrinsic motivation to the nature of the classroom learning task. It asks the question, "What kinds of tasks are most likely to induce and support learner interest, effort, and persistence?" PBL advocates the use of projects as the most appropriate vehicles for engaging learners. *Projects* have two essential components:

(1) they are built around a central question or problem that serves to organize and energize classroom activities, and

(2) they require learners to produce a product or outcome to successfully answer the question or resolve the problem.

Projects challenge learners with important (often real-world) problems and usually require them to draw on several diverse skill areas to solve them. A third-grade project, for example, built around the problem of nonrecyclable garbage, can involve the skills of reading, research, data gathering, data analysis, hypothesis-generating, and problem solving. Projects may be built around issues of current societal concern or questions of historical or purely intellectual interest. Good projects have the following critical characteristics.

- They are of extended duration (require several weeks to complete).
- They link several disciplines (math, reading, and writing skills, for example).
- They allow for a variety of solutions (the focus should be as much on process as on product).
- They involve the teacher as coach, and require small group collaboration to complete.

Blumenfeld and other proponents of PBL caution teachers that projects, by themselves, will not engage learners or motivate them to invest the effort necessary to investigate, acquire information, test solutions, and evaluate results. Rather, they must be used in a classroom milieu that supports thoughtfulness and sustained motivation.

There are, however, certain characteristics that projects must include if they are to capture the interest of learners and enhance intrinsic motivation. They must (1) present an authentic, real-world challenge, (2) allow for learner choice and control, (3) be doable—capable of being carried out within the time and resource limitations of the student and classroom, (4) require collaboration, and (5) produce a concrete result. Let's look more closely at each of these characteristics.

Present a Challenge

Both attribution and self-efficacy theory stress the importance of goals that learners want to achieve. PBL meets this important ingredient of intrinsic motivation when it offers learners an authentic, sometimes novel, and always challenging problem or question to investigate, resolve, and report on.

Allow for Learner Choice and Control

We learned about the importance of meeting learner needs for autonomy when we reviewed self-determination theory. Effective projects allow learners options regarding modes of investigation (reading, interviewing, observing, controlled experimentation), styles of reporting (written reports, audiotapes or videotapes, visual displays), solutions to problems, or types of products or artifacts to develop.

Be Doable

Learners will persevere and expend high amounts of effort if they see results (attribution theory). Similarly, they are more likely to believe that they can see a project through to a successful conclusion (self-efficacy) if it is time limited, requires readily available resources, and includes points along the way where they can receive positive feedback, make revisions, and generate further products.

Require Collaboration

Self-determination theory tells us that intrinsic motivation is nurtured in classrooms that allow learners to meet their social needs. Self-efficacy theory points out that learners acquire beliefs about their own capabilities from observing others. Projects that cannot be completed unless a small group of learners adopt different but essential roles are ideal vehicles for incorporating the principles of these motivational .e activities).

Result in a Concrete Product

Projects that give learners concrete goals to work toward are more likely to sustain intrinsic motivation. Moreover, products and the process involved in producing them allow for performance-based assessment. This type of assessment allows learners to see the connection between what they do in class and what their grades are based on. This gives learners a greater sense of control over their grades, and it better meets their needs for autonomy (as identified in self-determination theory) than grades based on paper-and-pencil tests alone.

The Role of the Learner

The key to developing intrinsic motivation is not simply a matter of finding the right activity or project. Educators since the time of John Dewey have urged schools to engage learners in "hands-on" learning activities as the best way to develop intrinsic motivation. Nevertheless, many educational reforms may have failed because they only described the activities to be completed—they did not consider the role of the learners' motivational beliefs and the teacher's encouragement of those beliefs to the overall activity. PBL recognizes that efforts to reform learners' tasks in school will fail unless instruction seeks to influence what learners think about the tasks and themselves. Consequently, PBL recognizes that learners will acquire important knowledge and skills from projects only if they

(1) attribute their success to effort,

(2) believe that they can accomplish the goals of the project, and

(3) perceive themselves as competent.

PBL also recognizes that learners are more likely to perceive themselves as competent if they have the prior knowledge, prerequisite skills, and learning strategies necessary for completing the projects before they begin.

The Role of the Teacher

PBL recognizes that the teacher is the last piece in the intrinsic motivational puzzle. The teacher's unique role in PBL is that of the supporter of intrinsic motivation. Consequently, Blumenfeld and her colleagues urge teachers to support their learners' interest, efforts, and achievements by:

- avoiding statements implying that innate ability is all that is required to complete a project
- focusing learners' attention on both the process of completing the project and the end product
- making encouraging statements to learners.

References

Cameron, J.; Pierce, W.D.; Banko, K.M. & Gear, A. (2005). Achievement-based rewards and intrinsic motivation: A test of cognitive mediators. *Journal of Educational Psychology*, 97, 641–55.

Case, R. (1985). *Intellectual development: Birth to adulthood.*New York: Academic Press.

Elliot, A.J. (1999). Approach and avoidance motivation and achievement goals. *Educational Psychologist*, 34, 169–89.

Sizer, T. R. (1984). *Horace's compromise: The dilemma of the American high school.* Boston: Houghton Mifflin.

Spaulding, C. L. (1992). *Motivation in the classroom.* New York: McGraw-Hill.

Bibliography

Alberto, P. & Troutman, A. (2003) *Applied behavior analysis for teachers* (6th ed.). Columbus, OH, USA: Prentice-Hall-Merrill.

Alderblum, E., (1950). "Beginning School-Guidance early". Mental Hygiene, U.S.A., Vol. 34, no. 4, Oct.

Alexander, W. P., (1943). *The Child Guidance Service in Principle and in Fact.* Sheffield, Education Committee.

Blacker, C. P., (1946). *Neurosis and the Mental Health Services.* Oxford. Oxford University Press.

Bloom, B. et.al., (1956). *Taxonomy of Educational Objectives: The Classification of Educational Goals, Handbook I. Cognitive Domain,* New York: Longmans.

Cameron, J.; Pierce, W.D.; Banko, K.M. & Gear, A. (2005). Achievement-based rewards and intrinsic motivation: A test of cognitive mediators. *Journal of Educational Psychology,* 97, 641–55.

Case, R. (1985). *Intellectual development: Birth to adulthood.*New York: Academic Press.

Cassidy, R. & Kozman, H. CL., (1947). *Counsefing Girls in a Changing Society,* New York & London. McGraw-Hill Book Co.

Clark, K., (1954). "The APA Study of Psychologists" *Amer. Psychology,* 9, 3, Mar, 117-120.

Cleugh, M. F., (1951). *Psychology in the Service of the School.* London, Methuen.

CWS, N. E., (1955). (Ed.) *School Psychologists at Mid-Century.* Washington

Daniel, R. S., Louttit, C. M., (1953). *Professional Problems in Psychology.* New-York Prentice-Hall.

Detterman, D.K. (1993) The case for the prosecution: Transfer as an epiphenomenon. In D.K. Detterman & R.J. Sternberg (Eds.), *Transfer on trial: Intelligence, cognition, and instruction*(pp. 1–24). Norwood, NJ: Ablex.

Elliot, A.J. (1999). Approach and avoidance motivation and achievement goals. *Educational Psychologist,* 34, 169–89.

Erickson, C. E. & Smith, G. E., (1941). *Organisation and Administration of Guidance Services.* New York and London, McGraw-Hill Book Company.

Furth, H.G. & Wachs, H. (1975). *Thinking goes to school: Piaget's theory in practice.* Oxford: Oxford University Press.

Gagné, R. M. (1975). *Essentials of Learning for Instruction,* Hillsdale, Ill.: Dryden Press.

Glover, J, & Ronning, R. (Ed.). (1987). *Historical foundations of educational psychology.* New York, NY: Plenum Press.

Gronlund, N.E. (2000). *How to write and use instructional objectives* (6th ed.). Columbus, OH, USA: Merrill.

Hamley et al., (1937). *The Educational Guidance of the School Child.* London, Evans Bros.

James, W. (1983). *Talks to teachers on psychology and to students on some of life's ideals.* Cambridge, MA: Harvard University Press.

Little, W. & Chapman, A. L., (1953). *Developmental Guidance in Secondary School.* New York, Toronto &London, McGraw-Hill Book Co.

Lucas, J.L.; Blazek, M.A. & Riley, A.B. (2005). The lack of representation of educational psychology and school psychology in introductory psychology textbooks. *Educational Psychology*, 25, 347–51.

Perkins, D.N. & Grotzer, T.A. (1997) Teaching intelligence.*American Psychologist*, 52, 1125–33.

Phillips, D. C., & Soltis, J. E. (1991). *Perspectives on learning* (2nd ed.). New York: Teachers College Press.

Resnick, L. B. (1987). *Education and Learning to Think,* Washington, D.C.: National Academy Press.

Schonell, F. J. & Wall, W. D., (1949). "The Remedial Education Centre", *Educational Review,* Vol. II, no. I.

Seifert, Kelvin & Sutton, Rosemary. (2009). *Educational Psychology: Second Edition.* Global Text Project, pp. 33-37.

Sizer, T. R. (1984). *Horace's compromise: The dilemma of the American high school.* Boston: Houghton Mifflin.

Slavin, R. E. (1988). *Educational Psychology: Theory into Practice.* Englewood Cliffs, N.J.: Prentice-Hall.

Spaulding, C. L. (1992). *Motivation in the classroom.* New York: McGraw-Hill.

Strang, R., (1948). *Educational Guidance: Its Principles and Pratice.* New York, McMillan.

Sulzer-Azaroff, B., et al. (1988). *Behavioral analysis in education,* reprint series, vol. III. Lawrence, KS: Society for the Experimental Analysis of Behavior, Inc.

Thorndike, E.L. (1912). *Education: A first book.* New York: MacMillan.

Wall, W. D., (1955). "Psychological Services for Children in Europe", *Yearbook of Education,* London, Evans Bros.

Whaley, D. L., & Malott, R. W. (1971). *Elementary principles of behavior.* Englewood Cliffs, NJ: Prentice-Hall.

Wjtmer, H. L., (1940). *Psychiatric Clinics for Children.* Oxford, Oxford University Press.

Woolfolk, A.E.; Winne, P.H. & Perry, N.E. (2006).*Educational Psychology* (3rd Canadian ed.). Toronto, Canada: Pearson.

Zimmerman, B.J. &Schunk, D.H. (eds.) (2003). *Educational psychology: A century of contributions.* Mahwah, NJ, US: Erlbaum.

Index

M

P

R

S

T